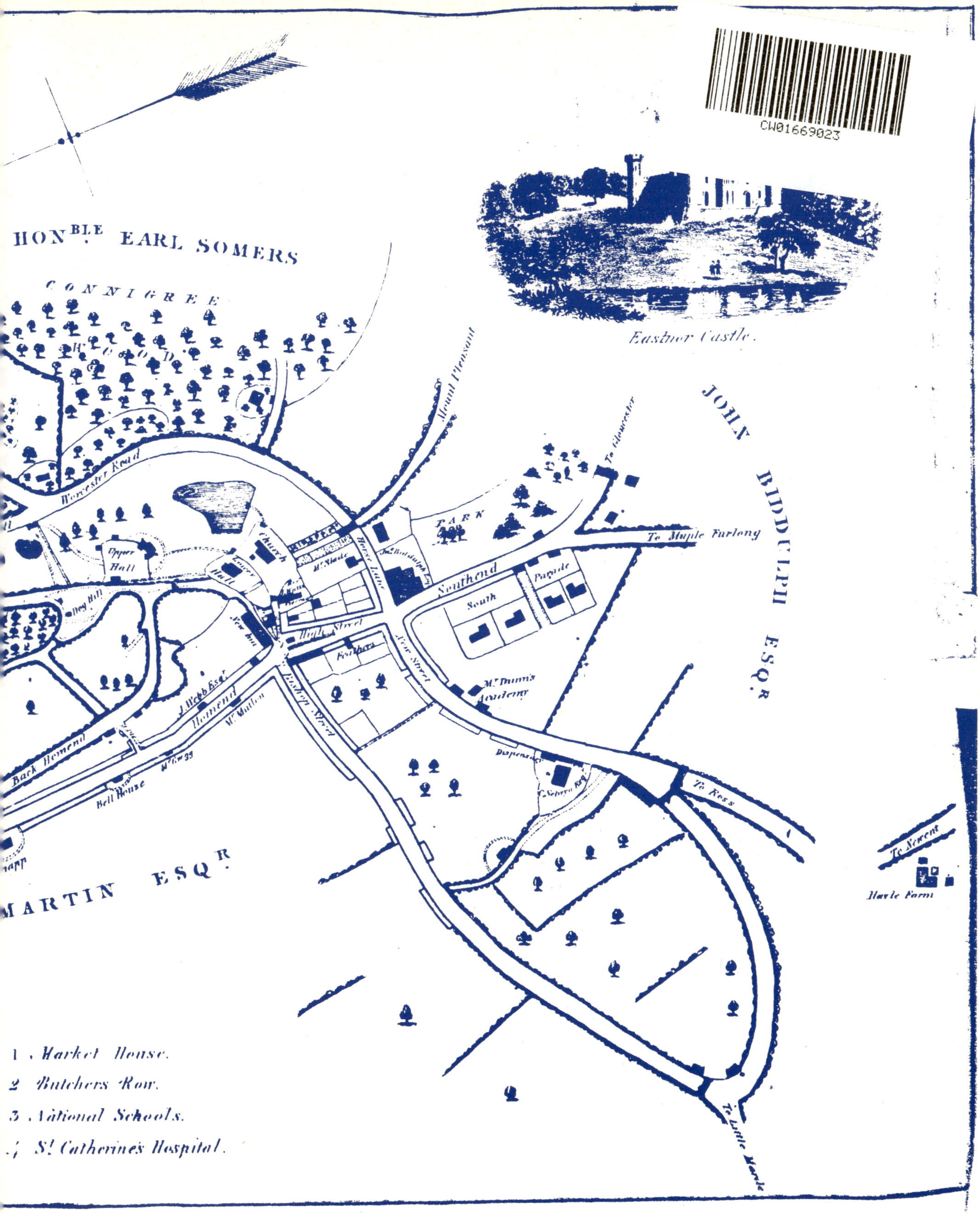

HON.BLE EARL SOMERS
CONNIGREE WOOD
Eastnor Castle.
Mount Pleasant
JOHN BIDDULPH ESQ.R
To Gloucester
PARK
To Maple Furlong
Worcester Road
Upper Hall
Church
Horse Lane
Southend
South
Parade
Dog Hill
New Inn
High Street
Feathers
New Street
Mr. Dunn's Academy
Dispensary
Bishop Street
J. Webb Esq.r
Homend
Back Homend
Bell House
To Ross
To Newent
Harle Farm
MARTIN ESQ.R
To Little Marcle
1. Market House.
2. Butchers Row.
3. National Schools.
4. St. Catherine's Hospital.

The Book of Ledbury 1982
has been published as a Limited
Edition of which this is

Number 109

A complete list of the
original subscribers is
printed at the back of the book

FRONT COVER: Middletown, the market place, with the Butchers Row. On the left are the pentices, under which corn was stacked until the coming of the turnpikes caused it to be sold by sample. T. Ballard, Engraving. (HCL/PC)
BACK COVER: Middletown after the Butchers Row had been removed. First there was a public subscription, opened in 1820, and then an act of parliament, in 1835. In the 13th century, before market encroachment, it would have looked much the same. T. Ballard, Engraving. (HCL/PC/)

THE BOOK OF LEDBURY

Church Street.

THE BOOK OF LEDBURY

AN ESSAY IN INTERPRETATION

BY

JOE G. HILLABY

Joe G. Hillaby.

BARRACUDA BOOKS LIMITED
BUCKINGHAM, ENGLAND
MCMLXXXII

PUBLISHED BY BARRACUDA BOOKS LIMITED
BUCKINGHAM, ENGLAND
AND PRINTED BY
HOLYWELL PRESS LIMITED
OXFORD, ENGLAND

BOUND BY
KEMP HALL BINDERY LIMITED
OXFORD, ENGLAND

JACKET PRINTED BY
CHENEY & SONS LIMITED
BANBURY, OXON

LITHOGRAPHY BY
CHAPMAN BROTHERS LIMITED
KIDLINGTON, OXFORD

DISPLAY SET IN BASKERVILLE
AND TEXT SET IN 10½/12 pt BASKERVILLE BY
BEDFORDSHIRE GRAPHICS LIMITED
BEDFORD, ENGLAND

ISBN 0 86023 125 9

Contents

Acknowledgements

Thanks are due to many people for help given over many years — firstly, to those who went before: the bibliography testifies to the scale of their contribution; secondly, to the many Ledburians and friends who attended the series of lectures on the history of Ledbury given during the winter months 1971-76 under the auspices of the University of Birmingham Department of Extramural Studies and the Workers' Educational Association, to whom thanks are also due. It was at these meetings that *The Book of Ledbury* was born. Even the energy crisis did not quench interest and enthusiasm. When rapidly diminishing fuel reserves forced the closure of the oil-fired central heating at the then County Secondary School in Mabels Furlong, first overcoats and gloves were worn, and then we moved to the luxury of the gas-fired heating at St Katherine's.

Many members will recognise in the text the questions with which we grappled and will, I trust, also recognise their contributions on some of the pages. My particular thanks are due to Miss S.R. Robinson, for much help in matters ecclesiastical and parochial; to the late Arthur Bayliss who, by his skill in languages, contributed much to our understanding of 13th century Ledbury; to Arthur Dew, for assistance with the history of the canal and railways, and to Peter Garnett who, as secretary to the group, helped us with many and varied difficulties — administrative and historical.

I am indebted to Miss Meryl Jancey, Miss Sue Hubbard and the staff of the Herefordshire County Record Office, to B.L. Whitehouse, Robin Hill and the staff of the Hereford City Library, to Miss Penelope Morgan and the late F.C. Morgan of the Hereford Cathedral Library, Miss Anne Sandford and the staff of the Hereford City Museum, Miss Kate Eggleston and the staff of the library of Hereford College of Education, and the staff of the British Library, the Bodleian Library and the Libraries of the Universities of Leeds, Bristol and Birmingham.

Almost all of the photographs have either been taken especially for inclusion or else they have been drawn from the major Herefordshire topographic collections: in the Hereford City Library there are the photographs of Alfred Watkins and F.C. Morgan (HCL/WMC) and in the Herefordshire County Record Office is to be found part of the large collection of photographs taken by Luke Tilley and Sons of Ledbury between about 1900 and 1925 (HCRO/AB/48). I am much obliged to Miss Tilley for permission to reproduce items from this collection. A small number of paintings and drawings of Ledbury are to be found in the Hereford City Museum (HCM). The reconstruction of the Iron-age hill-fort on Herefordshire Beacon by the late Brig R.H.H. Scott is reproduced by permission of Brig R.B. Scott and the photograph of the roof of the Magistrate's Court by kind permission of S.T. Walker. I should also like to record my gratitude to Paul Sumner for the photographs of the interior of St Katherine's Hospital and the parish church.

My particular thanks are due to Fred Druce of Ross-on-Wye and to Audrey, his wife, and Michael, his son, for printing the photographs to be seen in this book. They often had to work from old and difficult negatives. With skill and patience fine illustrations were wrought from this intractable material. The copy reader and typist had to battle with material that was almost as intractable. For that especial acknowledgement is due.

Foreword

By the Lord Bishop of Hereford, the Rt Rev J.R.G. Eastaugh

To understand the present rural communities in which we live we must have knowledge of past events which have shaped and influenced the quality of life in our villages and towns over a long period.

Folk memories, with roots deep in our history, still influence our behaviour, and the relationship of our agricultural communities with those engaged in commerce or in the professions, our attitude to the Church or those in authority, can only be understood if we know something of those events in the past which radically changed the lives of previous generations.

We are all greatly indebted to Mr Hillaby for his scholarly and very readable account of the history of Ledbury, which I have read with great pleasure and commend to all who value the history and traditions of the towns and villages in our county and diocese.

THE PALACE, HEREFORD

+ John Hereford

Introduction

Ledbury has been the Cinderella of the Herefordshire market towns. It is the only one for which there is now no full-scale written record. A newcomer or stranger curious about Ledbury can only turn today, as in 1898 when it was first published, to Ellen Tilley's admirable little *Guide* for assistance.

The present volume is intended to go some way to remedy the situation. It is not a history of Ledbury. This the conventions of the series do not permit. However, an attempt has been made to examine certain fundamental questions about the town. Why is Ledbury where it is? When and under what circumstances did it become a town? What factors explain its physical characteristics, in particular the shape and layout of its streets and buildings?

Answers to these questions are not merely of interest in themselves and of value for the light they throw onto the history of other towns. They are of vital importance for the future. If we value the beauty and individuality of the town bequeathed to us by our forebears we must ensure that their inheritance, and ours, is handed on to those who come after us. This obligation can only be fulfilled if we have some understanding of the nature of that inheritance.

The Book of Ledbury is, therefore, an essay in interpretation. This is why the mediaeval centuries dominate its pages and why relatively little is said about more recent times. It is hoped that the reader, bearing this in mind, will forgive the many and important omissions.

The Vision of William concerning

Piers the Plowman

In a somer sesun . whon softe was the sonne,
I schop me in-to a schroud . a scheep as I were;
In habite of an hermite . vn-holy of werkes,
Wende I wydene in this world . wondres to here.
Bote in a Mayes morwnynge . on Maluerne hulles
Me bi-fel a ferly . a feyrie me thouhte;
I was weori of wandringe . and wente me to reste
Vndur a brod banke . bi a bourne syde,
And as I lay and leonede . and lokede on the watres,
I slumberde in a slepyng . hit sownede so murie.
  Thenne gon I meeten . a meruelous sweuene,
That I was in a wildernesse . wuste I neuer where,
And as I beo-heold in-to the est . an-heiz to the sonne,
I sauh a tour on a toft . triz ely i-maket;
A deop dale bi-neothe . a dungun ther-inne,
With deop dich and derk . and dredful of siht.
  A feir feld ful of folk . fond I ther bi-twene,
Of alle maner of men . the mene and the riche,
Worchinge and wondringe . as the world asketh.
  Summe putten hem to the plou . and pleiden hem ful seldene,
In eringe and in sowynge . swonken ful harde,
That monie of theos wasturs . in glotonye distruen.
  And summe putten hem to pruide . apparaylden hem ther-after,
In cuntinaunce of clothinge . queinteliche de-gyset;
To preyere and to penaunce . putten heom monye,
For loue of vr lord . liueden ful harde,
In hope for to haue . heuene-riche blisse;
As ancres and hermytes . that holdeth hem in heore celles,
Coueyte not in cuntre . to carien a-boute,
For non likerous lyflode . heore licam to plese.
  And summe chosen chaffare . to cheeuen the bettre,
As hit semeth to vre siht . that suche men scholden;
And summe murthhes to maken . as munstrals cunne,
And gete gold with here gle . giltles, I trowe.
  Bote iapers and iangelers . Iudas children,
Founden hem fantasyes . and fooles hem maade,
And habbeth wit at heor wille . to worchen zif hem luste.
That Poul precheth of hem . I dar not preouen heere;
Qui loquitur turpiloquium . hee is Luciferes hyne.

William Langland
Prologue, 'A' Text, c1362

The Child of the Church

Ledbury was the child of the church. To understand its origins, one has to go back almost 1,300 years, to about 690 when the diocese of Hereford was founded to serve the spiritual needs of the *Magonsaetan,* the people or folk who lived west of the Severn.(1)

The boundaries of the diocese of Hereford and those of the sub-kingdom of the *Magonsaetan* were the same. They stretched from the Severn at Minsterworth, northwards up the Leadon to the ridge of the Malverns, to the Teme near Knightsford Bridge and along the Abberley Hills back to the Severn. Thence they took in almost all of Shropshire to the south of the Severn before they returned by way of the foothills of the Radnor and Clun forests, the vale of Ewias, the Monnow and Wye, once more to the Severn. This was a vast area.

The responsibility of a bishop then was essentially pastoral and peripatetic. He was expected to visit every part of his see each year to rule and feed Christ's sheep. It is not surprising, as Bede tells us, that there were 'many hamlets and steadings of our nation, lying amongst inaccessible mountains and bosky valleys, where in the passage of many years no bishop hath been seen, which should perform some ministerial act or bestow some heavenly grace'.(2)

To help him fulfil his pastoral responsibilities, the bishop sent out small groups of priests to strategic sites within the diocese, which thus became mission centres. The priests were drawn from the bishop's own *familia,* the community of clergy that lived with him at Hereford. In this way, the diocese came to be sub-divided into smaller and more easily managed units, called *parochia.* At the centre of each *parochia* a minster church was established. Such a minster was not usually a monastery. It was usually the church served by a small group of secular priests sent there to complete the process of conversion and to tend to the spiritual needs of local people, particularly the administration of the sacraments of baptism, marriage, extreme unction and the mass. The minster was also referred to as *matrix ecclesia,* the mother church of its district. One was established at Ledbury.

It was built to one side of the crossroads where the major east-west and north-south routes met, in a commanding position in the Leadon valley where one of these routes, from Hereford to Worcester, passed through the range of hills that stretch from Dingwood Park in the south to Oyster Hill in the north. This route's early importance is clearly shown by Wall Hills, an Iron-age hill fort of some 36 acres.(3) It retained its importance for a long time. Henry III visited Ledbury twice, in October 1231 and August 1256, using the bishop's palace there as a convenient resting place on his way from Hereford to Worcester.

It would seem that the minster at Ledbury was founded by the bishop of Hereford in the early 8th century to serve the people who lived 'in the district called *Lydas*'. These were a shadowy folk, for they appear only once in history, when they are referred to in the *Life of St Mildburga* of Much Wenlock, who died about 720, close to the probable date of foundation. The *Life* tells us that she received a considerable estate in the district called Lydas, 'to be forever at her disposal.'(4) However, the lands came into the hands of her diocesan, the bishop of Hereford, possibly as a result of her subsequent gift.

Place-name evidence may support this. Ledbury is usually taken to be the 'bury' or *burh* on the

Leadon. However, only once is the place-name Ledbury found with an 'n', *Lindeberia,* in 1167. Eilart Ekwall has commented that this extreme rarity of early forms with the 'n' is remarkable.(5) Perhaps the first element is derived, not from the Leadon, but from the district of the *Lydas?* If so the word *burh* was not used in its original sense of a place of defence but in a later sense, to denote the site of a religious house, a minster, as at Westbury on Trym and Tetbury in Gloucestershire, Fladbury in Worcestershire and Malmesbury in Wiltshire.(6) Tewkesbury seems to be yet another example, where the first element is derived from *Teodec,* the traditional founder of the great monastery. If this is so Ledbury would mean 'the religious enclosure of the minster of the Lydas district'.

Ledbury's importance as an ecclesiastical centre is reflected in the size and grandeur of its church. Sir Nikolaus Pevsner described it as the premier parish church of Herefordshire. Strangely, in the twelfth century there was a firm tradition that Ledbury had once been the centre of the diocese. After Gilbert Foliot, Bishop of Hereford (1148-63), became Bishop of London, he wrote a letter to his successor at Hereford, pleading that he should confirm the rights of the church of Ledbury as he, Gilbert, and his predecessors had done, 'for the sake of the episcopal see which it had held long since and out of reverence to the holy bishops whose bodies lie there'.(7) Unfortunately, there is no further documentary evidence to support this remarkable statement.

Most Norman bishops showed scant regard for their Saxon predecessors. It is likely that in the second Norman rebuilding of Ledbury minster, about 1180, Gilbert Foliot's worst fears were realised and all trace of the burial place of the earlier bishops was lost.

In the middle ages Ledbury minster (as a non-monastic church) was only outmatched by the cathedral itself. 187 feet in length, it compared creditably with the cathedral at 255 feet. This extraordinary length was attained within almost a century of the Norman Conquest, for the present church is essentially a late Norman structure of about 1180. The only major alterations and additions achieved by later generations were the rebuilding of the north and south aisles and the construction of St Katherine's chapel and the detached tower.

An earlier church of similar design and proportions preceded it. The evidence passes unnoticed by all but the most keen-eyed of visitors. At the foot of the north-westernmost columns of the north arcade of the nave are the conglomerate stone bases of four columns of an earlier arcade. Circular in shape and some five feet in diameter, they are the last vestiges of an earlier church, possibly of about 1120. This earlier nave arcade must have been similar, if not quite as grand, as those still to be seen at Hereford, Tewkesbury, Shrewsbury and Great Malvern. They are all of about the same date. The size and architecture of Ledbury parish church in the early 11th century is important, for it clearly confirms its stature as a minster or mother church, a *matrix ecclesia.*

There is other evidence. Ledbury was a portionary church. The earliest record of the appointment of a portionist is in 1201 when, the see being vacant, the King granted William, archdeacon of Hereford, 'that portion in the church of Ledbury which Henry Bannister held'. There were two such portionists. Each enjoyed quite distinct portions of the endowments and revenues of the church. These came to be known as the Upper Hall or Over Court and the Lower Hall or Nether Court estates. By 1311 it was accepted that the two portionists were sinecure rectors:(8) appointed by the bishop, their only duties were the nomination of the vicar and the payment of his, usually meagre, stipend.(9) The cure of souls was the responsibility of the vicar.

In the Domesday entry for Ledbury, these estates of the church were considerable: 'two and a half hides of land worth fifty shillings'; far more than would be associated with a mere parish church. By contrast, the two knights at Ledbury held between them merely one hide. The two and a half hides were the endowment of the ancient minster. By 1201, they had become the portionists' estates of the Upper and Lower Halls.

Taken together the evidence is conclusive. Ledbury originated as an early centre of missionary activity. The first priests may only have raised a large cross in the open air on the site of the present church — such crosses can still be seen in many parts of the country. It was eventually replaced by the first minster, of which no trace now remains. All this took place long before any parish churches had been founded in the district.

The precise site which they chose for the church is puzzling. Why does it lie in the lowest part of the churchyard? This necessitated the diversion of the stream that flows from the pond in the grounds of the Upper Hall, the former Grammar School, along the higher ground to the south of the churchyard, as Viscount Torrington observed when he visited the town in 1781. 'The churchyard is flanked on one side by a wet fossē and on the others by well-built houses (the Upper and Lower Halls), which gives it the look of a cathedral close'.(10) Did the first missionaries to the district of *Lydas* heed the advice of Pope Gregory the Great to St Augustine in 601, that on no account should the pagan temples be destroyed? The idols should be removed, the temples themselves 'to be aspersed with holy water, altars set up and relics enclosed in them'. Gregory hoped that the people, 'seeing that its temples are not destroyed may abandon idolatry and resort to these places as before, and may come to know and adore the true God'.(11) It is difficult to find any other explanation for the decision to build the church on the course of a stream — unless it was to use a site already sacred to a local deity of the area.

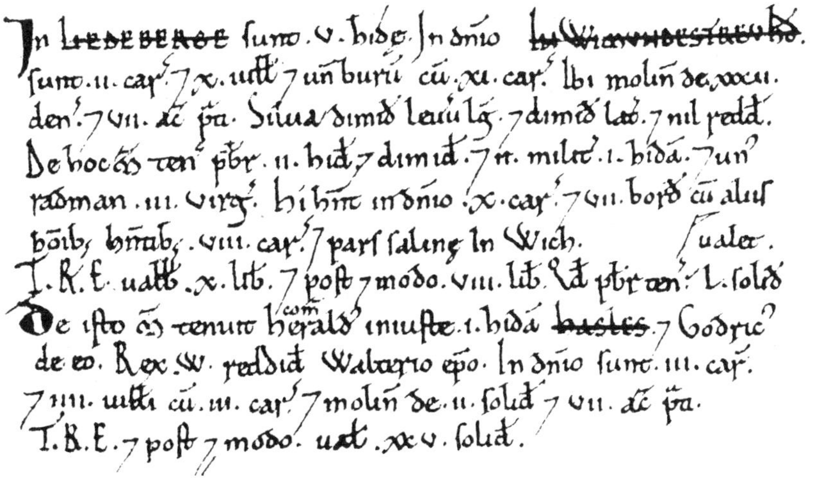

Facsimile of Domesday survey for the Bishop of Hereford's manor of Ledbury, 1086.

The existence of a minster church explains all that followed. Ledbury became the natural hub for all activity in the area. Because this was a wholly rural society, the religious centre became first the trading and later the administrative centre of the district. Hereford was too far away. For the people of the Ledbury district, a visit to Hereford would be one of life's high points, whether on pilgrimage to the shrine of St Ethelbert or while serving in the *fyrd,* the county militia.

It was only natural that attendance at church should be combined with all sorts of marketing. Each Sunday, and on the great days of the Christian calendar, Easter, Whitsun and Christmas, the Lower Cross and the lane leading up to the church would be the scene of intense activity. The area would be full of cattle, sheep, poultry, and farm produce of all kinds. Specialist craftsmen and pedlars would vend their wares. Such open air markets far removed from any town can still be seen in much of the third world today.

Even more important for trading purposes was the annual patronal festival, the feast of the dedication, 'originally kept on the same saints day annually unto whose memory the church was dedicated'. At Ledbury the dedication, as mediaeval records show, was not to St Michael and All

Angels but to St Peter, one of the most ancient of dedications. Sir William Dugdale explains how these occasions fell from grace. 'People cam to the Chirche with candellys brennyng and wold wake, and coome with light toward night to the Chirche in their devocions; and aftir they fell to lecherie and songs, daunses, harping, piping, and also to glotony and sinne, and so tourned the holinesse to cursydnes.'(12) Thus the Holy days became market and fair days and also holidays.

Church and king joined forces, quite ineffectively, against the growing evil of trading on the Sabbath, for the earliest extant charter for Ledbury, in 1138, records the grant by King Stephen of a market to be held each week on the Lord's Day, on Sundays. The problem remained 250 years later. In 1386, Bishop John Gilbert had to admonish the chantry chaplains at Ledbury not to celebrate their offices on Sundays and holy days before high mass had begun and the gospel had been read, as certain parishioners were wont to attend the low mass, celebrated in the chantries in the morning, and then to pass the rest of the day in dissipation or business.(13)

Just as the district or *parochia* served by the minster at Ledbury became an economic as well as an ecclesiastical unit, it developed in late Saxon times into a local government area for taxation and the administration of justice, called a hundred. The men of the hundred which included Ledbury met at Wygmund's tree. The name, now lost, was still in use in 1288, when a mill of that name was mentioned in a survey of Ledbury manor foreign. It was probably situated on the banks of the Leadon in the extreme southern part of the parish, at a place subsequently called Leather Mill, a mile to the south of the Full Pitcher. This Wygmundstree hundred disappeared after the Conquest in a general re-organisation of the Herefordshire hundreds, when it was combined with Radlow hundred.

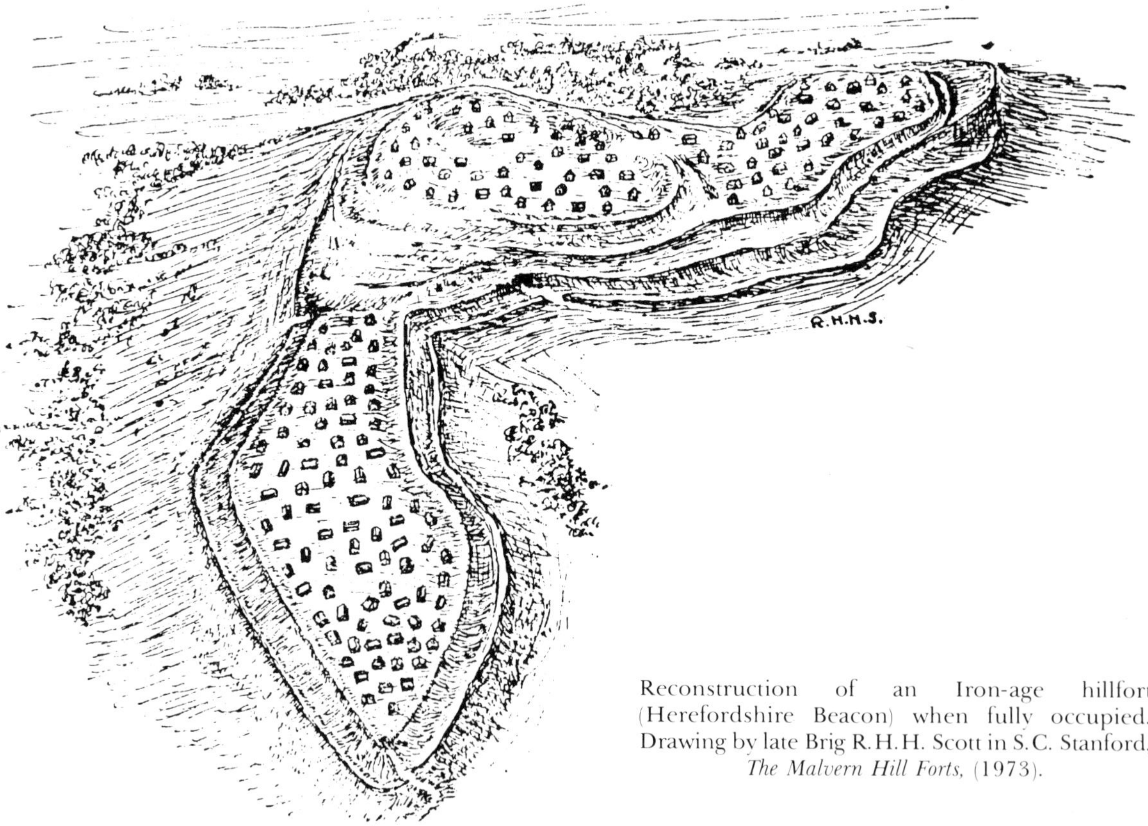

Reconstruction of an Iron-age hillfort (Herefordshire Beacon) when fully occupied. Drawing by late Brig R.H.H. Scott in S.C. Stanford, *The Malvern Hill Forts*, (1973).

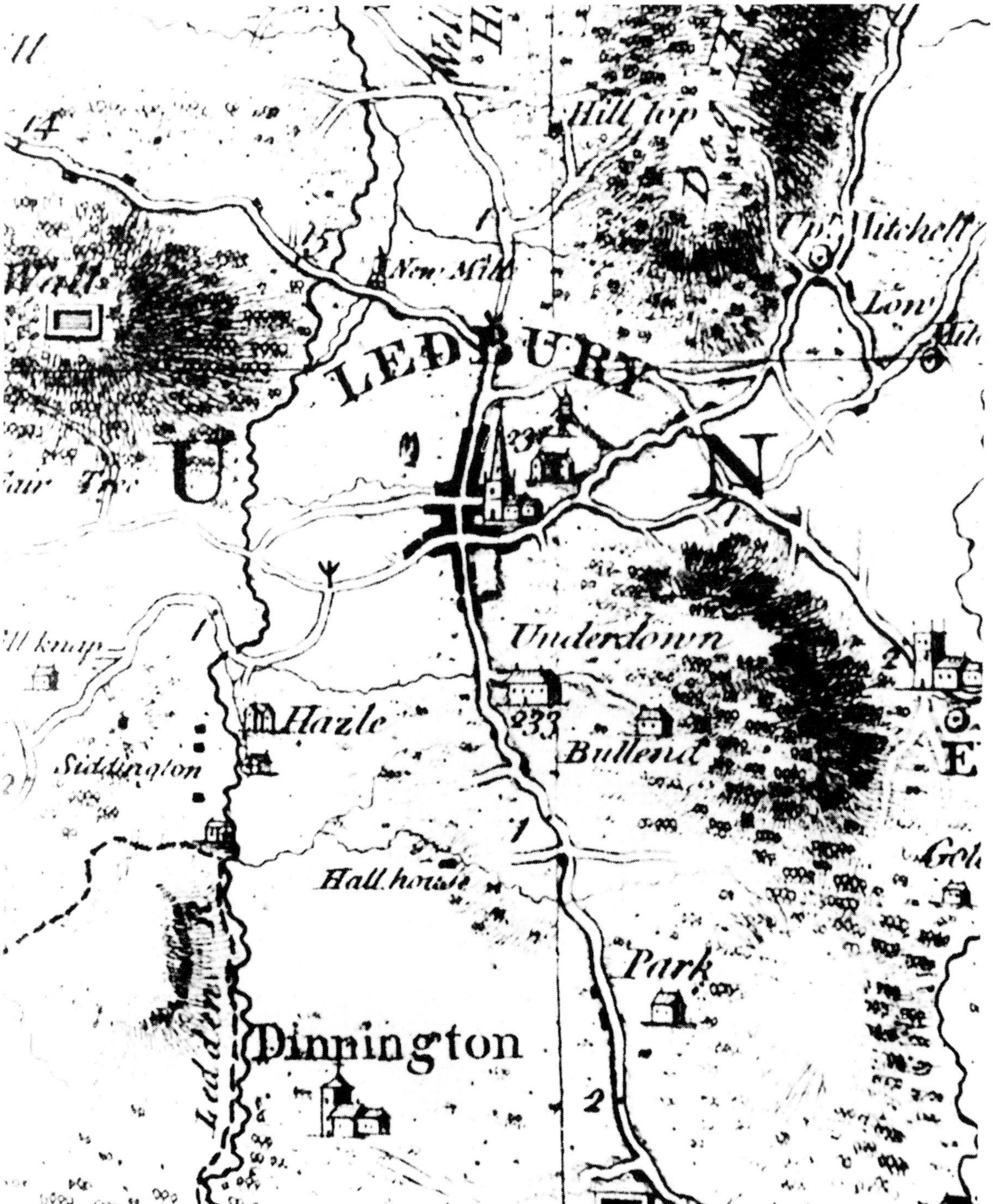

Isaac Taylor's *New Map of the County of Hereford* (1754). The minster was in a commanding position over the Leadon valley, and by a gap in the hills to the east.

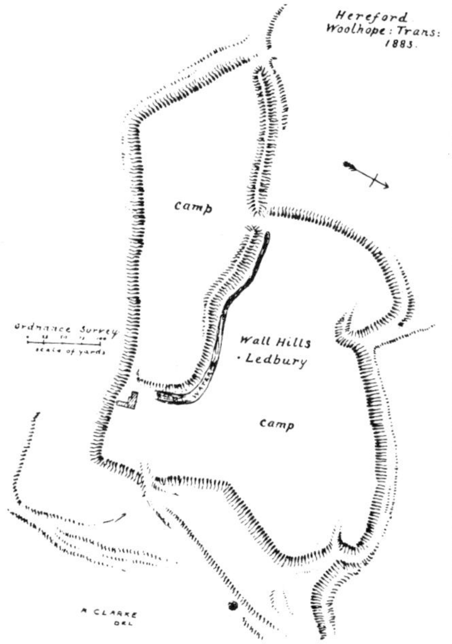

An Iron-age hillfort stood as a sentinel at the end of the gap. LEFT: Plan of Wall Hills. RIGHT: King's Ditch, Wall Hills, September 1942. (HCL/WMC/8765). BELOW: C. Price's *Survey of the Hazle Estate* for Jacob Tonson, 1730, showing Wall Hills. (HCRO,J95/1)

Ledbury, the site: ABOVE: the site chosen for the minster was close to a crossroad where the route from Hereford to Worcester crossed over Dog Hill by the ancient track, or green lane, that still exists. BELOW: Two views of Dog Hill. (HCL/WMC/554 and HCM)

Matrix Ecclesia, the mother church or minster of St Peter, Ledbury: ABOVE: Reconstruction of St Peter's after the second Norman rebuild of about 1180. LEFT: South chancel arcade and external wall above with circular clerestorey lights and corbel table of second Norman rebuild, now incorporated in south chapel. RIGHT: Evidence of the earlier, first Norman church of c1120. Conglomerate stone bases, five feet in diameter, carried a north nave arcade with circular piers.

LEFT ABOVE: West front prior to restoration in 1895. (HCL/WMC/580) BELOW: West doorway of second Norman rebuild prior to restoration, encasing earlier Norman facade. (HCL/WMC/581) RIGHT ABOVE: Chevron or zig-zag ornament of two of the four orders of the arch and capitals decorated with foliage; inner capital with a mask at the base which bites the shaft, c1180. BELOW: West front, 1980.

The axes on which the new borough was created: ABOVE: The road from Hereford proceeded in a south-easterly direction at Wallers Green to skirt the western flank of Wall Hills where even today much of the road, called Falcon Lane, follows the parish boundary, a sure sign of antiquity. It then made its way into Ledbury through Bye Street. LEFT: After crossing the water-splash at the Lower Cross, it continued up Church Street, which ironically came to be Back Lane in the 19th century. This was called the Hall End, for the road passed the Lower and Upper Halls before climbing Dog Hill. RIGHT: The north-south route from Bromyard and Bosbury through Ledbury to Newent and Gloucester.

The New Town

'In LIEDEBERGE are 5 hides. On the (bishop's) demesne are 2 ploughs, and 10 villeins and 1 burus with 11 ploughs (of their own). (There are) there a mill worth 32d and 7 acres of meadow. The wood (is) half a league long and half broad, and renders nothing.

Of this (bishop's) manor a priest holds 2½ hides and 2 knights (hold) 1 hide, and a radman (riding servant) 3 virgates. They have on (their) demesne 10 ploughs and (there are) 7 bordars with other men having 8 ploughs. Part of a salt-pit in (Droit) wich (belongs to the manor).

T.R.E. (In the time of King Edward the Confessor) it was worth £10, and afterwards and now £8. What the priest holds is worth 50s.

Of this manor Earl Harold held 1 hide unjustly (called) Hasles, and Godric (held it) of him. King William restored (it) to bishop Walter. On the demesne are 3 ploughs and 4 villeins with 3 ploughs, and a mill worth 2s and 7 acres of meadow.

T.R.E. and afterwards, as now, it was worth 25s.'(14)

As it is thus described in Domesday Book, Ledbury is a typical rural settlement, with a village nucleus between the church and the Lower Cross, and a number of lesser settlements, knightly estates such as the Hazle, beyond. How did it become a town? When was the borough founded? Who was responsible?

In terms of origins, most towns are classified as organic, or planned. Planned or new towns are characterised by regularly laid out market places and streets, with long narrow strips of land, called burgage plots, on either side. The first post-Conquest new towns, such as Chepstow and Ludlow, were founded for defence. They supplied additional manpower for a castle. It was soon realised that towns brought considerable profit to their lord, whether lay or spiritual. In the 11th century financial incentive became the principal motive for borough foundation.

Although Ledbury was a primary marketing centre centuries before the Conquest, it was still no more than a village in 1086. Nevertheless, its topography shows that it clearly is a planned borough. At some time after 1086 a new town was grafted onto the much earlier village nucleus of four elements — an important crossroads, a minster church, a village settlement and an episcopal manor house and estate.

The first recorded Ledbury market charter was issued by King Stephen (1135-54) to Bishop Robert de Bethune (1131-48). It reads: 'Stephen, King of England to his justices, barons and sheriffs and all his ministers and lords, French and English, of Herefordshire, greetings. Know that I grant Robert, bishop of Hereford, may have a market on Sunday of each week in his manor of Ledbury. And I ordain that all men going there and coming back may have my peace. In Witness John the Marshall, at Hereford.'(15)

At the same time Stephen granted a market charter to Bishop Robert for Ross. There the market was to be held on Thursdays. We know from the names of those who witnessed the two charters that they must have been issued by Stephen when he attended High Mass at the cathedral in Hereford on Whit Sunday, 1138.

It has been wrongly suggested that these market charters represent, not merely the origins of the market, but also the foundation of the boroughs at Ledbury and Ross.

Trade and towns could only prosper in times of peace and stability. This was no such time in Herefordshire and the neighbouring counties. On the death of Henry I in 1135, 'the kingdom was convulsed; peace and justice vanished. Immediately fierce and mad designs are revealed from the hearts of many. They prey upon one another, they slay, they burn'. Such is the contemporary description by Robert de Bethune's biographer, William of Wycumb.(16)

Just as the reign of Stephen was most certainly not the time, so was Robert de Bethune not the person to found boroughs and markets. They were founded for economic reasons by lords moved by the prospect of financial gain from the tolls, the rents and the profits of justice. Yet Robert de Bethune was one of the most ascetic figures to occupy the see of Hereford. His life and rule were characterised by humility, charity, vigour, great personal and moral courage and an intense personal austerity. He always wore a hair shirt next to his skin, carried the 'rods of correction' with him at all times for self-chastisement and died of syncope brought on by the meagreness of his diet.(17)

If the times were so inimical, and he himself was so lacking in concern for such worldly matters, why did Robert de Bethune press Stephen to issue the two market charters on Whit Sunday 1138? The answer lies in the last sentence of the charter, 'I ordain that men going there and coming back may have my peace'. This is a charter of ratification, not foundation. Robert's concern was to safeguard the lives and property of those who looked to him, as their feudal lord as well as their diocesan, for protection in such troubled times. Through the charter he got the new king to underwrite the peace of the market place itself, symbolised by the market cross, and of those who journeyed there and back.

One of the many miracles Robert de Bethune wrought during his life occurred in the market place at Ledbury, at the entrance to his palace or manor house, now St Katherine's hospital. It is important, not only in its own right, but because this passage from William of Wycumb's biography is the earliest story we have of life in the little town.

'The man of God came to his palace at Ledbury. There, in the multitude of paupers dying in front of the gates, lay one wretched man extraordinarily afflicted, by the devil, with the falling sickness. Like a smith tempering red hot iron in a forge, he ceaselessly beat his head on the ground. The bishop looked at him and passed on . . .

'Inside the gates, one of his priests, bolder than the rest, asked, "Why did you pass by? Why did you not place your hand upon him, calling on the Lord, so that the devil would leave him?" The bishop could scarce restrain his tears. When he had dismounted he blessed water and calling the priest he said, "Hasten and sprinkle the epileptic and make sure that he drinks the remainder of the water in the name of the Father, the Son and the Holy Ghost". The priest sprinkled the man. The crazed head rested, his eyes opened, he began to speak and hear. The priest poured the remaining water down his throat. Immediately the sick man sat up. After he had eaten he departed, free from his sickness'.(18)

There is little doubt that the real founder of the new town of Ledbury was not Robert but his immediate predecessor, Richard de Capella, Bishop of Hereford (1121-27). From about 1107 to 1121 he had been keeper of the Royal seal. He had been responsible for all the secretarial work of the king's *scriptorium* which issued Royal charters, including those granting or confirming rights to hold markets and fairs. During his first years of office, a spate of such grants had passed through his hands, especially to cathedrals and monastic churches. He was, therefore, fully conversant with the means adopted by the more enterprising and well-connected ecclesiastical landowners to profit from the rising agricultural production and expanding trade that characterised early 12th century England. Within three months of his election, Richard de Capella had persuaded the king to grant him a charter conceding a 'fair for three days at Hereford on the feast of St Ethelbert the martyr'.(19) This we now call the Bishop's Fair. We also know that the bridge at Hereford, a major stimulus to trade in the city and the shire, was built by Henry I on the advice of Richard de Capella.(20)

Having acted in co-operation with the king, Richard then struck out on his own. At Ledbury, Bromyard and Ross he found weekly trading activity associated with the mother churches that served the eastern part of the shire. Whether he obtained Royal market charters or not we shall never know. Early 11th century market charters are few and far between. However, in all three manors he put the centuries old informal market activity on a completely new footing.

A model was close at hand, at Hereford. There a new town had been created immediately after the Norman Conquest by William fitz Osbern who had been appointed Earl of Hereford by William the Conqueror about 1067.(21) At the centre of that new town was a vast wedge-shaped market place, of which the present High Town represents only a part, for it must originally have included all the area, now built-up, between Union Street and Commercial Street.

Although the difference in size between the new towns at Hereford and Ledbury is great, the parallels are important. At Hereford, the nucleus onto which fitz Osbern grafted his new town was the Saxon city. At Ledbury, the nucleus onto which Richard de Capella grafted his new town was the almost equally ancient precinct of the minster church. In both places the fundamental topography of the planned town was dictated by the combination of old-established routeways and original nucleus.

At Ledbury, Richard de Capella adopted the Hereford wedge-shape for his new market place. This was located at right angles to the earlier pre-Conquest market area which was on the land leading up to the south porch of the minster, now Church Lane. The broad end was placed at the Lower Cross because this was the original crossroads. It was only in the late 17th and early 18th centuries, when vehicular traffic rapidly increased, that the more gradual incline out of the town, Horse Lane, became the main road to the east, and it was only in the 20th century that it was finally dignified with the title of Worcester Road.

The road from Hereford through Ledbury to Malvern and Worcester then turned south-east at Wallers Green to skirt the western flank of Wall Hills, where even today much of Falcon Lane follows the parish boundary, a sure sign of antiquity. This route is clearly shown on Emanuel Bowen's mid-18th century map of Herefordshire. It then made its way into Ledbury through what was to become Bishop Street, now Bye Street. After crossing a water-splash at the Lower Cross, which was only culverted in the early 19th century, it continued up Church Street which, ironically, in the 19th century came to be called Back Lane. Originally, this was called the Hall End, for the road passed the Lower and Upper Halls before it crossed over Dog Hill by the surviving ancient trackway.This and the route which came north from Gloucester and Newent provided the axes on which the new borough of Ledbury was created by Richard de Capella's surveyor.

The market place was the heart of the new town. Here one would have expected burgage plots to be at a premium. Yet more than half of the western side of the market is occupied not by burgages but by St Katherine's hospital, founded by Bishop Hugh Foliot in 1232, more than a century after the foundation of the borough. Either a considerable number of shops and houses were demolished in 1232 to make way for the hospital or the site was already in use prior to the foundation of the borough. It is inconceivable that Hugh Foliot dispossessed townsmen already established on the site. That would have been a difficult task and an unnecessary one, for St Katherine's was not a commercial institution and did not need a market frontage. In fact, it would have served its purpose better elsewhere, removed from the hurly-burly of the market place. The hospital must have been given a site previously used for some other non-commercial purpose — the ancient bishop's palace, or manor house, the place where Robert de Bethune, almost 100 years earlier, cured the man 'vexed by the devil with the falling sickness'. With the growth of the town, the old palace site must have become more and more uncongenial. The noise, smell and lack of privacy all made a move imperative. In or slightly before 1232 a new site was chosen for the palace, above the Upper Cross. This ensured not only privacy but also direct access to Ledbury

Park and the Chase beyond, where the bishop and his guests could hunt at their pleasure, as far as the uppermost ridge of the Malvern Hills.

The hospital also took over all the buildings associated with the management of a great estate. Only a small part of the great square plot of land was occupied by the hospital; the rest was covered, as an inventory of 1316 shows, with barns, byres, malt houses, cider houses and the like — almost a third of the market place.(22)

This had an important impact, for shortage of market space led to rapid expansion of the town into the Homend and the western side of the Southend. Only later did the hospital relinquish part of its market frontage. The 1966 25 ins OS plan clearly shows the northern part of the Feathers, and 26 and 27 High Street, which bears the date 1695, as encroachment.

It would be wrong to portray Richard de Capella's foundation merely in physical terms. There was then a fundamental difference between those who lived in the countryside and those in the town. The peasant was bound to the land. He owed such personal services to his lord as ploughings and carryings, week work and boon work. These services were the hallmark of those who worked on the land. Rural tenure was servile tenure but urban tenure gave a man freedom from service on the lord's land, to move at will, to marry, to leave his goods and lands to whom he wished. The town dweller had to be free, because successful trade was dependent upon personal freedom. In mediaeval parlance, 'town air makes free'.

There was, in consequence, a clear distinction in legal status between those who lived within a borough and those who lived without. Landholding in the borough, with all its privileges, was based on burgage tenure. The lord merely received a money payment, normally 12d a year, from his burgesses. In return, they usually had freedom from all services, except suit of court, as well as the tenure of their burgage plots. Free from labour service and all the other restrictions associated in mediaeval times with work on the land, the burgess could devote most of his time and energy to a trade or craft.

Because of this fundamental difference in way of life and in legal status, the newly-founded borough of Ledbury had to be clearly marked off from the old manor of Ledbury from which it had been carved. The distinction between the two had to be precise and clear-cut in a geographical as well as in a legal sense. So the former manor of Ledbury was now divided into two parts, one the manor denzein or borough, the other the manor foreign; the areas within and without.

The geographical bounds of the borough continued to be clearly defined until the late 19th century. They appeared in their final form on the 25 ins OS plan of 1887. The next year, with the passing of the Local Government Act, Ledbury borough disappeared.

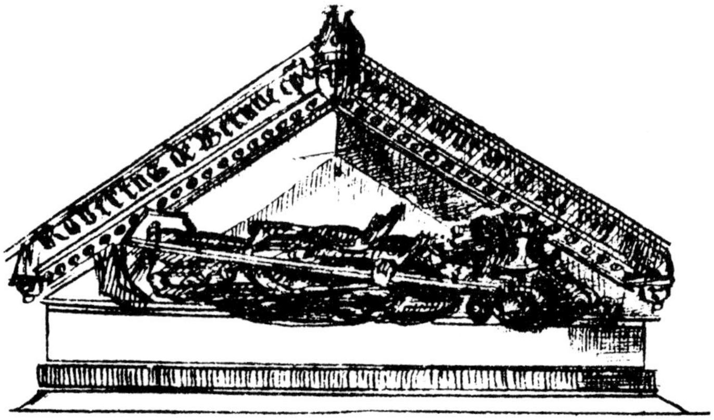

Robert de Bethune's monument in Hereford cathedral, c1684. T. Dingley, *History from Marble (Camden Soc* 1857), I, clxxii.

LEFT: The market area that was supplanted. CENTRE: Informal trading activity — fish stall, 1907. (HCL/WMC/6089) RIGHT: The broad end of Richard de Capella's new market c1125 was placed at the Lower Cross, for this was the original crossroads and was adjacent to the earlier market area. BELOW: Where the trees now stand were the gates to Robert de Bethune's palace. Here, among the multitude of paupers, lay the man afflicted with the falling sickness.

'Town air makes free!' Free from all labour service in the fields to his lord, the burgess could devote his time and energy to a trade or craft.

Burgages and Houses

The small town founded by Richard de Capella between 1121 and 1127 faced harsh times in the Great Anarchy of Stephen's reign, 1138-53. Thereafter it grew with extraordinary rapidity. Yet for almost a hundred years the records are quite silent. From the market charter of 1136 to the foundation of St Katherine's hospital in 1232, we have no documentary evidence to illumine the development of the town. The records of the first half century of St Katherine's throw little light on Ledbury's early history. To find out how the town developed in the first century and a half of its existence we must turn to the *Red Book* of the bishops of Hereford.(23)

From this we can draw a detailed picture of Ledbury in the closing years of the 13th century, when it had reached the climax of its mediaeval growth. We can describe in detail the topography and economy of the town and the origins and occupations of the burgesses.

In the last decades of the 13th century detailed surveys were made, probably on Bishop Richard Swinfield's orders, of all the episcopal estates, to provide a clear record of what money and services were due from his tenants. In the 16th century all these surveys were bound together, with a number of other records relating to the rights and estates of the see, in one volume bound in red leather. We know from a passage in the text that the survey of Ledbury borough and manor foreign was drawn up by the bailiff, Robert ffurches, in the year 1288.(24)

The *Red Book* gives details of the tenants, customs and value of all of the bishop's manors and the five small market towns founded on their estates. There were 282 tenancies at Ledbury, 255 at Bromyard, 105 at Ross, 46 at Bishops Castle in Shropshire (originally referred to as Lydbury North) and 30 at Prestbury, near Cheltenham, in Gloucestershire. This is a clear indication of their relative size and importance.(25)

The normal holding was either a whole or a half of a burgage plot, although quarter or even smaller plots are encountered in the survey of Ledbury. The burgage was a plot of land to which were attached specific liabilities and privileges. They varied from borough to borough according to custom or the foundation charter but they all had as a common basis the payment of a money rent and little or no liability for personal services.

In many mediaeval boroughs the area of the original burgage plots is known from the foundation charters. At Salisbury, the New Sarum, the plots were 3 perches by 7 perches; at Altrincham, 2 by 5 perches; at Stratford-upon-Avon, 3½ by 12 perches; at Burton, 4 by 24 perches; at Knutsford, 2½ selions, or open field strips. In other cases we are given only the area. This varied from the ⅓ of an acre granted at Wotton-under-Edge, based upon 'the customs and uses' of the neighbouring borough of Tetbury, to the full acre granted at Salford about 1230.(26)

As there is no extant foundation charter for Ledbury, one has to search elsewhere for help in assessing the size of the original burgage plots. If the various editions of the 25 ins OS plan of the town are examined carefully, a certain regularity of lay-out is evident. This is most obvious on the east and west sides of the Homend but the plots on the west side, which are on falling ground, are longer, with an average length of somewhat more than 200 feet. The same regularity is evident on the eastern side of the market place. The burgage plots on the eastern sides of the market place and the Homend are some 200 feet, equivalent to the mediaeval measure of twelve perches, or three chains, as at Stratford.

The width of the original burgage plots is not so easily established. There are two major difficulties. The first arises from the process of fragmentation, and to a lesser extent amalgamation of plots which has taken place over the centuries. The second arises from the presence of alleyways down the sides of many of the plots.

The fragmentation of burgage plots began early. In 1288 there were more than 130 half burgage plots and nine quarter plots as well as reference to ⅛, ⅜, ⅝ and ¾ plots. Most of the smallest holdings were in the market place where, for example, John Chibenol, Matilda Waleys and William of Eastnor all held tenancies described by the scribe as 'half of a quarter'. Even earlier, in 1232, a grant made by Bishop Hugh Foliot to his newly founded hospital included 'half a burgage . . . bought of Margaret daughter of Gilbert Fraunceys, rendering each year 6d.'(27)

The amalgamation of two or more whole or part burgages to give a wider street frontage is seen most clearly in the building of the larger inns during the great period of reconstruction in the late 16th and early 17th centuries. The Feathers and the Talbot are good examples. In the late 19th and the early 20th centuries the banks were great offenders. Webb's Ledbury Old Bank, now Lloyds, belongs to this category. Today it is supermarkets.

The process began at an early date, and frequently in a humble manner. Sometimes merely a fraction of a burgage would be added. As well as double and treble burgages, the *Red Book* mentions tenancies of 1¼, 1½ and 1¾, even 1⅛ and 1⅝ burgages in Ledbury. In 1232, half a century before the *Red Book,* there is the record of a grant by Bishop Hugh Foliot of 'a burgage and a half which we bought of John, son of Gersant, rendering the bishop 18d'.

The second difficulty arises from the existence of side alleys. Once the frontage was fully developed, almost all the outbuildings and gardens behind the houses and shops in the principal streets had to be served by such alleyways. There was no other way of obtaining rear access. Many have since been built over, leaving no trace. Elsewhere, burgesses encroached upon their neighbours' or their joint alleyways. No precise calculation, based on the width of the existing buildings, can therefore be made.

Looking at those plots which appear to have retained their original width suggests that, at the time of foundation and during subsequent expansion, the bishop's surveyor may well have laid them out at twenty two feet intervals along the street, giving plot widths of ⅓ of a chain. The chain, like the perch, was not merely a linear measure, it was also a measure of area. A burgage plot one third of a chain in width and three chains in length would be one chain in area, that is one acre, 4,840 square yards. The original Ledbury plots were thus rather similar in size to those described in the foundation charter of Salford but three times as generous as those at Wotton-under-Edge and at Tetbury. However, belief in mathematical precision was not a marked mediaeval characteristic.

The calculation of the mediaeval burgage plot, its length and width, the degree of consolidation and fragmentation, may appear to the layman a rather arid academic exercise. Yet much of the interest and charm of Ledbury today comes from the combination of regularity and variety that arises from the pattern of development, established in the early twelfth century and maintained ever since. You have only to look along the east side of High Street. There you will see twenty buildings on plots of virtually the same width. Yet each frontage is quite different. There is a wide variety of building materials, such as timber, stone, plaster, brick, etc, and an equal variety of design.

In this Ledbury is much more fortunate than other ancient market towns where, by contrast, out of scale development of a bland uniformity, making no concessions to local building materials and traditions, has destroyed almost all sense of the past. One has only to look at the branches of two major national stores that have been built in the High Town of Hereford to see the nature of the problem. This Ledbury has so far avoided and this is why it is thronged with admiring visitors each summer. However, even if redevelopment does not present a threat, the promiscuous use of white paint does. The current trend for painting or rendering natural materials, particularly brick and stone, could yet do much to erase the charm and variety and with it the fundamental character of Ledbury's market place, established more than eight and a half centuries ago.

As it is only concerned to record the money and services due to the bishop, the *Red Book* tells us nothing directly about the buildings of the town in 1288. Each entry gives the name of the tenant, the type and size of his holding, and details of the rents. The first entry for High Street (Middletown), which is quite typical, reads: 'Juliana of the Cross for one burgage owes at the feast of St Andrew 3d; at the Annunciation 3d; at the feast of St John 3d; at the feast of St Michael 3d.'(28)

This shilling rent was the standard for boroughs of early foundation. As it was a chief rent, plots could be bought and sold freely. For example, William, son of Robert Joye, sold one burgage in Ledbury to John Gersant for 100 shillings of silver.(29) Yet the burgage rent remained constant at a shilling throughout the mediaeval period. Inflation was not a concept for which allowance was made.

The burgess paid rent for his land. He then constructed his own house on the plot though development was frequently taken in stages. In 1358, a grant by John le Seneger to Robert le Mulewarde refers to a burgage of land 'one quarter built and three quarters not built', extending from the highway to the bishop's field. Another grant in 1444-45 refers to a burgage *'non edificatum'* in the Homend.(30) The *Red Book* does not specify whether burgages are fully developed or not. However, as there are references to two curtilages (pieces of land or courtyards) in New Street and to a 'vacant place' and a 'croft' elsewhere, it is assumed that each plot had been built upon, although in the case of the larger holdings the entire frontage was not necessarily occupied.

What we know of houses on these sites depends on examples to be seen elsewhere, for only the vestiges of one mediaeval secular building can be found in the whole of Ledbury: part of the roof structure of the Chandos Cafe in Bye Street. These houses were of timber, in-filled with wattle and daub, but in no way as substantial or elaborate as the 16th and 17th century buildings which still abound.

Built at right angles to the road, most had a frontage of only one bay, for this was dictated by the width of the burgage plot. Indeed, many mediaeval town houses were 12 feet or less in width. On the other hand, they could extend back from the street as far as they wished. Shops were open to the street throughout the day with a tilted plank to provide display and trading space at the front. This feature can still be seen at the 15th-century Priory Cottages at Tewkesbury. In most cases the ground floor was a workshop rather than a store, for most craftsmen would manufacture their wares on the spot. In the more substantial premises, one room to the rear, the hall, would serve the whole household — family, servants and apprentices or journeymen. According to size, there would have been a room, or rooms above, reached by ladder.

The more spacious plots permitted houses parallel to the road. A splendid four-bay 14th century house of this type stood in Bye Street, the last of Ledbury's mediaeval secular buildings. Nicknamed the 'Bishop's Palace', no doubt from when the palace occupied the St Katherine's site, it later fell to the bottom of the social ladder, for it was too close to the noise and smells of the cattle market in the open road further down Bye Street. In the 19th century it was divided up into four 'cottages', one a Temperance Lodging House for men. Then, in the 1930s, three of the 'cottages' were demolished. The smoke-blackened 14th century roof of the Chandos Cafe in Bye Street is all that remains.

The description given by the inspector of the Royal Commission on Historical Monuments indicates the full nature of Ledbury's loss.(31) It consisted of a four-bay building of which the bay nearest the Lower Cross may perhaps have acted as the service wing and the adjoining bay, the screens passage. Next to it was the hall. This we know was a single-storey building open to the roof and with a great open fire, because the floor and chimney stack which were there when it was demolished were of late 16th or early 17th century date. Of the 14th century roof the inspectors were able to find only two trusses, the timbers which bridge the roof space at the end of each bay, but these were adequate to give a clear impression of the quality of the building. One of the original windows of the hall remained as well. It was of timber, unglazed, with five gothic ogee-headed lights with moulded uprights and small rosettes carved as decoration in the spaces above. For Ledbury in the 14th century, this represented life on a grand scale. It is a tragedy for the town that it should have been destroyed.

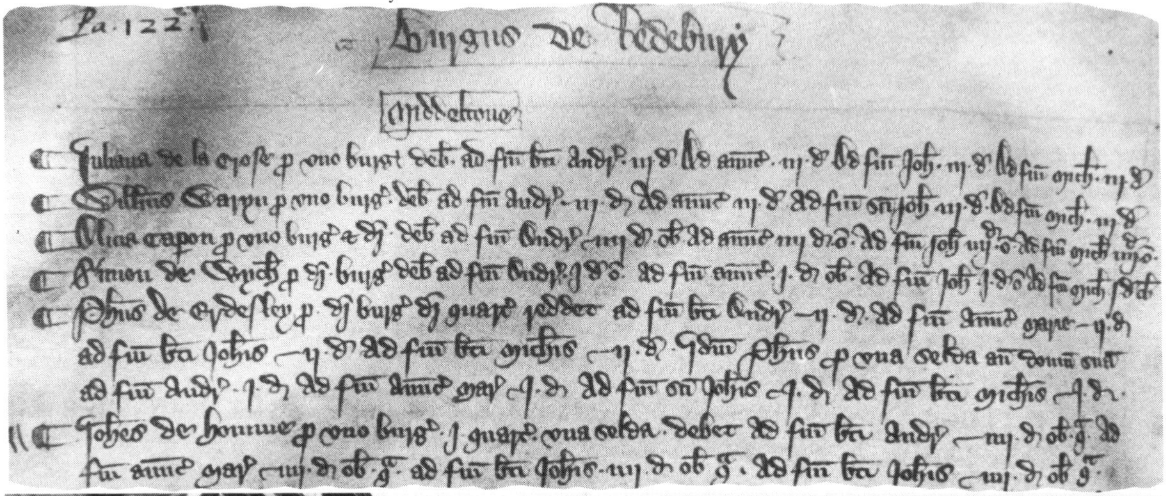
Pa. 122

Burgus de Ledebury

Middeltone

ABOVE: The *Red Book* of the Bishop of Hereford gives the name of each of his tenants in the borough of Ledbury in 1288, together with the type and size of his holding and details of the rents due. The first entry for Middletown (High Street) reads: *Juliana de la Crose p(ro) uno burg(agio) deb(et) ad f(estu)m b(ea)ti Andr(ee) iijd. Ad ann(u)c (iacionem) iijd. Ad F(estu)m Joh(annis) iijd. Ad F(estu)m mich(aelis) iijd.* BELOW: The amalgamation of burgage plots can be seen in the larger inns and banks.

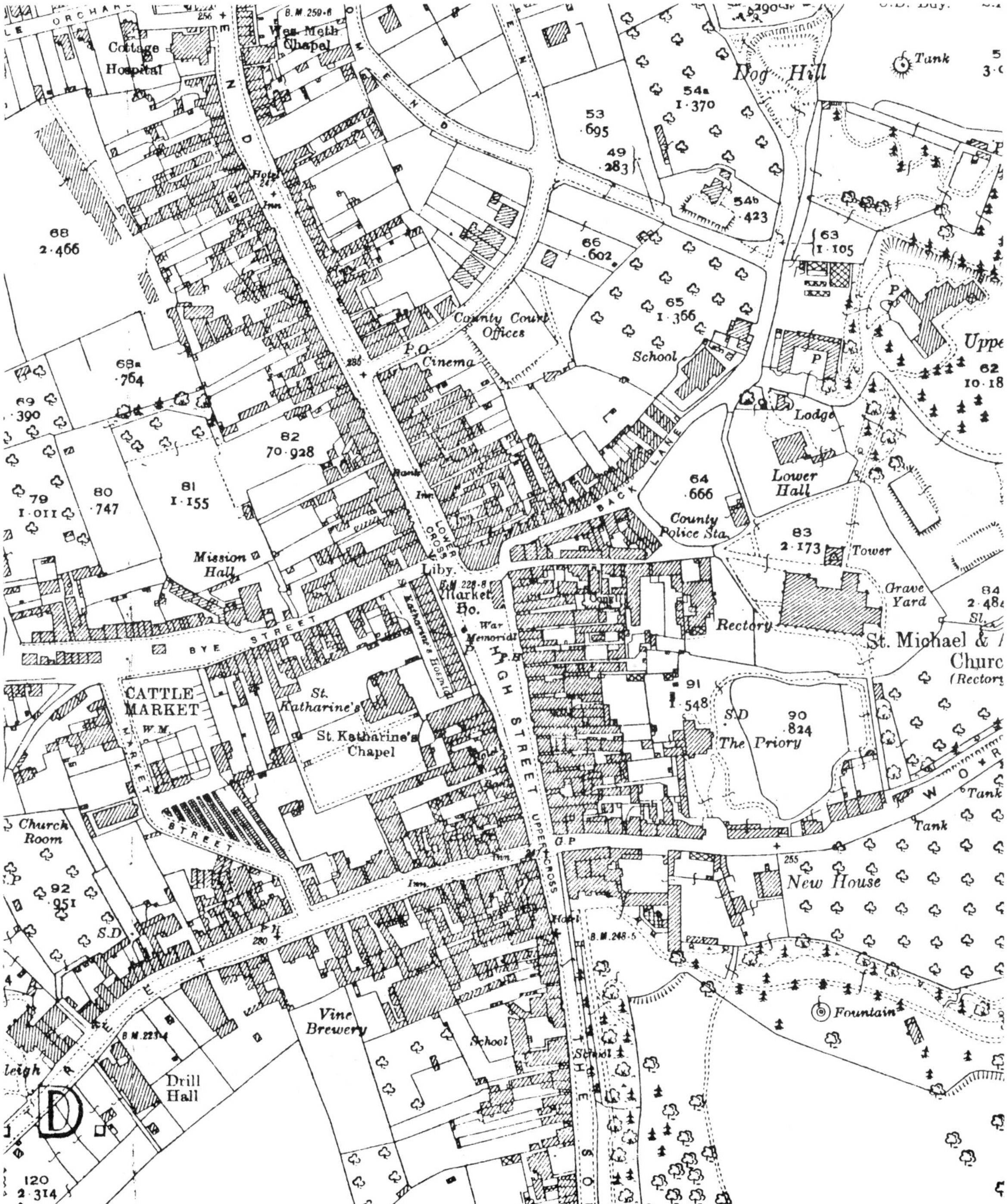

2nd ed 25 ins OS plan, Ledbury (1928). A certain regularity of layout is evident, especially on both sides of the Homend and the east side of High Street.

The width of the original burgage plots is difficult to calculate because outbuildings and gardens behind the houses and shops had to be served by alleyways. These are full of charm today.

Much of the interest and charm of Ledbury comes from the combination of regularity and variety that arises from the pattern established in the early 12th century.

INSET: 19th century population pressure subjected rear gardens or back sides of burgages to intensive development. ABOVE: 52-62 and BELOW: 43-65, the Homend. LEFT and BELOW: Painting or rendering natural materials could erase the charm and variety of the market place. RIGHT: More spacious plots permitted houses parallel to the road. This four-bay 14th-century house, nicknamed the Bishop's Palace, struck bad times. Divided up into four cottages, three were demolished in the 1930s.

People, Places & Occupations

The personal names and surnames of Ledbury borough and foreign, as given in the *Red Book,* add considerably to our knowledge of the town and district.(32)

The restricted range and character of the personal or first names may come as a surprise. Nine names were extremely popular and form a dominant group. They were borne by 90 per cent of the men in the borough and foreign. The range was even more restricted than this suggests, for 50 per cent of the men bore one of three personal names — William, Richard or John. William and John were soon to become joint favourites, a distinction which has continued to the 20th century. Among the women, three names stand out — Alice, Matilda and Juliana. These account for more than half the total.

Within the restricted group of nine male personal names, the Christian predominance that one would have anticipated within a community where the church and thus the font loomed so large, is not to be found. Only two — John, which was third in order of popularity, and Adam, which was ninth — can be described as Christian in character, for both are Hebrew in origin. All the seven others had come to England at the time of the Norman Conquest. They were Normanised forms of Teutonic names, with a decidedly martial flavour. No personal names of Anglo-Saxon or Celtic origin are to be found within the dominant group.

Table 1. Personal Names in Ledbury Borough and Foreign, 1288

	Male	*No*	*%**
1	William	42	17.5
2	Richard	39	16.25
3	John(1)	38	15.8
4	Robert	28	11.6
5	Roger	19	7.9
6	Walter	15	6.25
7	Galfridus (Geoffrey)	12	5.0
8	Gilbert	9	3.75
9	Adam(1)	8	3.3
10	Others	30*	12.5
		240*	100.0

	Female	*No*	*%**
1	Alice	10	22.7
2	Matilda	8	18.1
3	Juliana	6	13.6
4	Others	20*	45.4
		44*	100.0

*Approximate
(1)Names of Christian and Hebrew origin

This restricted group of nine personal names has given us some of the most popular surnames in use today. When a man was described as the son of his father, rather than add 'son', in many cases the transformation was achieved merely by the addition of the possessive 's' to give Williams, Richards, Johns, Roberts and so on.

It is quite wrong to regard the bearers of such names as being necessarily Welsh in origin. Indeed, an official list of the incidence and distribution of surnames, based on the 1851 census, showed that Williams was the third most common surname in England, with Roberts ninth and Johns tenth. Walters, Richards and Rogers were still particularly common as surnames in the West Midlands and the Marches of Wales.

The pagan Teutonic predominance was already under assault in Ledbury borough by the time that the *Red Book* was being compiled. Among the minority group — the townspeople who did not bear a personal name taken from the popular nine — a new and overwhelmingly Christian order is to be found.

Surnames fall into four main categories — relationship, occupation, locality and nicknames.(33) Surnames of relationship derived from first names, such as those already referred to — Williams, Roberts and Johns. This was a development which was only just beginning in Ledbury borough in 1288. In High Street, Agnes Philip held half a burgage, while in the Homend, Juliana Philippes, who held a full burgage, is the only person to have a surname carrying the possessive 's'. Other patronymics include *Willelmus* and *Ricardus Budde,* who both carry their father's Old English personal name, and *Willelmus* and *Johannes Waryn,* possibly the two sons of *Warinus le Chaloner* in New Street. This form developed later into Waring. *Johannes Colitt* bore a particularly interesting name, a double diminutive derived from Nicholas, while one man bore a metronymic, *Willelmus filius Mabille.* Metronymics appear always to be written in full. *Alicia* and *Christina filia Pistoris* held half a burgage in the Homend next to their father, *Johannes Pistor.* In the same street was *Matilda filia Tibbe.* The surname most calculated to surprise us was borne by *Ricardus filius Capellani.* One of the most lowly in the ecclesiastical hierarchy, the chaplain was the hired assistant who looked after the cure of souls. He served his vicar or rector, in his absence celebrating mass, hearing confessions and administering the last rites. Here was one whose son bore his name as a constant reminder to the townsfolk of his father's failure to observe the celibacy required of the clergy.

The occupation or status of a person, or of his forebears, was often used as a ready means of distinguishing him or her from those with similar personal names, an important consideration where the range of first names was so restricted. These occupational surnames were rendered in Latin, French (in which case they are prefaced with *le* or *la)* or Middle English. On occasions there is a not altogether unexpectedly strange mixture of languages. Thus *Robertus Tharcener* derived his surname from the combination of 'the' not *le,* with the French term *harcener,* saddler. *Johannes le Webbe* combines all three languages, Latin, French and Middle English in that order, *Webbe* meaning weaver. Already the *le* or *la* is coming to be dropped. In the Homend, for example, we find *Robertus le Tynkere* and *Robertus Tynkere, Adam Webbe* and *Adam le Webbe.* Elsewhere there were *Walterius le Gerlaundor* and *Ricardus Gerland.* All show that the process of surname formation was at a crucial stage.

These surnames indicate six main occupational groups — textiles, leather trades, metal workers, woodworkers, food trades and clerical.

In this respect Ledbury is quite typical, for these were the trades that dominated the economy of the mediaeval town. In the larger urban centres, not only would the range be wider, the degree of specialisation would be greater. All towns drew in raw materials from the countryside they served and to a lesser extent from further afield. These they processed to provide clothes, specialised building materials, food, drink and luxury goods. In the latter category, at Ledbury, the needs of the horse stood high. The saddler, the spurrier and the farrier all served the affluent, for the plough team was dependent on the ox, while the horse was the animal of swift passage and of the gentlemanly pursuits of war and sport. The two garlanders, makers of circlets or chaplets of gold and silver, served a restricted luxury market.

Geoffrey the goldsmith, with a *selda* in the Shop Row and a house on a half burgage plot in the more salubrious Southend facing the bishop's palace and park, served a similar clientele. To his shop in the market place would have come the sons of the knightly class and the more affluent farmers of the district. In many cases it might have been their parents, for, according to both civil and canon law, espousal, the plighting of troths could take place at the end of infancy, at seven years of age. Matrimony could be contracted when the 'woman' was twelve and the 'man' was fourteen.(34)

However, Geoffrey's trade in wedding, as opposed to engagement rings had carefully prescribed seasons for during the middle ages

'Advent marriage doth thee deny,
But Hilary gives thee liberty.
Septuagesima says thee nay,
Eight days from Easter says you may.
Rogation bids thee to contain
But Trinity sets thee free again.'(35)

Table 2. Occupation names in Mediaeval Ledbury

Textiles		*Metalworkers*		*Leather Trades*	
le taylur	tailor	*aurifaber*	goldsmith	*pelliparius*	skinner or
cissor (2)	tailor	*la coteler*	cutleress	*skinnare*	pelterer
le parmynter	tailor	*plumber*	plumber	*tharcener*	saddler
schereman	tailor	*lorimer*	spurrier	*glovere*	glover
le ffolur (2)	fuller	*marescall*	farrier, shoeing smith		
textor	weaver				
le webbe	weaver				
le chaloner	blanket maker	*le tynkere*	mender of kettles, metal pots, etc	*Wood Workers*	
capron	hood maker			*carpentarius*	carpenter
tredegold	embroiderer			*rotarius*	wheelwright
le mercer	dealer in textile fabrics, etc			*wheolire*	wheelwright
				le cupere	cooper
Clerical		*Food Trades*		*Miscellaneous*	
capellanus	chaplain	*pistor*	baker	*le croupere*	potter
clericus	cleric	*le polter*	poulterer	*le ffauconer*	falconer
deaconus	deacon	*le saltere*	maker or seller of salt	*le leche*	physician
vicarius	vicar	*molendinarius*	miller	*telemon*	tiler
		muleward	miller	*le tilere*	tiler

A small group of Ledbury surnames refers not to occupation, but to an office. *Thomas Ballivus, Galfridus Praepositus* and *Richardus Camerarius* all bear such names. While bailiff, provost or reeve and chamberlain may well describe the offices held by them or their forebears, other names present difficulties. What is one to make of *Cecilia Kyng, Walterus Legat, Willelmus Shirreve* and *Willelmus Chastelayn* in the borough; *Philippus Kyng, Ricardus le Bisshop* and *Robertus* and *Willelmus Bisshop* in the manor foreign? There are at least three possible explanations: that they refer to office held under the authority of such august personages, patrons whose badges they may well have had to wear; that they are nicknames, or that they are pageant names. Do we have evidence here of a procession with pageants in mediaeval Ledbury such as, if on a much grander scale, took place on the feast of Corpus Christi in Hereford? Within the borough there were a number of other people who bore nicknames as surnames — *Ricardus* and *Margaret Baset* (short, small, perhaps even dwarf), *Rogerus Rouheved* (rough-head), *Ricardus le Hog, Ricardus Partrich, Ricardus Prat* (astute), *Willelmus Scharp, Johannes Wrey* (nook, corner, remote or isolated place). It should be remembered that nicknames frequently come from opposites; *Ricardus Baset* may in fact have been very tall, and the more offensive forms, such as *le Hog,* were frequently used endearingly as marks of affection.

It is difficult to say when such surnames became hereditary. Although hereditary surnames were fairly frequent at the time of the *Red Book* among the middle and lower classes in the towns, non-hereditary and hereditary names did exist side by side. Certainly among the tenants of the Butchers Row there are occupation names indicating quite different trades. Even if these surnames have in some cases become hereditary, handed down from father or grandfather, we still have a fair indication of the economy of Ledbury at the end of the 13th century — the striking preponderance of craftsmen and traders in textiles, metal, leather and wood, together with victuallers.

The local or place surnames form the largest of the four categories. The place of origin, either of the owner or of his forebears, was usually preceded by the French preposition *de,* occasionally by its English form *atte* or *ate. Willelmus de Hereford* held two burgages in Bye Street and *Nicholaus ate Rugge* held one and a half burgages in High Street. As with occupation surnames, so with local surnames, already the *de* is coming to be dropped.

Some local names refer to humble topographical features, others to towns, villages and settlements. These are particularly valuable as they give some indication of the origins of Ledbury's population, for all but the largest English mediaeval towns drew their population from close at hand. It is possible that the hereditary factor is stronger among the local than the occupation names. The family's place of origin, once it became incorporated in a surname, was not as liable to change as that of an occupation.

The growth of hereditary surnames does not at this stage throw into serious doubt their value in establishing origins, especially since, from its foundation in the early 1120s, Ledbury's population continued to grow. The town recruited, not only for growth, but also, given the high urban death rate, for replacement of population. *Galfridus le Newecomene* bore a name which, fortunately for us, was not taken by the generations of other newcomers who came to seek their fortune, however modest their expectations, in their local market town of Ledbury. If they had taken such a name we should have lost most of the evidence of immigration.

Nevertheless, the interpretation of place surnames is fraught with difficulty. While many places can be identified with a degree of certainty, with others it is not so easy. Is *Willelmus de Ledene's* surname taken from Upleadon in Bosbury parish, Leadon Court in Bishops Frome, or even Upleadon further south in Gloucestershire, at the junction of the Leadon and the Glynch brook? Did *Simon de Wich,* or his forebears, come from the Wyche above Colwall on the Malverns, or the great salt centre of Droitwich? What of *Philippus de la Berwe* and *Johannes de Berwe?* Can we assume that *Berwe* refers to Bromsberrow, or to Berrow near Birtsmorton, in Worcestershire? Did *Matilda* and *Rogerus Clenge,* who lived next door to each other in the Southend, originate from Clenchers Mill or from some other place on the Glynch brook, which was still referred to in a Gloucester Abbey charter of the 13th century as *Clenche?* What of *Robertus de la Grave* and *Rogerus* and *Juliana de Hope?* Can we assume that the surnames are derived from Groves End and from Hope End, which in the early 19th century became the childhood home of Elizabeth Barrett Browning? With others, such as *de Bosco, de la Hulle* and *de la Hurste,* we have no chance. In drawing up a distribution map and table of local surnames, given alternative localities within the immediate neighbourhood, that which is closest has been accepted for inclusion. Some clear conclusions can be drawn from such a map and table.

Ledbury borough drew its population overwhelmingly from an area within a seven and a half mile radius — that is the area which it served through its craftsmen and traders, its weekly markets and annual fairs. It is virtually the same area as the *parochia* of the pre-Conquest minster and the Domesday hundred of Wygmundstree. Despite the ambiguities, the majority of the names can be easily recognised on the 1:50,000 Ordnance Survey map today, eg: Catley, the Frith, Groves End, the Hazle, Hope End, the Knapp, Lilly Hall, Massington, Plaistow and Underdown.

Only seven of the surnames refer to places outside the county and only ten indicate an origin beyond that seven and a half mile radius that Ledbury served. The majority came from within three miles of the Lower Cross. All those places outside the seven and a half mile radius, except Abinghall, Deerfold, Martley and Melksham, are trading centres immediately beyond Ledbury's own district — Hereford, Ross, Weobley, Eardisley, Malvern and Worcester. Only Bromyard and Leominster are major omissions.

Table 3. Local or place surnames in Ledbury Borough, 1288

Within 3 miles	*3-7½ miles*	*Over 7½ miles within Herefordshire*	*Outside County*	*Neighbouring Trading Centres*
Clench	Bromsberrow	Deerfold	*Gloucestershire*	Eardisley
Eastnor	Catley	Eardisley	Abinghall	Hereford
Frith	Cradley	Hereford	Preston	Malvern
Groves End	(Up)leadon	Ross	Bromsberrow	Ross
Hazle	Marcle	Weobley		Weobley
Hope End	Mathon		*Worcestershire*	Worcester
Knapp	Wych		Malvern	
Lilly Hall			Martley	
Massington			Worcester	
Petty France				
Plaistow			*Wiltshire*	
Preston			Melksham	
Underdown				
Wall Hills				
Wellington				
Woolpit				

Some of these surnames represent recent arrivals, already established in trade, from the nearby market and county towns, for a number were men of substance. *Nicholaus de Wygornia* (Worcester) had, except for St Katherine's hospital, the largest holding in the town. He held one burgage in the market place, three in Bye Street and two stalls in the Shop Row. *Philippus de Erdesley* was not quite so high in the urban hierarchy but his holding was nonetheless impressive. We know that he was no absentee, that he lived in a house on a one burgage plot in High Street, for we are told that he paid rent for ⅛ of a stall *ante domum suam,* in front of his house. In addition he held another burgage in Bye Street and he had two further stalls or shops, possibly in the same street. *Willelmus de Hereford* and *Willelmus de Melksham* both held two burgages.

The *de Birminghams,* father and son, who between them held four tenancies in the Homend amounting to a total of two and ⅞ burgages, at first appear to have belonged to this small group of affluent outsiders but this is not so. They were representatives of a cadet branch of the *de Birmingham*s who held land by knight service from one of the great noble families of the localities, the *de Grandisons* of Stretton and Ashperton. There they had a mansion for which, three years before the Ledbury section of the *Red Book* was compiled, they had obtained a licence from Edward I to crenellate and convert into a castle.

De Birmingham was not the only knightly name to appear in the list of the burgage holders. There were two *Esegars, Alicia* and *Roger,* and a *Gersant.* Both of these families figure prominently in the list of witnesses to gifts of lands to St Katherine's hospital in its early years, lists which include the *Alkrugges* or *Alchurges,* who had held land of the bishop by knight service for more than 120 years, and the *Pauncefots* and *Walintones* who had held lands by knight service at the Hazle and Wellington respectively, some 150 years earlier. These notable local families were the peers of the Gersants and the Esegars. A William Esegar was to be one of Ledbury's representatives in Edward I's 1305 Parliament. *Matilda de ffurches,* who held burgages in the Southend and New Street, was of the same family as *Robert de ffurches,* the bishop's bailiff who was responsible for drawing up the *Red Book* survey for Ledbury. Surnames, therefore, indicate a broad social mixture in the borough, with a number of its members drawn from local knightly families. The links between town and country were intimate in a social as well as an economic context.

Although the great majority of its burgesses were drawn from that district which it had already served for some five centuries, a small number came from further afield. This was not a one-way traffic. In the 13th and 14th centuries references can be found to Ledburians living, working and misbehaving far beyond its immediate district. In 1244 *Nicholas de Ledbury* was a canon of Llandaff cathedral. In 1283 *William de Ledbury* was prior of Great Malvern. In 1292 *Roland de Erle* received a Royal commission to deliver the gaol of Oxford castle of *John de Ledbury* and in the same year *John le Taylur* of Ledbury escaped from Worcester gaol with four other malefactors, 'which men the sheriff of Worcester beheaded in pursuing them'. One wonders whether this was the *Johannes le Cissor* listed in the *Red Book* as tenant of a one burgage plot in New Street.

Among the list of London citizens of 1311, we find *Robert de Ledbury, pessoner,* that is fishmonger. Fourteen years later we find him, or possibly his son, arraigned before the courts for 'besieging *Henry de Polynton* in the house of *Robert de Gumby* in Flete Strete, breaking the house, assaulting him and carrying away his goods'.(36) In 1316, nine years after he served as one of the members of the Commons for Ledbury, *William Esegar* of Ledbury, merchant, was exchanging lands in Northleach, Gloucestershire, for a house and land at *la Hulle* in Ledbury foreign. The other party to the exchange is described as 'of Northleach', yet bore the local name of *John de la Hasele.*(37) Ledbury men served even further afield for in 1324 a *Ralph de Ledebury* was 'going to Gascony in the King's service'.(38)

All these men, once they had left the town, were distinguished as *de Ledebury,* which, as the 14th century passes, slowly becomes Ledbury in the records. They left behind their nicknames, their local or occupation names. The only exception was *John de la Hasele,* but the Hazle was itself an exceptional place — 'unjustly held by Harold' at the time of the Conquest, it had always been a home of one of the knightly families of the district. Clearly, a *de la Hasle* could look a *de Ledebury* in the eye.

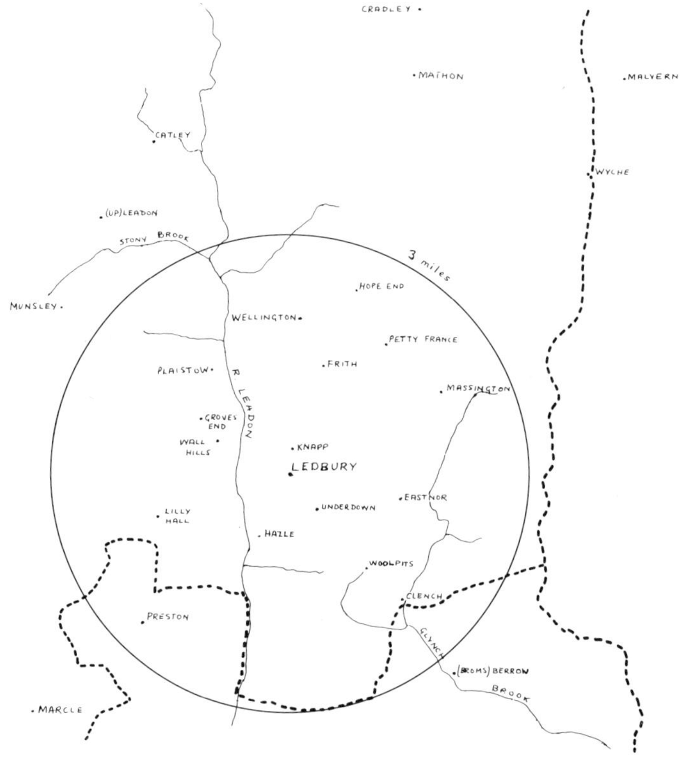

(Map A) The sketch map shows the three mile radius of place names around Ledbury.

GENTRY.

Brydges Mrs. Mary, (F.)
Biddulph Michael, Efq. (F.)
Hammond Mrs. Sufannah, (F.)
Higgins Mrs. Ann
Hill Mr. James
Hill Mr. Richard, (F.)
Jarvis Mrs. Ann, (F.)
Pewtrefs Mrs. Ann, (F.)
Reece Mrs. Elizabeth
Rodway Mr. George, (F.)
Skipp John, Efq. (F.)
Williams Mr. John, (F.)
Whitcome Mifs Frances

CLERGY.

Birt Rev. James, *Canon of Hereford, and Mafter of Ledbury Hofpital*
Powles Rev. Michael, (F.) *Juftice of the Peace*
Rogers Rev. Rowland, *Curate*

PHYSIC.

Grinnell Richard, *Druggift*
Hill Thomas, (F.) *Surgeon, Apothecary, and Man-midwife*
Jarvis Jofeph, (F.) *Surgeon, Apothecary, and Man-midwife*
Woodward George, (F.) *Apothecary*
Woodyatt George, (F.) *Surgeon, Apothecary, and Man-midwife*

LAW.

Holbrook William, *Attorney*
Nott Thomas, *Attorney*
Reece William, *Attorney*
Rickards Samuel, *Attorney*
Seward William, (F.) *Attorney*

TRADERS, &c.

Amey Rd. *Victualler, (Royal Oak)*
Andrews Jofeph, *Houfe-carpenter*
Bowkett Benj. *Shoemaker*
Bowkett Jofeph, *Shoemaker*
Burgefs Thomas, (F.) *Hatmaker*
Boulter John, *Baker*
Baylis P. *Peruke-maker & Hair-dreffer*
Baylis Thomas, (F.) *Maltfter, Baker, and Farmer*
Baylis Thomas, *Tanner and Hatmaker*
Baylis William, *Baker*
Baylis Stephen, *Currier*
Bennett Ann, *Milliner*
Bennett George, (F.) *Cider-merchant*
Bennett John, *Mafter of the Grammar School*

Bennett

Bennett Richard, *Tanner*
Brown Jof. *Watch and Clock Maker*
Brown John, *Victualler, (Talbot)*
Bofley John, *Hair-dreffer & Victualler*
Bofley Richard, *Brightfmith*
Bellers William, (F.) *Maltfter*
Bibbs Benjamin, (F.) *Butcher*
Bibbs John, (F.) *Shoemaker*
Beddoe Ann and Eliz. *Milliners*
Beddoe John, (F.) *Mercer*
Butt James, *Bafket-maker & Shopkeeper*
Bond John, *Collar-maker*
Bowler John, *Shoemaker*
Barnes John, (F.) *Houfe-carpenter and Farmer*
Bufley Mary, *Shopkeeper*
Barrett John, *Flax-dreffer*
Bofworth Thomas, *Baker*
Bofworth Mary, *Milliner*
Crump William, (F.) *Cabinet-maker*
Creece William, *Staymaker*
Cotton Thomas, *Currier*
Cotton Thomas, *Ironmonger*
Cotton Eleanor, *Shopkeeper*
Carwardine William, *Shopkeeper*
Cooper James, (F.) *Ironmonger*
Cooper Samuel, *Tanner*
Cooper John, *Currier*
Cooper Edw. (F.) *Baker and Farmer*
Crifp John, (F.) *Baker*
Cale Martha, *Butcher*
Cale John, *Butcher*
Cale John, (F.) *Butcher*
Cox Edward, *Shoemaker*
Chandler John, *Tallow-chandler*
Dance Mary, *Innkeeper, (New Inn)*
Drew John, (F.) *Cider-merchant*
Denton William, (F.) *Butcher*
Edy Ann, *Milliner*
Edy Thomas, (F.) *Maltfter & Grocer*
Evans Rich. *Victualler (Seven Stars)*
Evans Samuel, *Taylor*
Fox James, *Breeches-maker*
Fifield Edward, (F.) *Maltfter and Cider-merchant*
Greenaway Wm. *Victualler, (Unicorn)*
Grundy Thomas, *Mafon*
Grundy John, *Cider-merchant*
Glover Wm. *Clock and Watch Maker*
Griffiths James, *Collar-maker*
Gregg Jas. (F.) *Mafon & Stone-cutter*
Gurney John, (F.) *Houfe-carpenter*
Hill John, *Shoemaker*
Hill Charles, *Victualler, (Bell)*
Hill John, *Baker*
Hill Charles, *Collar-maker*
Hill Mary, *Shopkeeper*
Hooper Wm. *Joiner and Victualler*
Smith Jofeph, *Victualler, (Fox)*
Smith Henry, *Victualler*
Simmons Richard, (F.) *Gardener*
Stephens Ann, *Schoolmiftrefs*
Thomas William, *Innkeeper, (George)*
Tully John, (F.) *Hop-merchant*
Tomlins John, (F.) *Shoemaker*
Tandy William, *Victualler, (Harrow)*
White Giles, *Shoemaker*
Webb Richard, *Butcher*
Hooper Ann, (F.) *Shopkeeper*
Hooper Levi, (F.) *Shopkeeper*
Heath John, *Cooper*
Hodges William, *Butcher*
Hutchens John, *Breeches-maker*
Hatton John, *Peruke-maker*
Hope Thomas, *Taylor*
Juckes William, *Houfe-carpenter*
Jenkins George, (F.) *Staymaker and Shopkeeper*
Jones Richard, *Houfe-carpenter and Victualler, (Lion)*
Johnfon Mary, *Ironmonger, &c.*
Johnfon Abfalom, *Shoemaker*
Kings William, *Wheelwright*
Kirk Benj. *Taylor and Shopkeeper*
Lucy Edw. *Grocer & Tallow-chandler*
Lane Thomas, *Mercer*
Lowe William, (F.) *Brickmaker*
Loton Francis, *Grocer*
Mafon Nathaniel, *Stone-cutter*
Morton William, *Victualler*
Morris Luke, *Innkeeper, (Feathers,) Poft and Excife Office*
Morris William, (F.) *Shopkeeper and Victualler, (Plough,)*
Maddox Richard, (F.) *Blackfmith and Victualler*
Mutlow James, *Cooper*
Mutlow Wm. (F.) *Banker & Tanner*
Milton John, *Peruke-maker and Shopkeeper*
Merrick Simon, *Sadler & Collar-maker*
Mathews John, (F.) *Ironmonger*
Mathews Francis, *Gardener*
Millard Elizabeth, *Victualler*
Mafon Jofeph, (F.) *Mafon*
Nott Jofeph, (F.) *Plumber & Glazier*
Nafh Jas. (F.) *Patten and Heel Maker*
Nicholas John, *Glazier*
Pynock Rich. *Grocer and Linen-draper*
Paine William, *Houfe-carpenter and Victualler, (Horfefhoe)*
Pool Thomas, *Butcher*
Phillips Richard, *Blackfmith*
Pearce Richard, *Peruke-maker*
Powell William, *Staymaker*
Price John, (F.) *Shoemaker*
Raynolds Job, *Blackfmith*
Rofton Edward King, *Mercer*
Ruffell Wm. (F.) *Patten & Heel Maker*
Ruffell Thomas, *Wheelwright*
Slade Tim. *Houfe-carpenter and Joiner*
Slade John, *Houfe-carpenter and Joiner*
Smallridge Thomas, *Cider-merchant*
Spencer Tim. *Taylor and Shopkeeper*
Scott Gilbert, *Grocer, Tallow-chandler, and Soap-boiler*
Webb John, (F.) *Butcher*
Webb Benjamin, (F.) *Skinner and Cider-merchant*
Webb George, (F.) *Tallow-chandler*
Woodyatt George, (F.) *Maltfter*
Woodyatt William, *Cider-merchant*
Wood Jofeph, (F.) *Shoemaker*
White John, *Taylor*
Watts John, *Sackmaker, and Mafter of the Houfe of Induftry*

Ledbury trades, 1793-98: *The Universal British Directory.*

LEDBURY, HEREFORDSHIRE.

Market Day, Tuesday.

BAYLIS, Stephen, *Tanner*
Bellers, William, *Corn-dealer and Cheese-factor*
Binnett, George, *Corn-dealer and Cheese-factor*
Chandler, John, *Grocer, Tallow-chandler, and Soap-boiler*
Church, Antipas, *Attorney*
Coldwell, William, *Leather-dresser*
Cooper, James, *Ironmonger and Tanner*
Crisp, John, *Corn-dealer and Cheese-factor*
Denton, Benjamin, *Grocer, Tallow-chandler, and Soap-boiler*
Drew, John, *Cyder Merchant*
Edy, Thomas, *Grocer and Maltster*
Fifield, Edward, *Grocer, Cyder and Hop Merchant*
Hankins, Sarah and Richard, *Linen, Woollen-drapers, & Mercers*
Hartland, John, *Tanner*
Hartland, Benjamin, *Tallow chandler and Soap-boiler*
Hill, John, *Corn-dealer and Cheese-factor*
Hope, Thomas, *Grocer, Tallow-chandler, and Soap-boiler*
Holbrooke, William, *Attorney*
Hunter, Thomas, *Linen, Woollen-draper, and Mercer*
Lucy, Charles, *Timber Merchant*
Lucy, Edward, *Grocer, Tallow-chandler, and Soap-boiler*
Matthews, John, *Ironmonger*
Morris, Luke, *Innholder*, Plume of Feathers
Mutlow, William, *Cooper and Timber Merchant*
Mutlow, William, jun. *Timber Merchant and Tanner*
Nott, Thomas, *Attorney*
Philpotts, John, *Corn-dealer and Cheese-factor*
Pynock, Richard, *Grocer and Haberdasher*
Rickards, Samuel, *Attorney*
Tully, John, *Brazier, Tinman, and Hop Merchant*
Wellings, Edward, *Linen, Woollen-draper, and Mercer*
Woodyatt, William, *Cooper and Cyder Merchant*
Woodyatt, George, *Grocer and Maltster*

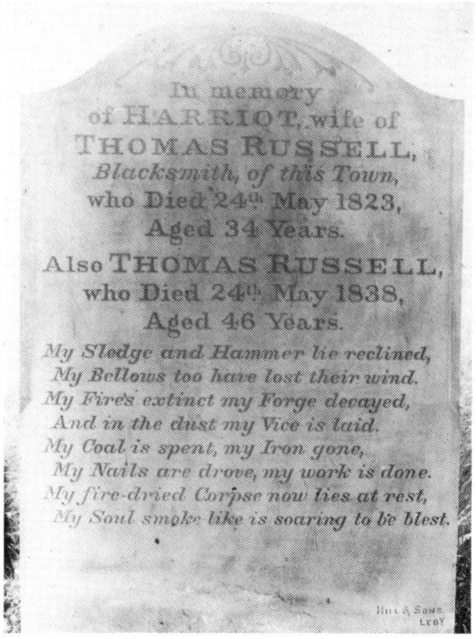

LEFT ABOVE: Ledbury trades, 1783: Bailey's *Western and Midland Directory*. BELOW William Hampton, 'Family boot and shoe maker', was established in the Southend in 1876 and still there in 1902, 'sole agent for the waterproof "K" boot'. (HCRO AB48/B10) RIGHT ABOVE: At the sign of the Iron Kettle, High Street. (HCL/WMC/566) CENTRE: At the sign of the Plume of Feathers, High Street, and BELOW: 'The carved heads in the church looked down/On Russel, Blacksmith of the Town'. John Masefield, *The Everlasting Mercy*. (HCL/WMC/577)

ABOVE: The motor trade in the '30s. (HCL/WMC/573) LEFT: William Madders, Grocers, established in the Homend by 1890. The building retains the sign 'Madders, Bacon Curer, Corn Flour and Meal Stores' today. RIGHT: Projecting iron sign holder brought into the age of the internal combustion engine.

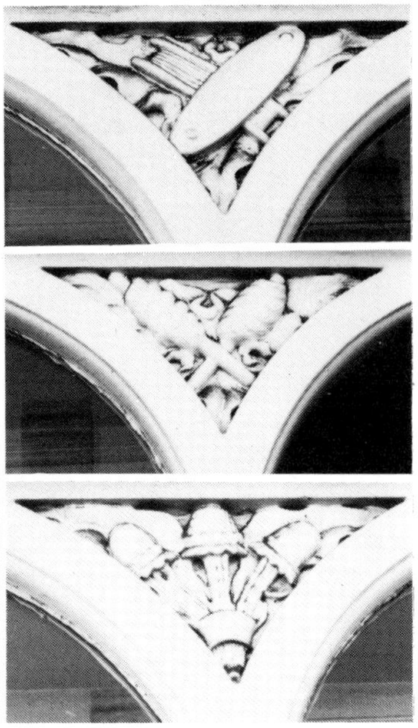

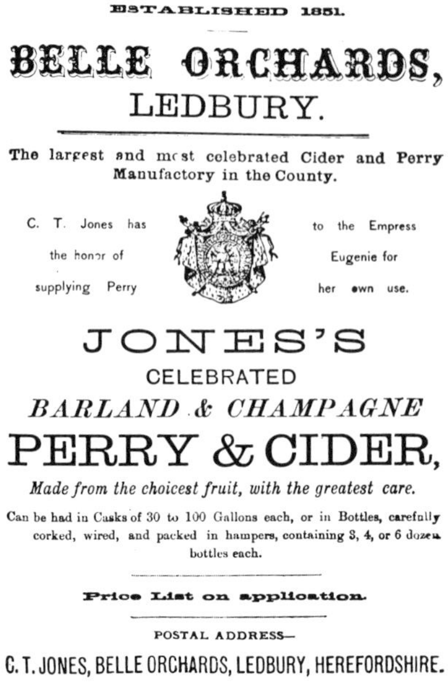

ABOVE LEFT & CENTRE: The Homend, spandrels of the charming turn-of-the-century shop-front, embellished with the signs of country crafts. RIGHT: Advertisement for 'Jones's Celebrated Barland and Champagne Perry and Cider', as drunk by the last Empress of the French. BELOW: The Tannery at the corner of the Homend and Bye Street used the water from the stream which flowed down from the Upper Hall. This building, apparently built 1600, gave way to the Barrett Browning Memorial Institute in 1895. (HCM)

The Red Book, 1288

If an impression has been formed of the original building plots, the burgages, and the houses and shops found on them prior to the great rebuilding of the town in the late 16th and early 17th centuries, what of the general layout of the town in 1288 and how far should we recognise it today? The answer is quite surprising.

The topography of Ledbury in 1288 can be pieced together by analysing the *Red Book* entries, observing closely the existing layout of the town and relating what is found to the series of town plans available from the late 18th century. These include J. Lydiard's *Plan of Ledbury* of 1788, the Enclosure map of 1816, the Tithe map of 1841, the plans in the *Ledbury Guides* of 1824 and 1831, and the 25 ins OS plans of 1887, 1928 and 1966. The 1788, 1824 and 1831 plans are of particular value even though they have serious shortcomings cartographically.

Each entry in the *Red Book* represents one tenancy, usually a burgage holding, but there are other holdings such as booths, shambles, crofts, curtilages, etc. The scribe listed 215 of these tenancies under five street headings. He then went on to list 67 more tenancies, of which half were not burgages but *selda* or booths, but he placed no street name at the head of this last list. These, it will be seen, were located in various streets.

Table 4. Tenancies in Ledbury by streets, 1288

	Tenancies		
	Total(1)	*Burgage*	*Other Holdings*
le Southende	20	20	———
Newestrete	35	34	+ 1 (2 curtilages)
Middeltoune	26	26	includes 4 booths(2)
le Homende	78	78	includes 1 croft
Bysshopestrete	56	56	———
	215		
Unassigned	67	33	includes: 23 booths(2) 14 butchers' booths 5 shambles 2 places 1 oven 1 dyke
Total	282	247	

(1) 'Burgage Tenancies' + 'Other Holdings' do not necessarily = 'Total' because of multiple ownership
(2) Booths or stalls = *selda*

Let us follow the scribe on his journey around Ledbury and identify the particular character of the streets he names and see how far they retain that character today.

le Southende. The survey begins in the Southend where 20 tenants are named. All would have lived on the west side of the street, for the bishop's palace and park lay on the eastern side. Nowadays, it is guarded by a tall brick wall. In 1288 it would have been protected by a timber pale. The original pattern of the burgage plots cannot be clearly distinguished on the 1887 25 ins OS plan. The Enclosure map shows that even in 1816 the built-up area extended only a third of the distance to Mabels Furlong Lane. It would seem that development of the Southend came to a halt at the end of the 13th century and that, if it did not contract, at least it remained static until after 1816. The extent of subsequent 19th century development is clearly indicated by the 1887 25 ins OS plan.

Newestrete. The name clearly indicates later development. This is corroborated by topographical evidence. New Street has a narrow neck and only opens out by the Talbot after a distance of some 200 feet, that is twelve perches or three chains — the length of the burgage plots of the adjacent sections of High Street and the Southend. Even today, 21 High Street, Hobbs the ironmongers, extends for four bays down New Street and 3-15 New Street appear to have been squeezed into what must have been the rear garden of its original burgage plot. The street was called new in the *Red Book* but it must have been laid out with burgage plots before 1232, for one of the three burgages given by bishop Hugh Foliot to St Katherine's hospital in that year was described as being *in novo vico* — in the new street, a name which it has retained for 750 years.

As the principal crossroads is today at the Upper Cross, it may seem strange that New Street was the last of the mediaeval streets to be developed. But Ledbury grew up at the meeting point of two important routes at the Lower, not the Upper Cross. In the middle ages New Street was out on a limb.

The 1816 Enclosure map shows uneven development, with a particular emphasis on the north side. A similar impression is gained from the 1824 plan. Certainly, the 35 tenants would have been quite easily accommodated in that wide stretch of the street which now ends by Hopkins' Garage. The straightness of this stretch of road supports the suggestion that this was planned mediaeval development.

Middeltoune, the Stalls, the Butchers Row and the Shop Row. Although the name Middletown has now totally disappeared, its place in the survey, between the Southend and the Homend, as well as the name itself, make it quite clear that this is now High Street. The earliest reference to the new name, High Street, is in a grant of 1461 which gives the Latin form, *alto vico.*(39)

Even though Ledbury quickly outgrew its original wedge-shaped market, Middletown retained its position as the chief market of the borough. At the entry to the Homend would have stood the market cross, and possibly at the entry to the Southend another, the upper cross. These were the physical expression of the peace of the market place which Robert de Bethune sought to strengthen when he persuaded Stephen to grant the Royal peace to all who travelled to or from Ledbury market. From these crosses some Ledbury families took their names. The first in the list of tenants for Middletown is *Juliana de la Crose* and the fifteenth is *Agatha de Cruce.*

There were only 26 tenants in High Street. Even today, it only bears postal numbers to 27. The number of tenancies was low because the bishop's palace occupied the greater part of the western side of the market place until 1232 when St Katherine's was founded. The 1887 25 ins OS plan clearly shows that the site was almost square in shape. Part of the Feathers and the buildings to the right represent later encroachment onto the original frontage.

The demand for properties would always have been high in this central market area, especially in the century or so of vigorous expansion between c1150 and 1288. Yet the supply was abnormally constrained by St Katherine's. The result was threefold: firstly, there was a much higher degree of fragmentation of plots in Middletown than in the other streets; secondly, it was not long before additional market facilities had to be found, in Bye Street; finally, it led to more rapid encroachment of buildings on the market place itself.

On market days and fair days Middletown would have been filled with stalls and animals. Originally these stalls would have been erected for the day and taken down, under the close supervision of the bishop's bailiff, at the end of the day. Due to a combination of neglect and slowly-established custom, they gradually became both substantial and permanent structures — first booths and then a row of buildings running down the centre of the street. The process is well described by John Stow in his *Survey of London,* 1598. 'In old Fish Street,' he tells us, 'the houses, now possessed by fishmongers, were at the first but moveable boards (or stalls), set out on market days, to show their fish to be sold; but procuring licence to set up sheds, they grow to shops, and by little and little to tall houses, of three or four stories in height, and now are called Fish Street'.(40) This market encroachment, as it is called, is still an outstanding feature of some of our market towns. At Ludlow, for example, the whole of the built-up area between the entrance to the castle, Castle Square, and the Tolsey and the Bull Ring is market encroachment.

The *Red Book* shows the process at work in Middletown. By 1288, even though they were still described by the old term, *seldae,* the temporary stalls and booths were giving way to permanent structures. Within a century, official terminology had caught up with the change and they were called *schopa,* shops.

Only three of the tenants in Middletown were described as booth-holders. These were *Philippus de Erdesley,* who payed 1d each quarter day for a *selda* 'in front of his house', *John de Homme,* who had one quarter (sic) of a *selda,* and his immediate neighbour, *Nicholaus de Wygornia,* who held one burgage with two *seldae.*

However, in the last of the six sections of the 1288 survey relating to the borough, that section which bears no street name, the scribe records five shambles or slaughter houses. They all belong to one person, *Roudulfa Joye.* This is then followed by 14 individual entries of *seldae macetrarie,* butchers' booths. This is the Butchers Row shown so clearly on the 1816 Enclosure map and the plans of 1824 and 1831, as well as in drawings and prints of the period. Because of the nuisance that was always associated with the slaughtering of animals, the shambles can be placed at the northern end of the Row, close to the supply of running water at the Lower Cross. So serious was this nuisance in Hereford in Elizabeth's reign that the City Council ordered that 'all offal and refuse from the slaughter houses should be carried away in the night and taken to Wye Bridge, there to be cast in at the place accustomed, between eight and nine o'clock in winter, and nine and ten in summer'. At Ledbury, 'the disagreeable practice of slaughtering pigs in the street' was only abolished in 1830.

Table 5. Distribution of Unassigned Tenancies in Ledbury Borough, 1288

	Middletown					
	Butchers Row	Shop Row	Bishop St	Church St	Church Lane	Total
Burgages				———33———		33
Booths		———23———				23
Butchers' Booths	14					14
Shambles	5					5
Places			———————2———————			2
Oven		———1———				1
Dyke			1			1

For a further 550 years, the Butchers Row continued to serve the town. When an 'Act for the Improvement of the High Street' was passed in 1835, it referred, not to five shambles and 14 butchers' stalls, but only to 'certain houses, buildings and erections, fifteen in number', for some of the shops in the Row had already come down. By 1840, they had all been swept away and the market place once more resembled the unencumbered open space originally laid out by Richard de Capella's surveyor in the 1120s.

The Butchers Row was not the only market encroachment in Middletown. Running parallel to it along the eastern side of the market place, but probably not extending so far towards the Upper Cross, was the Shop Row. Here were to be found some, but not all, of the remaining 23 *seldae* listed in the sixth, undesignated section of the survey. The first direct reference to this other market encroachment is to be found in 1370, when John Wynch, the master, and the brethren of St Katherine's hospital leased *unam schopam in vico vocato Shopperewe* to William Schereman and his wife Alice, for their lives, at rent of 10s a year. A grant of 1402 details certain lands and tenements including *unam Schopam in Ledebury in vico Schoparum.*(41) Little is known of this second free-standing row except that it was pulled down at the beginning of the 17th century to make way for the Market Hall.

It is not possible to provide any firm date for the third area of market encroachment in Middletown, now 1 and 3 the Homend, which look respectively into the market place and down Bye Street. They are significant in terms of the evolution of the town's street plan because their encroachment has distorted the original line of the old east-west routeway, creating a dogleg curve at the entrance to Church Street. Early 19th century illustrations show clearly how the western side of the timber-framed 3 the Homend was refaced in brick so that Spencer's store looked west down Bye Street rather than into the market place and then how 1 the Homend and the adjacent part, now the side of 3 the Homend, were later rebuilt in brick as well.

Middletown was paved as early as 1365 when Edward III granted 'to the bailiff and good men of Ledbury', for '40s paid into the royal hanaper', the right to charge pavage for five years.(42) This was a local tax, not unlike the later turnpike tolls, levied on incoming traffic to defray the cost of paving. It was usually related to the weight of goods. Often pedestrians were not charged. The usual method of paving was to pitch a gravel bed to the kennel in the centre of the road. Then pebbles or stones would be tapped into the gravel until bedded at the right level, when the whole surface was rammed tight.

le Homende. By far the largest number of holdings was in the Homend, 78 in all. Their position on either side of the street can be clearly seen on all the 25 ins OS plans. What is not clear is how far they extended down the Homend. If there was equal development on both sides of the street, the burgage plots would have extended almost twice as far down both sides of the Homend as they extended down the west side of the Southend, for there were nearly four times as many tenancies in the Homend as there were in the Southend. On this assumption the Homend would have been built up as far as number 66, formerly the Fox Inn, and certainly no further than number 78. This fits in neatly with other topographical evidence, for the Homend is quite straight and of uniform width to the Fox. Just beyond, at 78 the Homend, the road begins distinctly to curve to the east. All the evidence points to a carefully planned mediaeval layout.

The Enclosure map shows that the east side of the Homend, even in 1816, was only built up as far as the land on which the Infants' School now stands and that the west side was still not built-up much further than the Fox. In terms of length, 500 years had brought little change to the street.

Bysshopestrete. There were 56 tenancies in *Bysshopestrete,* now called Bye Street. It was the second largest street in the town. On the plans of 1824 and 1831 it is still entitled Bishop's Street yet it is referred to in the text of both guide books by its contracted name, Bye Street. Ledbury was more fortunate than Hereford, where the name Bishop Street was, in 1855, abandoned altogether in favour of Commercial Street.

The topography of Bishop Street is of particular interest. The eastern end, some 200 yards, is narrow. Here, the road is less than half the width of the Homend. In this respect it is almost identical with New Street — and with similar implications for traffic today. The reason may well be the same, that the burgage plots of the south-western end of the Homend extended over 200 yards down Bye Street, suggesting that, like New Street, this is later development.

By the Elim chapel Bye Street debouches; it widens out considerably, and follows a different, more northerly alignment, confirming the view that the street is later than the Homend. In this wider part of the street the 56 tenancies were situated.

19th century maps and plans show two distinct features. Firstly, there were buildings in a series of islands down the middle of the road. A few buildings in the road yet remain, between the cattle market and the railway bridge. These formed another Shop Row, similar in appearance and origin to that in Middletown. Here would have been situated the remainder of those 23 *seldae,* mentioned in the sixth section of the survey, but not already allocated to the Shop Row in Middletown.

Secondly, the 1788 and 1824 plans show a stream running down the middle of the street. It flowed from the Upper Hall and formed a water splash at the Lower Cross, by which time it had become an open drain, a gullet or kennel. It is described in a mediaeval document wherein *Richard le Wyte* of Ledbury granted to *William de Notrone* and Alice, his wife, for two marks of sterling silver, a certain plot of land in Church Lane, between the home of Richard Long and the 'stream flowing from the Upper Hall to the garden of the Lower Hall and then to the king's highway'. This stream served the tannery which stood at the corner of Bye Street and the Homend. The tannery disappeared in 1895 to make room for the Barrett Browning Memorial Institute and Clock Tower, now the County Library, and the water splash was culverted in the general improvement of the town in the 1830s.

These two features indicate that Bye Street was a secondary market area. With the rapid growth that took place after 1120, Middletown was no longer large enough to cope with the requirements of expanding markets and annual fairs. In the middle ages it was the custom for one or more of the major roads, either within or just outside the walls or borough limits, to be used as overflow market areas — an interesting example is to be seen just outside the north gate of Chepstow. The stream flowing down the middle of Bishop Street was important since it provided drainage for the cattle market. Only in the late 19th century was an off-street market built, on a site adjacent to that which had served Ledbury for so many centuries.

The stream served another purpose. In the last section of the survey, *Johannes le Webbe* is recorded as paying the bishop 1 d a year rent for the privilege of using a *fossato,* that is a dyke or mill leet. It is highly probable that John's water wheel stood at the head of Bishop Street, on the tannery site, for his name is also to be found among the tenants of that street. Unfortunately, there is no internal evidence to suggest the location of the *furnus* for which *Robertus Mereb* paid an annual rent of 6d. Normally, the lord retained suit of oven to himself. Thus the 1230 Salford charter states that 'no burgess should bake bread for sale except at my oven on payment of reasonable dues'. At Ledbury, by 1288, the bishop's oven had been leased to Robert.

The remaining tenancies of the last section of the 1288 survey, 33 burgage tenancies, were almost certainly situated in Church Street and Church Lane. There are a number of mediaeval records relating to houses where the streets are variously described as *vico ecclesiale, vico vocatur le Halle-ende* and *le Church-ende.* (43) The majority of the burgages would have been on the north side of Church Street, which remained the principal route out of the town to the east until the 18th century. Until 1967, the houses fronting the street were numbered up to 27.

Here, close by the entrance to the minster, was the site of the pre-Conquest Sunday market and the Domesday village. This was not planned settlement; it had evolved over the centuries by gradual encroachment on the lands of the church and stood in marked contrast to the new town, situated about the market place with its four carefully laid out streets. Nevertheless, when the borough was created, those who lived here had to be accorded the same legal status (as free burgesses) as the newcomers — even though the shape of their holdings bore little relationship to those of the long narrow burgage plots newly pegged out by the bishop's surveyor. The triangle of land between the streets remained in the hands of the parish, originally as an ecclesiastical, but after the mid-16th century, as a civil body.

The Booth Hall and Hundred House. Almost all the important business of the town, as a community, was conducted in the Booth Hall, but it finds no place in the 1288 survey, for it belonged to the bishop as lord. It was the meeting place of the borough court, presided over by the bishop's senior officer, the bailiff. The court was charged with the duty of punishing all who infringed borough regulations, such as 'those bakers, inn-keepers, victuallers, regraters, forestallers and other transgressors' accused by Bishop Spofford in 1442 of violating his assize, that is the fixed measure and price, of bread, ale and wine.(44) The responsibilities of the bailiff's office are clearly illustrated by a Royal indictment of William Colyer, in 1390, 'for that after he had arrested there on Monday after Michaelmas one Robert Pyon of More by Ludlow for felony in stealing a cow value 8s of William Boteler at Cors . . . he allowed him to escape . . .'(45)

The Booth Hall is also described as the Hundred House and on a number of occasions the hundred of Radlow and Ledbury, as it was sometimes called, met there, although the traditional open-air meeting place continued to be used as well. The last recorded meeting of the hundred, in Radlow field just west of Tarrington, was in 1652.

In 1295, Edward I, faced with a French invasion, a Scots war and a Welsh revolt, summoned the so-called Model Parliament. Representatives from even the smallest towns were called to Westminster on the basis that 'what touches all, should be approved by all'. The Booth Hall was no doubt the scene of the election of Roger Caperun and John Baskervylle in 1295 and of William Esegar and Roger Fetherick in 1305. Subsequently Ledbury, like Bromyard, Ross and, after 1306, Weobley, declined the privilege of further representation due to the borough's inability to pay its members the statutory wage of 2s per day.

The early 14th century saw the quantity of English wool exported reach an all-time record. In the half century after 1280 this trade was dominated by such Florentine merchant houses as the Bardi and the Peruzzi who were at the height of their power. They bought, in particular, the short wool used to make cloth of a heavy texture. This was produced on the Yorkshire moors, the chalk downs, and in Herefordshire and the whole of the Welsh March between the Severn and the hills of Wales. Thus, in September 1328, we find 'men . . . of the Society of the Peruzzi bringing to London wool bought under licence from the king — 120 sarplars at Hereford, 15 at Lyddebury, 35 at Wyggemor, 16 at Upton and 20 at Swyndon, Berks . . .'. At the same time, the Society of the Bardi bought '100 sacks from the county of Hereford'.(46) Such transactions would have taken place at the Booth Hall. The sarplar was a large sack or cloth of coarse canvas which would contain 80 tods of wool, each tod weighing 28 pounds. In the 14th and 15th centuries the export trade in wool was transformed. England ceased to be simply the supplier of the primary product; instead, she became the major exporter of manufactured cloth.

A grant of 1375 enables us to locate the site of the Booth Hall, for it refers to a piece of vacant land in Ledbury 'between the main building of the hospital and the hundred house of the town'.(47) The Booth Hall therefore stood on or near the land now occupied by the Feathers. In 1400 Bishop John Trefnant granted 'all that messuage called *le Bothehalle* in Ledbury denzein' to Richard Glover on a lease for 40 years at an annual rent of 6s 8d, but the bishop reserved to himself free access to 'the place where the hundred and borough court has been held' and also to 'that small place in the same building used for locking up and guarding prisoners'.(48) *Aluredus de la Frithe,* one of the tenants in the foreign, as part of his service to the bishop, had the 'custody of thieves within the court of Ledbury', being answerable to the court if they escaped. This duty he combined with responsibility for the bishop's standing corn in the fields in autumn.(49)

As part of the contract for his 40-year lease on the Booth Hall, Richard Glover undertook to build from his own resources a structure of three bays and four roof trusses, with a chamber above, where the court could be held. The bishop engaged to supply one oak but transport was Richard's liability. Furthermore, Trefnant insisted on the payment of 40 silver shillings as security that the work would commence the next year. There is no way of knowing where the new Booth Hall stood, unless it was in the Southend, on the site referred to in the 19th century as the Old Court House.(50) This would certainly have been more convenient for the bishop.

The 1288 survey, together with details derived from the bishop's registers and the remarkable collection of mediaeval deeds relating to the property of St Katherine's, has enabled us to appreciate the rapidity with which Richard de Capella's borough grew in the 150 years after its foundation. Analysis of the survey also shows that within 100-150 years of foundation Ledbury had assumed, not merely a topography which we should easily have recognised, but also a town plan which remained virtually unchanged for some 500 years. This was the case in the Southend, New Street, the High Street, the Homend and Church Street or the Hall End. Even in Bye Street, despite the construction of the canal and the railway and the creation of the off-street cattle market with all its attendant demolition, the fundamental character of the street, established prior to 1288, has not been seriously eroded.

Table 6. Relative Size of the Bishop of Hereford's Boroughs, 1288

	Ledbury	Bromyard	Ross	Bishops Castle	Prestbury
Burgage Tenancies	247	229	96	46	30
Burgage and other Tenancies	282	255	105	46	30
Bishop's annual Receipts	£27.10.7½	£23.1.6½	£10.15.0		

The pattern that emerges is of rapid growth between 1120 and 1288 and then apparent stagnation. If one looks at population, a similar picture emerges. An assessment of the relative size of the five episcopal boroughs described in the *Red Book* is quite simple. (Table 6.) To assess their population in absolute terms is more difficult. Debate over the average number of persons in the mediaeval household, the so-called multiplier, has been long and involved. In 1948, J.C. Russell suggested 3.5. More recently, 4.5 or even 5 has been proposed as a more accurate multiplier.(51) For urban households, which in many cases would have included servants and possibly journeymen or apprentices as well as the immediate family, this last figure seems more acceptable.

Table 7. Population Estimates for Ledbury, 1288

		Multiplier		
		3.5	4.5	5
Burgage Tenancies	247	864.5	1111.5	1235
Burgage and other Tenancies	282	987	1269	1410

Table 7 gives the results, which range from 864, using a multiplier of 3.5 applied only to burgage tenancies, to 1,410 using a multiplier of 5 for all tenancies. Obviously there is plenty of room for error. It may well be that some of the burgages were not built up. On the other hand, some of the burgage tenancies, such as that of six burgages held by St Katherine's, may well represent more than one household, and these estimates ignore the important ecclesiastical households. In 1801, at the first census, the population of the township of Ledbury was about 2,000. The pattern that emerges is again one of rapid growth between the 1120s and 1288, and then apparent stagnation.

This is in no way remarkable. Ledbury's fortunes reflected those of its hinterland. The years after 1288 were years of ever-increasing hardship and crisis. The early 1290s and the decade from 1310 were marked by bad harvests, with famine in 1316 and 1317. Finally, in 1348, the Black Death arrived in England.

The full impact was not felt in Herefordshire until 1349. This is clearly shown in the register of Bishop John Trilleck. For the years 1345-47, presentations to benefices, for all reasons, averaged six per year. In 1349 that figure rose to 160. On many occasions the scribe no longer troubled to note the reason for the vacancy — death.(52)

From Trilleck's register we can trace the course of the great pestilence in Ledbury and its hinterland. The first of the clergy to be struck down, in March, were *John de Prato,* priest of the chantry of the Blessed Virgin at Ledbury, 'Sir Walter', priest at Cradley and 'Sir Adam' at Bishops Frome. John de Beverley, vicar of Ledbury, and the parish priests of Bromsberrow, Donnington, Canon Frome, Castle Frome, Munsley and Little and Much Marcle were all claimed by the plague before the year was out. At Evesbatch two priests, and at Bosbury three in succession, died during that catastrophic year. Colwall seems to have been the only parish in the locality that did not lose its priest, for there were presentations at Coddington in March and at Eastnor in August, 1350. It is estimated that between one third and a half of the population of England died in the outbreak.

Later outbreaks in the 1360s and 1370s, especially the major visitation of 1361, prevented a population recovery. Although, as a consequence, land was cheap, real wages were higher and rents were low, a significant change seems to have taken place in the age structure of the adult

population. On one West Midlands estate, 65 per cent of the tenants were in their twenties in 1350; by 1393 the figure had dropped to 38 per cent.(53) It has been said that 'it is doubtful whether (the) English rural population came up to its 13th century peak until the very eve of the industrial revolution of the 18th century'.(54) In this respect, Ledbury, in its topography and population, mirrored faithfully the countryside it served. By 1288 the topography of Ledbury as we know it was fully formed. All that happened after was little more than a postscript.

1st edition 25 ins OS Plan of Ledbury (1887).

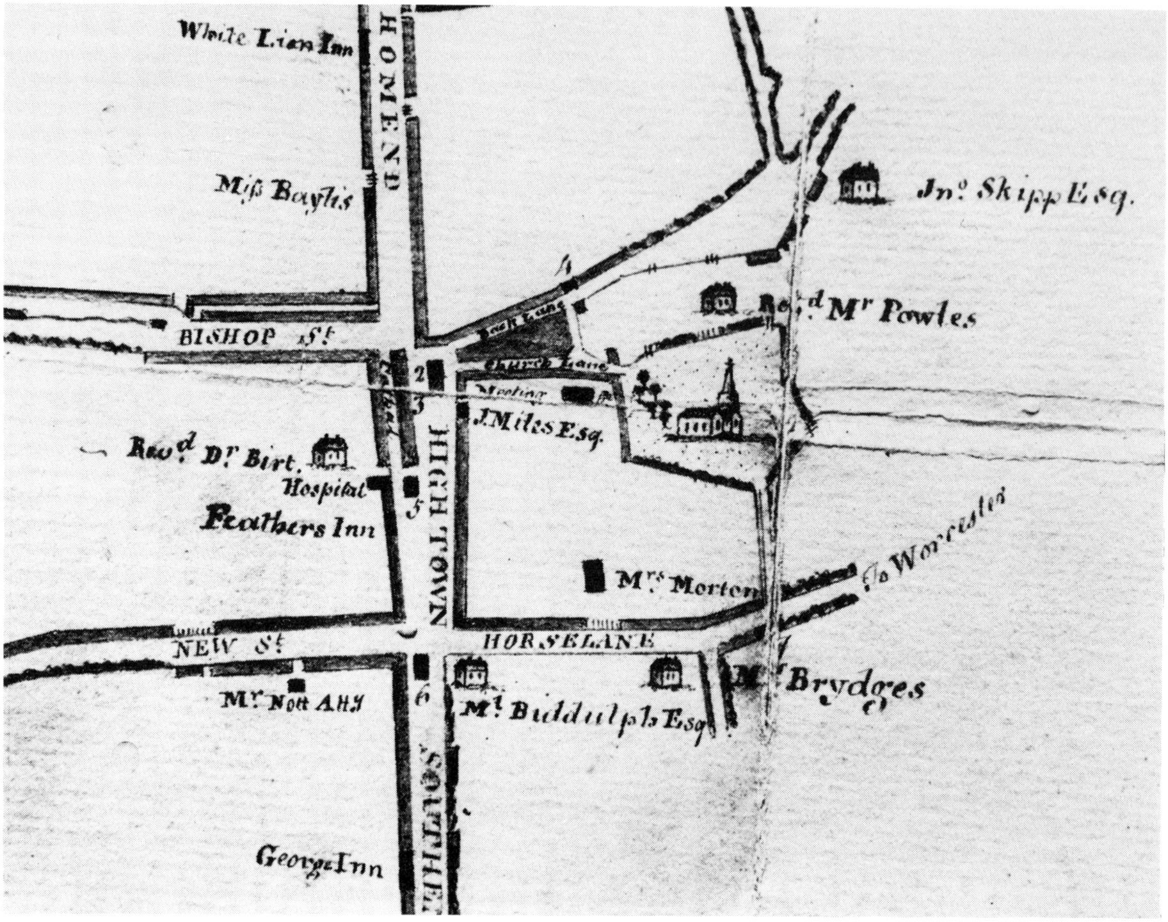
White Lion Inn
HOMEND
Miss Baylis
Jno. Skipp Esq.
Revd Mr Powles
BISHOP St
Church Lane
Meeting
J Miles Esq.
Revd Dr Birt.
Hospital
Feathers Inn
HIGH TOWN
To Worcester
Mrs Morten
NEW St
HORSELANE
Mr Brydges
Mr Nott Atty
Mr Biddulph Esq
SOUTHEND
George Inn

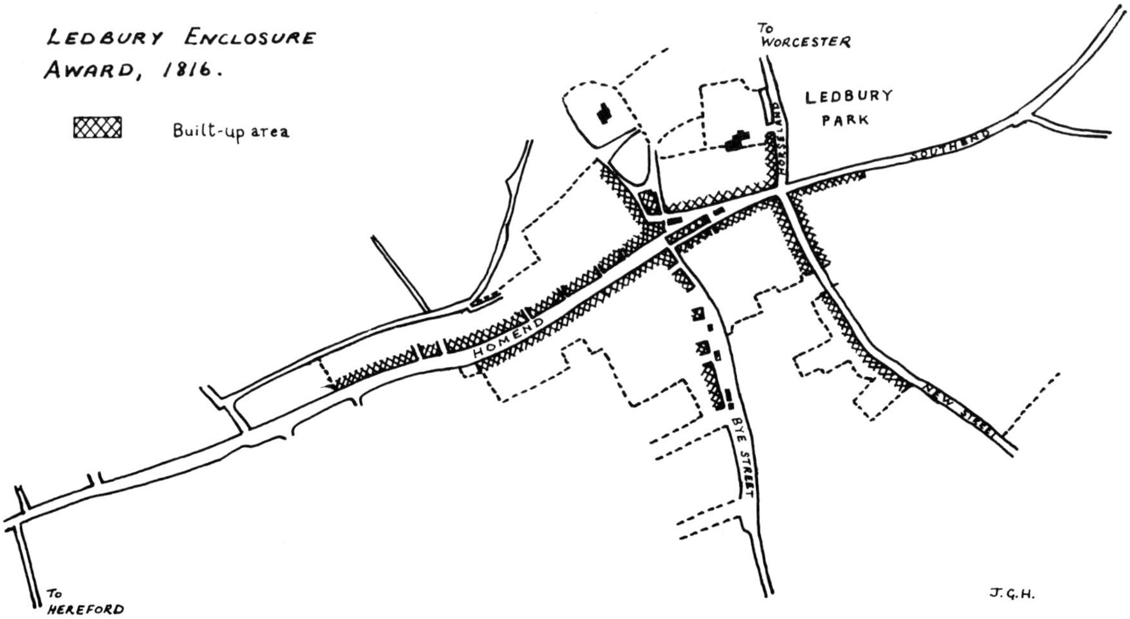
LEDBURY ENCLOSURE AWARD, 1816.
Built-up area
TO WORCESTER
LEDBURY PARK
SOUTHEND
HOMEND
BYE STREET
NEW STREET
TO HEREFORD
J.G.H.

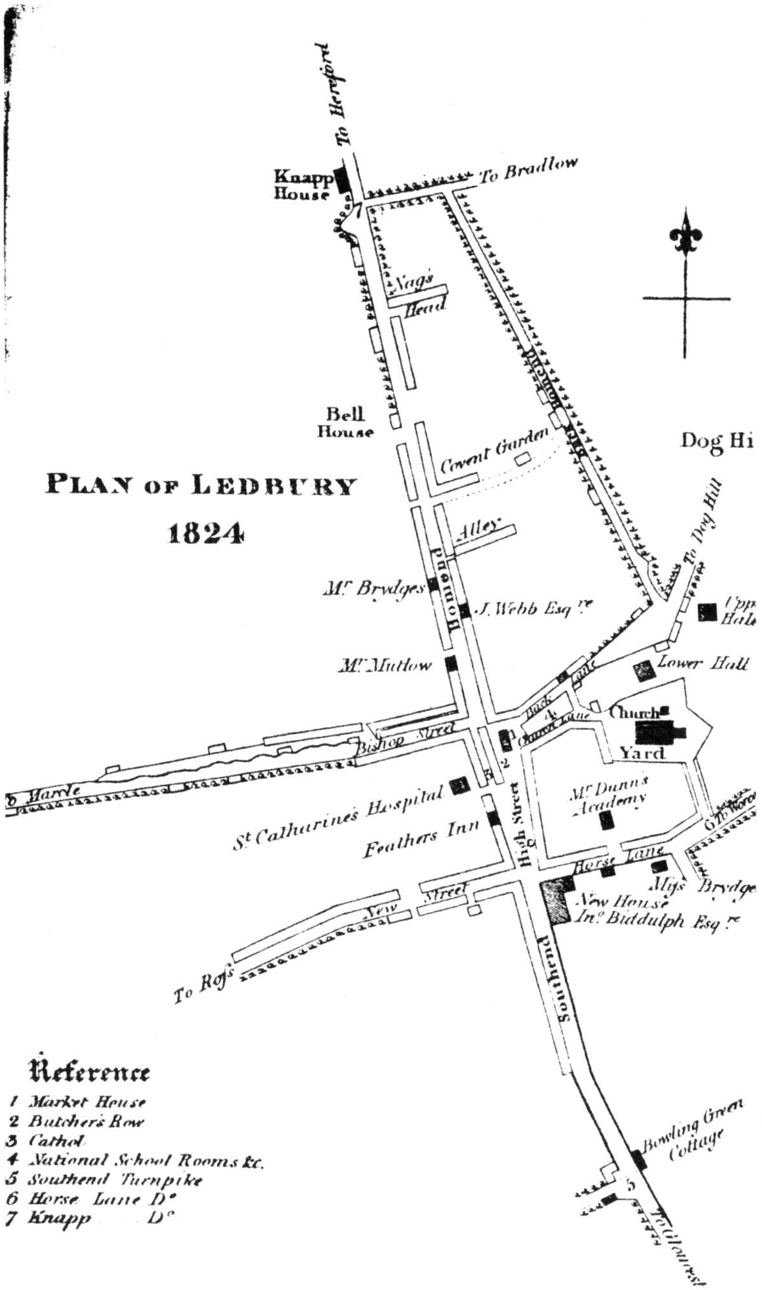

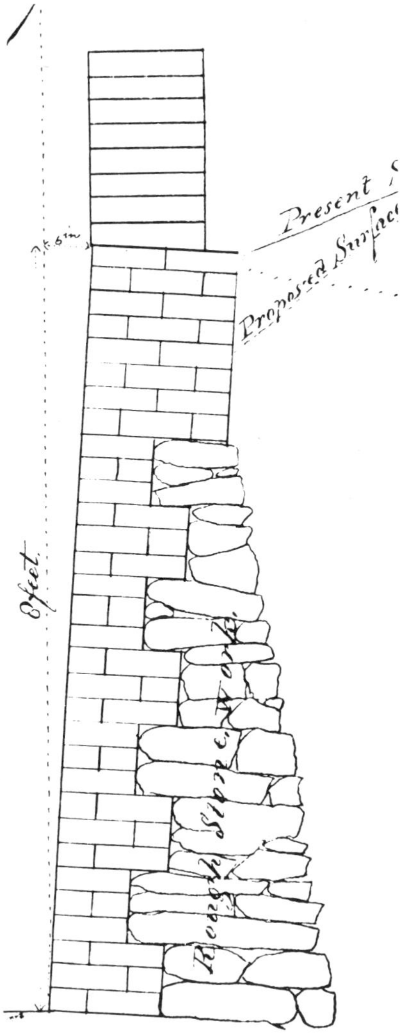

OPPOSITE ABOVE: *Plan of Ledbury,* 'dedicated to Micl Biddulph Esq by his most obedt Servt J. Lydiard, 1788'. (HCRO/G2) BELOW: *Ledbury Enclosure Map,* 1816, showing built-up area in wash on original and not visible on endpaper copy. (HCRO/Q/R1/25) LEFT: *Plan of Ledbury* from the *Ledbury Guide* 'describing the Picturesque Views and Beautiful Scenery of that Neighbourhood. Ledbury: Sold by John Devereum, 1824'. RIGHT: All the burgages lay on the west of the Southend. The bishop's park lay to the east and was protected by a timber pale. In 1832, John Biddulph built a brick wall along the line of the pale. (HCRO/G2)

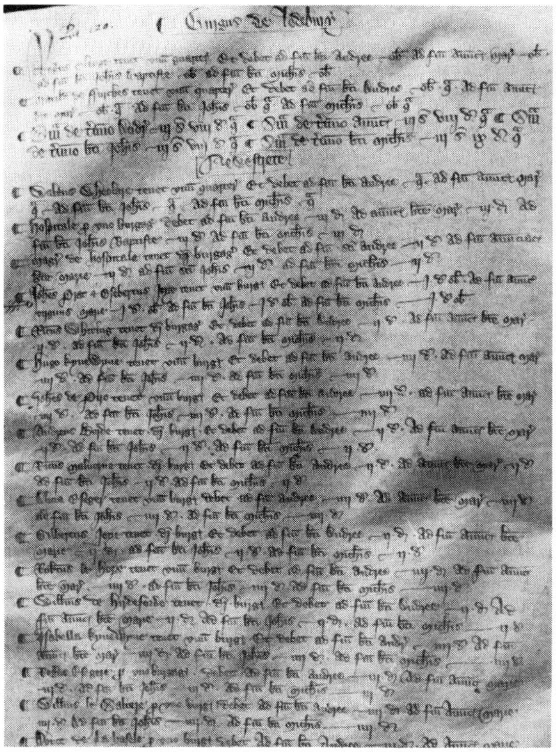

LEFT: *Newestrete,* so-called in the 1288 Survey, but certainly laid out before 1232. *Walterius Wheolare, Hospitale, Magister de Hospitale, Johannes Prat et Osebertus Joye* head the list of tenants. BELOW: New Street has a narrow neck. It only opens out after some 200 feet — the length of the burgage plots of the adjacent sections of High Street and the Southend. New Street c1890. Wm Palmer at the Old Talbot. (HCRO/AB48/B10) and RIGHT: New Street c1900. Edwin Carr at the Bell. (HCRO/AB48/B10)

ABOVE: New Street c1880. Sampson Walters was at the Vine Brewery Taps and James Wetson, who had been landlord of the Crown and Sceptre in New Street, had now taken over the Old Talbot. (HCL/WMC/571) BELOW: New Street a hundred years later. Half-timbering has been revealed, but the patina of old brick has been lost in a sea of white paint.

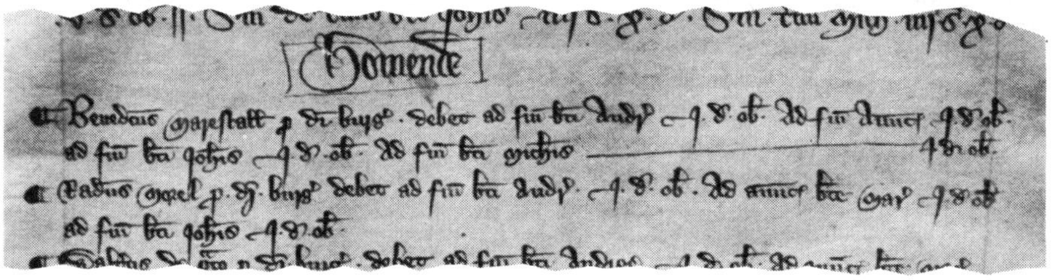
Homende

The Homend, a planned street of the 12th century: ABOVE: In the late 1880s. (HCL/WMC/567) and BELOW: About 1896. (HCL/WMC/568) CENTRE: *Benedictus Marescall, Radulfus Morel, Walterius de Prato, Rogerus de Piro, Rogerus Rouheued, Willelmus Joye iunior, Johannes de Byrmingham iunor* and 71 other tenants held burgages in 1288.

LEFT: Brewery Inn and the rear of the Bye Street Shop Row c1890. (HCL/WMC/558) RIGHT: The road called *le Halle-ende* remained to the 18th century the principal route to the east. Until 1967, the houses fronting the street numbered up to 27. Then these five 17th-century half-timbered houses, with their deep overhang, were demolished and the line of the road straightened to transform this part of Ledbury. A similar fate now threatens the Georgian brick buildings on the other side of the road. (HCL/WMC/556) BELOW: The front of Bye Street Shop Row c1900. The narrow neck of the street and the building nicknamed 'Bishop's Palace' in the distance. The new off-street cattle market on the extreme right. (HCL/WMC/559).

LEFT ABOVE: The hospital founded in 1232 by Hugh Foliot 'to the honour of the Lord and of St Katherine the Virgin', as drawn in 1865. (HCM) CENTRE: The splendid 14th-century roof, showing the curved braces between the tie beam and the collar. The partition is modern. BELOW: Another lancet window, now blocked, in the south wall. RIGHT ABOVE: The western or service end of the original hospital. BELOW: Two rows of curved wind braces give added strength to the timbering of either side of the roof.

St Katherine's Hospital

The hospital founded by Hugh Foliot 'to the honour of the Lord and of St Katherine the Virgin' in 1232 was a constant reminder to all in the market place of the need for prayer and works of charity. Hugh Foliot's motives are clearly outlined in the foundation documents.(55) It was built to provide for the spiritual as well as the material well-being of the poor and the aged, the sick and the distressed, of travellers and pilgrims. The founder was merely expressing in institutional form those duties and responsibilities incumbent upon all Christians, but most especially upon the bishop as shepherd of his flock, to be, in the words of Job, 'the father of the poor, eyes to the blind, feet to the lame'. Indeed, a century earlier, Robert de Bethune had maintained in each of his manor houses, at Ledbury as elsewhere, a definite number of paupers, 'for whom he provided not only a daily ration, but the requisite clothes and shoes, throughout the year'.

The government of the hospital was conferred on the dean and chapter of Hereford cathedral. They were to 'keep, maintain and defend its rights and possessions' principally by means of an annual inspection. 'The said dean and chapter are to receive 40s annually from the said hospital and are to devote all the remainder of the resources . . . to the support of the paupers and sick lying there'.

One chaplain was to be appointed to minister to the spiritual needs of the sick and the poor. 'If, by lapse of time and the blessing of God, the means of the hospital should be sufficient for their maintenance, there should be two chaplains. One should celebrate mass for the souls of myself and my predecessors and successors, and of the canons of Hereford, and of all the faithful dead. The other shall celebrate divine service for the living and for all the benefactors of the hospital. At the death of any one of the canons of Hereford, both chaplains shall sing a trental (a daily mass for a month after death) for the soul of the deceased.' Before the year was out, Hugh Foliot had provided for the second chaplain. A third chaplaincy was endowed in 1364 by Adam de Esegar, canon of Hereford, vicar-general of the diocese and one of the two men appointed by the king as custodians of the see after the death of Bishop Trilleck in 1360.(56)

Mediaeval hospitals were much influenced by the monastic life. Although they did not take the vows of poverty, chastity and obedience, the small company of brethren were to live a corporate life with the master. This was clearly expressed in the architecture. The building now called St Katherine's Hall is the original hospital. Although the Royal Commission on Historical Monuments describes this as 14th century, it is in fact 13th century. The east end was originally composed of three lancet windows of which only the two side windows remain. In the 14th century a large new window, of three trefoiled ogee lights with elaborate quatrefoil tracery in the head, was inserted in the place of the central lancet, to give more light for the priest to be seen when he was celebrating the mass at the altar below. The splendid timber roof with its curved braces is also of the 14th century. These two dominant elements give the impression of a 14th century structure but the two lancets at the east end and another at the eastern end of the south wall give the lie to this, showing it to have been originally Early English in style and therefore 13th century. The windows, now blocked, in the south wall also show that until the late middle ages at least the building was free-standing. The Hospital building has now been restored by the people of Ledbury for community use.

Internally, it was one great open hall. Hall and chapel were indivisible. They were consecrated to a common purpose. The 14th century timber truss between the two presented only a slight visual punctuation, for the existing partition is modern. The beds of the inmates were in two rows along the north and south walls. Thus all could participate with the chaplains in the daily services at the altar in the chapel. This arrangement can still be seen at the Hopital de Dieu at Beaune in Burgundy.

The foundation charter gives details of the first benefactors. Walter de Lacy, master of the castles at Weobley and Ludlow, and Lord of Meath, was described by the annals of Clonmacnoise as 'the bountifullest foreigner in steeds, attire and gold that ever came to Erin'. Benefactor of both Llanthony Prima and Secunda, he founded Craswall priory in 1225 and, with his wife, the nunnery at Aconbury about 1237. Possessed of considerable estates in the Frome valley, Walter de Lacy gave the hospital the tithes and the right of presentation to the churches of Weston Beggard and Larkhill. Geoffrey de Longchamps gave those of Kempley. The churches of Larkhill and Kempley were also charged with the provision of one pound of incense each year for use in the chapel.

Other benefactors quickly followed suit. By the end of the century, due in part to the generous grant of episcopal indulgences, the hospital's endowments were numerous. An inventory of 1316 refers to a collection of almost 250 'writings' kept in chests and deed-boxes in the sacristy, giving title to lands and tenements in Ledbury borough and at Ockridge and Massington in the foreign, at the Hyde in Cradley, at Eastnor, Colwall, Weston and Hereford, Berrow in Worcestershire and Kempley in Gloucestershire, as well as the water mill at Malmespool, 'worn out and almost collapsed'.(57)

The hospital, with its 'beds for master and brethren' and its sacristy, was situated amidst a wide range of service and farm buildings, as befits the centre of a considerable estate. The contents of the service buildings indicated the standard of living enjoyed by the master, chaplains and brethren. These included a '12 gallon bronze ale-measure' and '11 dishes and 11 saucers of pewter' in the kitchen, '4 ox carcasses and 20 salted bacons' in the larder and '18 silver spoons, 1 pewter salt cellar, 4 towels and 6 table cloths' in the cellar and brewhouse. There was '1 large trough divided for the brethren and community' in the wash-house. The farm buildings included stable, cattle-shed, byre with '120 sheep with hurdles for pens', piggery with '1 boar, 4 sows, 16 hoggets, 19 piglets', and a barn with '12 loads of corn, 8 of oats, 6 of peas and beans, and 4 waggon loads of hay'.

Given such temptations, the founder's 'public and solemn excommunication of all those who at any time should presume to subtract or misapply the estate and possessions of the said hospital contrary to his ordinance' had little effect. In 1322, Pope John XXII had to write from Avignon to the Abbot of Wigmore, instructing him to prevent the master from squandering the resources of the hospital by fraudulently granting long leases at low rents.(58) The Black Death exacerbated these problems. In 1353, Bishop Trilleck ordered Thomas Bellamy, his commissary, to punish those responsible for the 'errors and excesses' of the brethren. Two years later, he had to send his official to hear and decide the case between the brethren and William le Brut, master, about the dilapidation of the goods of their three appropriated churches.(59) In 1384, Bishop John Gilbert had to threaten with excommunication in all the churches of the diocese those who had despoiled the revenues and property of the hospital by improperly exacting the tax of 1/15, granted by the laity to the king, from its lands, 'unless restitution be made within 15 days'.(60)

In 1398, John Prophet, Dean of Hereford, hearing that the chaplains were neglecting their duties for paid services elsewhere and that the brethren and inmates were being forced to beg for bread, to the scandal of the hospital, published firm ordinances on future conduct. The master, if he was to retain his office, must be resident. The chaplains and brethren were to receive adequate food and fixed stipends. They were no longer to be removed from office by the master, but only by the dean and chapter.(61) Despite John Prophet's ordinances, threats to the revenue and property of the hospital continued to be one of the chief features in the history of St Katherine's until it was finally reformed under a private Act in 1819, at the then enormous cost of £3,974.(62) Having weathered such threats for some 700 years, the estates were finally sold off after 1945.

One of the results of insistence on the master's residence was his decision to have accommodation appropriate to his station in life. Elsewhere, new buildings such as those of the hospital of St Cross, refounded by Cardinal Beaufort near Winchester in 1445, show how a compromise was achieved between the earlier ideal of the communal life and the growing desire for privacy. At St Cross, separate dwellings were provided for the master and brethren around an inner court, while travellers and others received hospitality in the Hundred Mens Room in an outer court.

At Ledbury, change was more gradual. In the 15th century, the master removed himself from the common dormitory and hall to live in a newly-completed 'Mansion House'. This was built to the usual H-shaped plan of the period. The eastern cross-wing formed the service area with buttery and pantry. A screens passage gave access through a spere truss to the central hall which was open to the roof. Beyond, in the western cross-wing, was the master's solar with chamber above. There have since been extensive additions to the north and west while the principal facade to the south was rebuilt in advance of the line of the original hall and service wing in the 18th century. Nevertheless, this four-bay hall, with its two cross-wings, is still structurally intact within the existing building.

A century later, individual accommodation was also provided for the brethren and the sisters who had joined them within six years of the foundation. In all likelihood, these almshouses were the 'dilapidated old buildings' replaced after the passage of the 1819 Act and shown as 'Brethren and Sisters Houses' on the plan of the St Katherine's site drawn up in 1817.

LEFT: The seal of St Katherine's. SIGILL HOSPITALIS (SANCTE KATER)INE DE LEDEB(URY). The west front of (Hereford?) cathedral, crosses surmounting each bay and a central tower; St Katherine of Alexandria; below, a bishop (the founder, Hugh Foliot?). Original HD&CR. (Photograph. HCL/WMC/565) RIGHT: 14th- or 15th-century encaustic tiles in the chapel.

In this Room are also seen ye following devices seen in ye Glass.

This device is for the Reverend Thomas Thorneton Dean

1617.

Hugh ffoliot Bishop of HEREFORD founded thys Hospitall in the yeare of the Lord 1232 and QUEENE ELIZABETH reestablished the same in the xxiij^d yeare of her happy Raigne

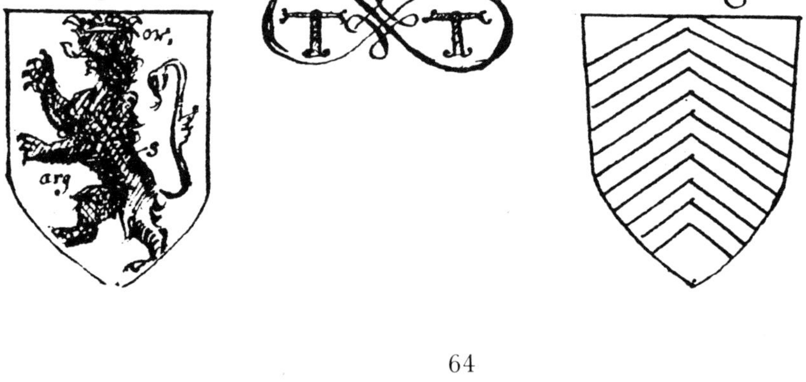

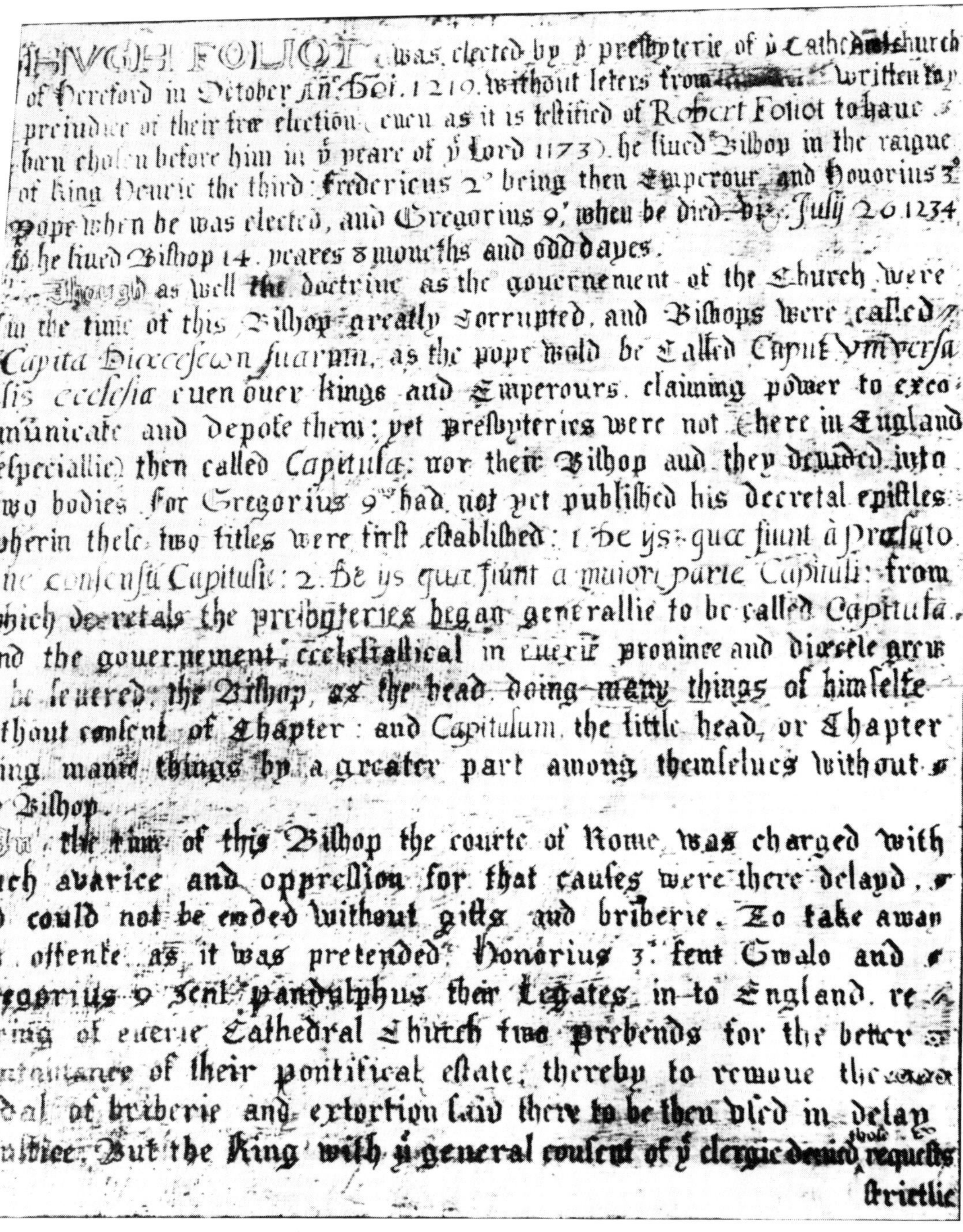

HUGH FOLIOT was elected by ye presbyterie of ye Cathedral church of Hereford in October An. Dni. 1219. without leters from [illegible] written to ye preiudice of their free election, euen as it is testified of Robert Foliot to haue bein chosen before him in ye yeare of ye Lord 1173. he liued Bishop in the raigne of king Henrie the third: Fredericus 2 being then Emperour, and Honorius 3 pope when he was elected, and Gregorius 9 when he died the July 26 1234. so he liued Bishop 14. yeares 8 monethes and odd dayes.

Though as well the doctrine as the gouernement of the Church were in the time of this Bishop greatly corrupted, and Bishops were called Capita Diœcesewn suarum, as the pope wold be called Caput vniuersalis ecclesiæ euen ouer kings and Emperours, claiming power to excommunicate and depose them: yet presbyteries were not there in England (especiallie) then called Capitula: nor their Bishop and they deuided into two bodies. for Gregorius 9 had not yet published his decretal epistles: wherin these two titles were first established: 1 De ys quæ fiunt a Prælato sine consensu Capituli: 2. De ys quæ fiunt a maiori parte Capituli: from which decretals the presbyteries began generallie to be called Capitula. and the gouernement ecclesiasticall in euerie prouince and diocesse grew to be seuered: the Bishop, as the head doing many things of himselfe without consent of Chapter: and Capitulum, the little head, or Chapter doing manie things by a greater part among themselues without the Bishop.

In the time of this Bishop the courte of Rome was charged with much avarice and oppression for that causes were there delayd, and could not be ended without gifts and briberie. To take away this offense, as it was pretended, Honorius 3. sent Gwalo and Gregorius 9 sent Pandulphus their Legates in-to England, requiring of euerie Cathedral Church two prebends for the better maintainance of their pontifical estate, thereby to remoue the scandal of briberie and extortion said there to be then used in delay of Justice. But the King with ye general consent of ye clergie denied those requests strictlie

OPPOSITE ABOVE: Hugh Foliot. This late 16th-century painted panel was placed above the fireplace of the solar by Edward Cooper, master 1562-74 and 1580-96. His initials and the date, 1588, were carved on the frieze above. In 1953 it was said, 'May the present trustees of St Katherine's be worthy of their distinguished predecessor!' Within a few years, the panel had been taken down and left in an outhouse with general lumber. Its rescue was entirely due to the interest and determination of Miss S. Robinson. BELOW: Stained glass placed by Thornton in the window of the solar of the Master's House, 1617. Seen and drawn by T. Dingley c1684. ABOVE: A late 16th-century view of the papacy and the Roman church.

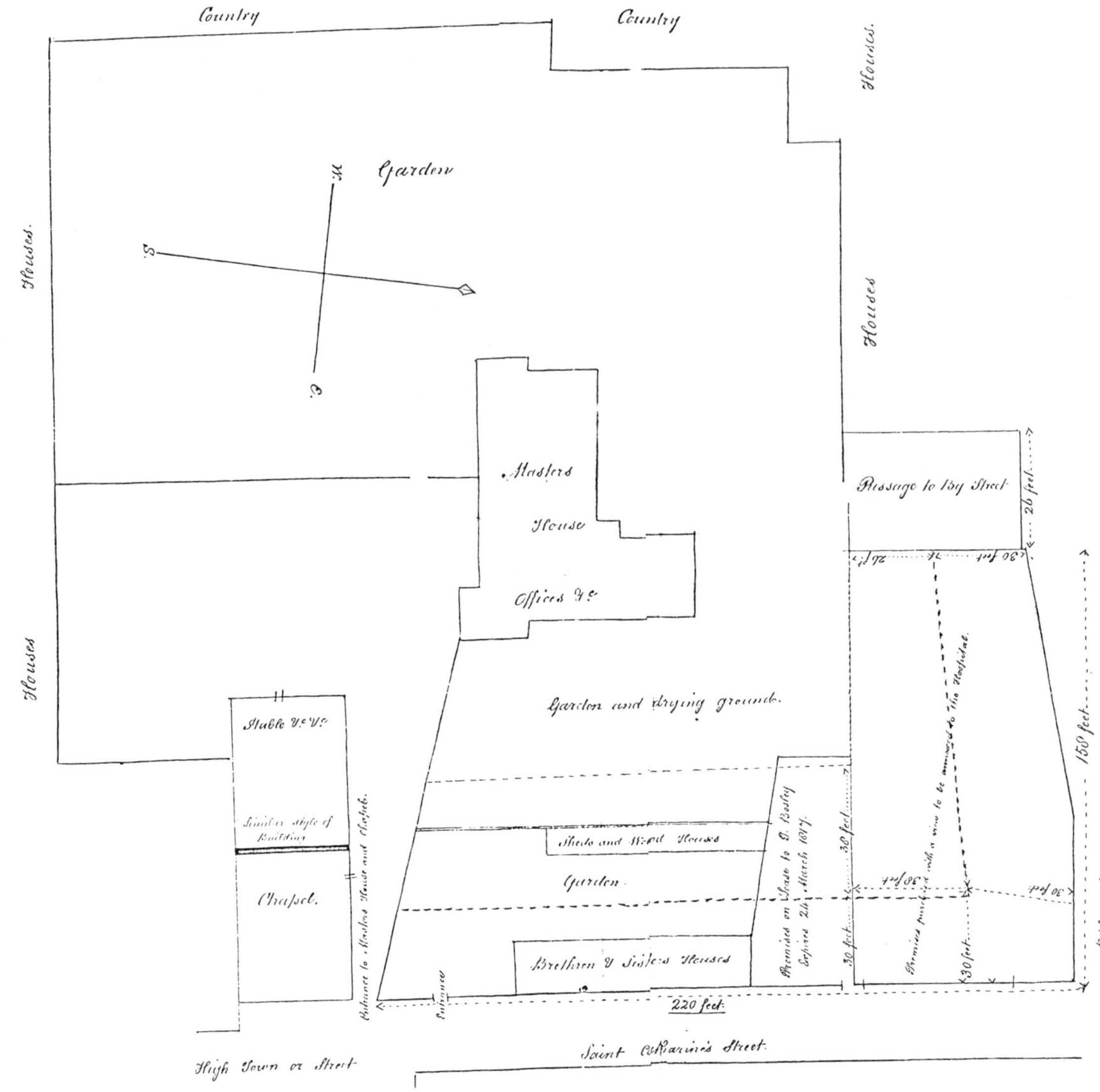

ABOVE: Plan of St Katherine's, 1817, showing Butchers Row, St Catherine's Street (the Cathol) and the 'wretched buildings', the earlier half-timbered almshouses. (HCRO/G2) BELOW: The Mansion or Capital House from the south. The left wing is a 19th-century addition. The three windows to the right of it represent the solar wing of the H-shaped house built in the 15th century and refurbished by Cooper, 1580-96. The service wing is on the extreme right under its own pitched roof. The screens passage is still marked off by the small projecting block to the left of the service wing. The hall, lit by the three large ground floor windows, lies in the centre. (HCL/WMC/10107).

LEFT: Edward Cooper's memorial, as portrayed by T. Dingley c1684. RIGHT: Thomas Thornton, Master 1612-29. (HCL/WMC/8758) BELOW: Rear of the almshouses, 1822 and 1866, the older northern part designed by Smirke, the architect of the British Museum and Eastnor Castle.

ABOVE LEFT: West front of St Peter's prior to restoration of 1895, showing earlier window tracery, and south aisle of 1210-20. The detached tower beyond is of 1230-40 but the bell turret and spire were the work of Nathaniel Wilkinson of Worcester, 1727-34. RIGHT: Brass to Thomas Caple, d 1490, depicted in armour of the period, his feet resting on a horse. Dingley c1684. BELOW LEFT: Window tracery of the Katherine chapel, c1335. RIGHT: From the outside, St Peter's appears to be wholly of the 13th and early 14th centuries. Apart from some internal reconstruction, perpendicular work is absent. Drawing by Philip Baylis b1809.

The Church of St Peter

Despite the outstanding success of Richard de Capella's foundation, trade and industry and the secular spirit never held unchallenged sway within the borough. The great minster church and the bishop's palace were potent symbols of the power and authority of the mediaeval church.

One of the principal spiritual responsibilities of the bishop, as diocesan, was the ordaining of men to holy orders. Our first record of such a ceremony at St Peter's, Ledbury, is in the register of St Thomas Cantilupe, when the bishop ordained 24 men to acolytes', 26 to sub-deacons', 26 to deacons' and 15 to priests' orders in 1280. These numbers are not at all unusual. Lewis Charlton ordained 62 men at Ledbury in 1366, 64 in 1367 and 53 in 1368. His successor, William Courtenay, made 70 ordinations there in 1370 and a similar number were present for John Gilbert in 1385. In 1345, John Trilleck held two quite unprecedented ordination ceremonies at St Peter's, on 24 September and 17 December, when 347 and 206 men respectively were ordained. Even these figures were overshadowed when, six months later, on 10 June 1346, 451 were ordained.(63)

On such occasions, the church of St Peter's came fully into its own. The large building would have been packed with the ordinands, their families and friends. The windows were filled with stained glass, giving an intensely rich and jewel-like appearance. Only a few fragments, such as the 13th century scenes of the 'Massacre of the Innocents' and the 'Flight into Egypt', now remain in St Katherine's chapel. The walls were painted with the iconographic scheme of the western church.

Above the bold colours of the great painted wooden screen which divided nave from chancel and laity from clergy, reflected in the light of hundreds of candles, was the rood, Christ crucified. On the chancel arch the great doom showed Christ seated in judgement on a rainbow, behind him the heavenly city painted as a mediaeval walled town. Angels sounded the last trump and the dead rose from their graves. To the right, fiends fed the damned, including some with crowns and mitres, into the maw of hell. On the left, the blessed were welcomed by St Peter himself at the gates of the heavenly city. Such dooms can still be seen at St Michael's, Mitcheldean and St Thomas', Salisbury.

Through these images of 'the poor man's bible', the church sought to spell out vividly the conflicts between 'the City of God and the city of man, eternity against time, perfection against sin'.

From behind the screen would be heard the full glory of mediaeval plainsong. The air would be suffused with incense. Standing out above all would be the figure of the bishop. The mediaeval glass in the east window of the church at Ross depicts St Thomas Cantilupe on such an occasion. Over his white alb he wears a white amice with red collar and a white chasuble edged with gold and powdered with gold roses above a red dalmatic with white ornamented border. On his head there is a jewelled mitre and on his feet sandals. In his right hand is the gilded crozier. His left hand is raised in blessing. The church thus used all the arts and assaulted all the senses. To both townspeople and countrymen, the sheer physical presence of the church must have been overwhelming.

The judgement scene, showing so graphically the terms of divine punishment, filled the hearts of great and humble alike with fears of the retribution to come in the life after death. However, such fears were alleviated by the belief in intercessory prayers and the recitation of masses, such as those enjoined by Hugh Foliot on the chaplains of St Katherine's in 1232. By the 14th century, the cult of masses for the dead found expression in personal endowments in parish churches, called chantries. There were three such chantries in St Peter's, Ledbury. The chantry of the Blessed Virgin Mary, first mentioned in 1317, was in the north chapel, but that of the Holy Trinity has not been located. For St Anne's chantry, which was in the south chapel, we have documents which tell the story of its foundation in 1384.(64)

The founders, John and Joanna Hope, obtained letters patent from the Crown, at a cost of 60s, to permit the alienation of land into mortmain, into what was regarded by the king as the dead hand of the church. The endowments in question were quite impressive — six messuages, one of which stood on the Homme House site, two shops, a windmill, 80 acres of land, six acres of meadow and the rent of 11 lb of cinnamon. However, John and Joanna died before the chantry was established and their executors, Roger Hunte and Alicia Pauncefote, had to complete the formalities before William Calew could be presented as chantry priest, on 21 April 1384. The missal Calew was to use was valued at 8 marks and the vestments at 40s, a sum considerably greater than his annual income from the chantry. His memorial brass can still be seen in the chancel, showing him kneeling in his academic robes, with the inscription,

'Saye Pater Noster for Sir William Calwe
That loved God well and All Halwe'.

The chaplains had to swear residence and on every holy day they had to offer a *placebo* and *dirige,* with the nine sections, for the souls of the founders, 'of whom they are ever to make special mention'. They were to be present at matins and the canonical hours in the church with the other chaplains, and were to live honestly and chastely. If any chaplain was absent for 15 days without urgent occasion, 'so that masses are not celebrated or through lapses of the body is defamed or convicted, and should a second time fall into the same sin he should be removed plainly, simply and without any noise'.

The so-called outer north chapel, or baptistery, was never a chantry chapel. Unlike the chapels of the Virgin and St Anne, it had no piscina (the little stone bowl, set in the wall, with its drain for washing the sacred vessels after the mass) which is a sure indication of the presence of a mediaeval altar. The date of construction, in the late 1330s, suggests that this was built as a shrine for 'the Blessed Katherine of Ledbury'. The provision of an external door, in addition to the entrance from the north chapel, indicates a design intended for the departure of pilgrims beyond the shrine.

According to local tradition, it was revealed to Katherine Audley that she would only find a resting place where the bells should ring of their own accord. The bells of Ledbury welcomed her in this way, for when her maid, Mabel, went to the belfry, she found it locked, with no ringers at hand. Here Katherine settled in 1313. She granted her estate of the castle and town of Llandovery, to James de Ferrers and was awarded an annual pension of £30 by Edward II. We know that she died after June 1323, for in that year the pension was £22 in arrears. The effigy of a lady in a wimple and long gown, on a tomb in the chancel, is not, as sometimes supposed, Katherine's. It is of later date and is the tomb of Ankaret, 1st Baroness Strange of Blake Mere, near Whitchurch, Salop, who died in 1413.(65)

Despite the sanctity of her life and her local reputation, Katherine Audley was never canonised. Nevertheless, the Katherine chapel has been described as 'the gem of Herefordshire ballflower work, for the intricacy of the tracery in its five majestic windows is complemented by the delicacy of the miniscule ballflower that ornaments them'.(66) Ballflower is the hallmark of the architectural decoration of the reign of Edward II and 'rarely has it been used with so much gusto' as in Herefordshire.(67) It is to be found in profusion on the nave at Weobley, the south aisle at Leominster priory and the north aisle of St Lawrence's, Ludlow, as well as at Ledbury. All were inspired by its use on the central and the, now lost, western tower of Hereford cathedral. However, the ballflower decoration is exceptionally small at Ledbury, confirming the work to be of the late 1330s. The window tracery indicates the additional influence of a school of masons at Lichfield. It is fitting that such a remarkable artistic achievement should be the last major addition to the church.

St Peter's also witnessed those occasions when the bishop, charged with the supervision of the spiritual welfare of both clergy and laity, came as judge, exercising his powers of visitation and correction — for 'the planting of virtue and the plucking and rooting out of vice'. Bishop Trefnant carried out such a visitation for the parishes of Ledbury, Little Marcle, Colwall, Munsley, Aylton, Pixley, Eastnor and Coddington at St Peter's on 26 May 1397.(68)

The visitation gives valuable insight into the life of the parochial clergy after 30 years of pestilence. Robert Prys, priest of Ledbury, was publicly charged with 'incontinence' with his servant woman, Alice Smith, and also with Maiota Crompe. The shortcomings of the master of St Katherine's were made public. At Munsley, the rector was not resident, divine service was neglected and Walter Bray had taken away a breviary which he refused to return. At Coddington, the rector was lukewarm and negligent in the divine services. He publicly maintained a concubine in the rectory. He kept his hay and calves in the tower of the church and his pigs in the churchyard. At Pixley, where the rector celebrated mass only on Sunday, 'John Smith, chaplain of Ledbury, is incontinent with Joanna Tyler'. At Eastnor, the rector was non-resident and the vicarage was in a ruinous condition. At Little Marcle, the chancel was ruinous and the rector lived with a Ledbury woman, Agnes Gatley. The moral lapses of the laity of the surrounding parishes were subjected to similarly detailed scrutiny. Only at Aylton could the parishioners say, 'All is well'.

In its architecture, St Peter's fully reflects the fluctuations in the economy of the mediaeval town — no 'wool church' this. Apart from some reconstruction, perpendicular work is wholly absent. Confined within its 12th century bounds, from the outside the church appears to the visitor to be wholly of the 13th and early 14th centuries — the detached tower (1230-40), north chapel (1250-60), north aisle (c1300), south aisle (1210-20), St Katherine's chapel (c1335), north porch (c1340). The only major work undertaken after the Black Death was the reconstruction of the south aisle. The rebuilding of the north aisle may well have taken place in the reign of Henry VII or VIII.

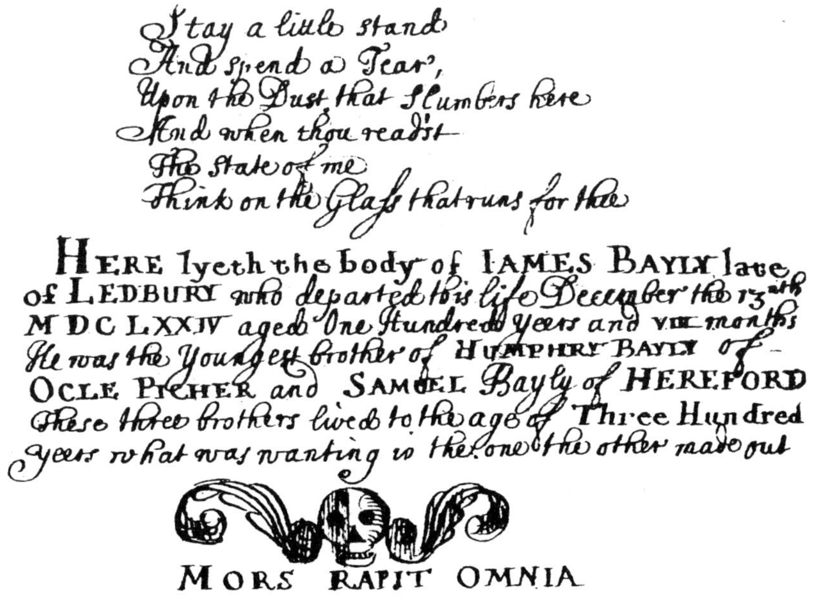
Stay a little stand
And spend a Tear,
Upon the Dust that slumbers here
And when thou read'st
The State of me
Think on the Glass that runs for thee

HERE lyeth the body of IAMES BAYLY late of LEDBURY who departed this life December the 13th MDCLXXIV aged One Hundred years and VIII months He was the Youngest brother of HUMPHRY BAYLY of OCLE PICHER and SAMUEL Bayly of HEREFORD These three brothers lived to the age of Three Hundred years what was wanting in the one the other made out

MORS RAPIT OMNIA

Longevity in Herefordshire — another lost Ledbury memorial.

LEFT: Badsey Walk with south chapel, formerly the chantry of St Anne, founded by wish of John and Joanna Hope in 1384. (HCL/WMC/557) RIGHT: Two chantry priests; ABOVE: Calew was the first chaplain to serve St Anne's chantry in 1384. The brass is in the chancel but the figure of St Peter above, shown by Dingley c1684, has now gone. BELOW: 'Here lyeth magister Roberde Preece who in lyffe tyme was counted wyse . . . for the love Peter and St Paul sey a pater nost. and one for magister Roberde Preece soule'. Brass of Robert Preece, chaplain of the Trinity chantry, now lost. T. Dingley c1684.

LEFT: St. Thomas Cantilupe as he would have appeared at the ordination ceremony in 1280. Mediaeval glass in the east window of Ross church, formerly at the episcopal palace at Stretton Sugwas. RIGHT: Splendid 14th-century roof in north aisle, similar to that in St Katherine's hospital but much longer. It extends for 15 bays. Like St Katherine's roof it has curved braces to the tie beam and curved wind braces but no collar beams. (HCRO/AB48/B10)

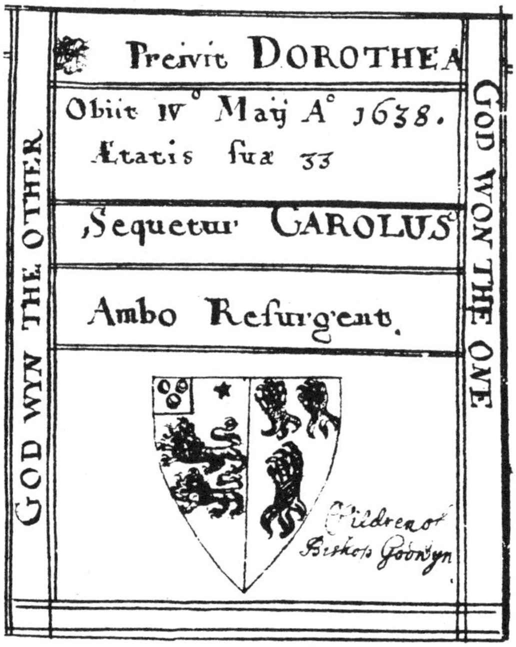

LEFT: Tomb attributed to Ankaret, 1st Baroness Strange of Blackmere, Salop, d1413. Her dowry included Wilton, Longhope, Huntley, Huntsham, Penyard and Eccleswall. There was also a close blood relationship between her family and that of Katherine Audley. (HCR/WMC/3782) BELOW: Interior prior to the restoration by J.L. Pearson, architect of Truro cathedral, in 1895. RIGHT: Gravestone, now lost, of Dorothy, d1638, wife of Charles Godwin, a son of Francis Godwin, Bishop of Hereford (1617-33), author of *De Praesulibus Angliae,* a catalogue with biographies of the English bishops. T. Dingley c1684.

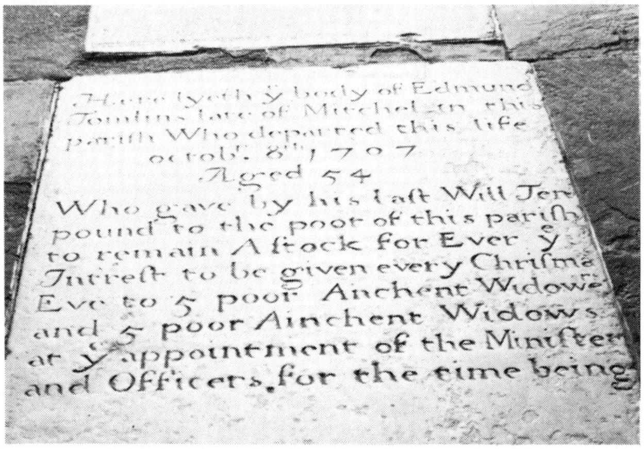

Within the church, ABOVE LEFT: 'Perhaps the finest monument in the church'. A priest of about 1280 in an attitude of prayer, the intensity of feeling fully expressed in his face. (HCL/WMC/3781) BELOW RIGHT: Monument to Edmund Tomlins, d 1707. In the churchyard, ABOVE RIGHT: two cherubic angels mourn Joseph Bond, d 1784. BELOW LEFT: The Hodges' monument in the later low-relief tradition.

The bounds of the chase in Trefnant's perambulation of 1394. From Primeswell spring west of the Wyche gap(1) it followed the shire boundary — by 'le Dedeorle', the Red Earl's dyke, to Charmill pool at the southern tip of the Malverns(2) and to Clencher's Mill.(3) Here it turned north along the ridge to meet Ledbury Denzein Park(4) and then via Eastnor Church,(5) the Ridgeway,(6) and Bartons Court(7) back to the Wyche.

Palace, Park and Chase

The bishop had no permanent abode. The palace at Hereford was never popular. It was used as a court rather than a residence. To fulfil his responsibilities for the spiritual well-being of the diocese, he had to spend his life on the move, constantly travelling between his many manor houses, some 24 in all. Before 1232, bishops such as Robert de Bethune would have been seen among the crowds in Ledbury's market place. Afterwards, the removal of the palace to its new site, beyond the Upper Cross, ensured the popularity of Ledbury as an episcopal residence. St Thomas Cantilupe (1275-82) used it quite frequently. Richard Swinfield (1282-1317) preferred Ledbury to all his other town residences, and it was a favourite of John Trilleck (1344-60).(69) However, the bishops never rested long at Ledbury. In 1280, Swinfield was there only from 17 to 20 December. He was back again on 23 February and left after a rather unusually long visit, on 3 March.

Here at the palace were also accommodated Royal visitors: King John for two days in 1211; Henry III *en route* from Hereford to Worcester in 1231 and 1256. After his capture at Llantrissant, the unfortunate Edward II was imprisoned by Bishop Adam de Orleton (1317-27) at Ledbury before he was taken to Kenilworth Castle, where he was forced to abdicate. It was from Ledbury that the writs were issued on 3 December 1326, summoning the Parliament which, under Orleton's leadership, was to give the crown to Edward II's son, prince Edward, who was himself to stay at Ledbury in August 1332.(70)

The bishop's arrival in Ledbury was an impressive spectacle. Normally, he had some 40 attendants with his squires at the head. Next came the serving valets, with the clerk of the chapel taking precedence over such other officers as the chief carter, the larderer, the porter, the stable groom, the butler, the chamberlain, the farrier, the head huntsman, the messenger and last, but by no means least, the falconer. The kitchen servants, the cook and baker and their helpers, the sumpterer and under-groom were of the third category. The lowest group, the underlings, included the page boys and the kitchen, bakehouse, stable and kennel attendants.

In the bishop's retinue were some 30 or 40 horses: nags — saddle horses; palfreys — small horses suitable for ladies; sumpters — pack horses to carry clothes and furniture, and draught horses for pulling the chamber and kitchen carts along the inadequate trackways. The maintenance of these horses was a continuous source of trouble and expense to the bishop.

At the greater festivals, the bishop, like any great feudal lord, kept open house for tenants and friends of the locality. On Easter Sunday 1281, at the Colwall palace, such a company ate 1¾ carcasses of fresh and 1½ of salt beef, 5 pigs, 4½ calves, 22 kids, 3 fat deer, 12 capons, 88 pigeons, and 1,400 eggs, with bread and cheese. They drank 60 gallons of wine, and beer without stint. It was not merely the duties of office, but also the problems of provisioning, that kept the bishop constantly on the road, for the major part of what was consumed was local in origin.(71)

Although the bishops may have had others, their vineyard on the slopes of Wall Hills was pre-eminent. Some 45 productive vineyards were mentioned in the Domesday Survey, but none was recorded in Herefordshire. The first such record is a letter of Gilbert Foliot (1148-63) granting one of his villeins, William, the son of Robert, his vine-dresser at Ledbury to Gloucester Abbey.[72] In 1266, Thomas Cantilupe instructed his seneschal to renew this vineyard. In the *Red Book,* the vineyard was 12 acres in area and was valued at 100s, the equivalent of 100 burgage plots.[73]

In 1298 the yield was seven pipes of white wine and almost one of verjuice, a drink made from crab-apples. The pipe was a large cask, usually of 52 sextaries, each equivalent to six bottles. The produce of the Wall Hills vineyard, which was stored in casks from which it was drawn directly, was equivalent to 2,200 bottles a year. Daily consumption varied from ½ to 11 sextaries. Red wine came from the continent and was bought at Bristol at about double the cost of the home product. In the late 17th century, George Skyppe grew red and white grapes at the lower estate at Wall Hills and in his garden at the Upper Hall. In 1687, 48 bottles of white and 20 of red wine were produced.[74] The same vineyard is shown on a survey of the Hazle estate drawn for Jacob Tonson by C. Price in 1730.[75]

The whole area from the Upper Cross and the palace to the top of the Malverns, the park and the chase beyond, was devoted to the bishop's sport and table. Within the chase, the bishops had parks at Eastnor and Colwall. The parkland character is still self-evident from near and afar. Let us hope that this ancient feature of Ledbury's townscape will not be subjected to development, whether of houses or caravans, and that the authorities will have the wisdom to ensure that this Denzein park, with its fine mature trees as far as the top of Coneygree wood, is retained for the peaceful recreation of present and future denizens of Ledbury. Here, in the middle ages, the fowler and the falconer had to give way to the huntsman. The hunting season for the hart or buck began at Midsummer; for the hind or doe, on Holyrood Day, 14 September. The season extended through Martinmas to Candlemas, 2 February.

Rights over such an extensive chase had to be jealously guarded. St Thomas Cantilupe was involved in a lengthy legal conflict with Gilbert de Clare, 8th Earl of Gloucester, because his predecessor, John le Breton, had failed to defend his rights to the Eastnor and Colwall areas of the chase. Such was the overwhelming influence of the great marcher lord, that three years elapsed before Cantilupe could get a hearing, at Candlemas 1278. In the words of an old rhyme:

'Ly eveske de Hereford	'The bishop of Hereford
Sout bien que ly quens fu fort,	Knew well that the earl was strong
Kant il prist l'affere:	When he took up the matter;
Devant ce esteit mult fer,	Before that he was very proud and
Les Engleis quida touz manger,	Thought to eat up all the English
Mes ore ne set que fere.'	But now he scarce knows what to do.'[76]

On the day, the Red Earl appeared with a force of armed retainers and, saying that no sorry shaveling would take from him what he and his ancestors had enjoyed so long, sought postponement. Before the jury could be dismissed Cantilupe, who had retired to a nearby wood, issued forth in full canonicals, his priests at his side, bearing lighted tapers. At the place of judgement, 'the candles being put out, he solemnly pronounced sentence of excommunication against all and everyone who that day hindered the church of Hereford's right in its woods and forests'. Faced by the full power of the church, the Red Earl rode off and the jury gave their verdict in the bishop's favour. The bishop then began a perambulation of the bounds, but 'divers of the Earl's men obstinately persisting to maintain the quarrel, shot at random very near his person . . . one of whom more injurious than the rest . . . shortly after, saith the record, was miserably drowned'. The Red Earl's dyke along the top of the Malverns, constructed by Gilbert de Clare in 1287, remains as witness to this epic encounter.[77]

It was not merely the mighty that the bishops had to withstand. Numerous cases occur in the episcopal registers, of trespass and poaching on the chase. In 1278 the sheriff summoned John d'Abitot of Redmarley to answer charges of poaching in the bishop's park at Ledbury. In 1346 the bishop threatened Thomas de Goldhull, a chaplain of Bosbury who had hunted over his land, with excommunication. In 1391 John Deynte and others pretended a right to the chase 'at the mountains of Malverne' but when Trefnant appeared at Ledbury 'at the vicaridge house, the said John Deynte cast himself upon his favour . . . and said that he had never made such pretence. Upon which the bishop received him into his favour and in testimony thereof kissed him'.(78)

Trefnant then sought to secure the rights of the see by carrying out a detailed perambulation of the chase in 1394. It began at a spring called Primeswell on the west side of the Wyche gap by 'le Dedeorle', the Red Earl's dyke, and then along the ridge of the mountains to 'Chenernisshepole', Chevernish or Charmill pool. Hence, following the county boundary, it extended to the mill called 'Clenchmille' before turning north to the church at Eastnor and along the Ridgeway as far as Frog Lane and Barton's gate by Barton Court to pass Brodley meadow south east of Brockbury before returning to the Wychegap.(79)

In the chase were '. . . harte and hinde, dove and bokke, Hare and fox, Catt and Brocke, Wylde foule with his flocke, Partrich fesaunt hen and fesaunt cocke, With grene and wyld stob and stock . . .'

From the park there was further provision. Rabbits are not mentioned in Swinfield's register but Coneygree wood stands witness to a coney or rabbit warren. By the late 13th century the rabbit, valued for its fur and its meat, was increasing in popularity. The Archbishop of Canterbury supplied 200 rabbits from his warrens for a Royal feast at Westminster in 1270. Before the mid-14th century, an enclosed warren with a professional rabbit keeper was established at Ledbury, for in 1346 John the Forester, priest of Ledbury, was convicted for poaching in the bishop's warren and after public penance in Ledbury church, swore not to repeat the offence and to abstain from all hunting for three years.(80)

Another prerequisite was a series of fishponds. Days of abstinence and fasting were numerous — Wednesday, Friday and Saturday each week and the days of Ember and Lent. An extraordinarily wide range of fish was eaten on such occasions, from salt water, rivers and stagnant pools. Pike and tench, for example, were kept in the stews of the Ledbury palace. These intimate details of the bishop's domestic arrangements have come down to us from the accounts of the household expenses drawn up by Richard Swinfield's chaplain, John de Kemeseye, between Michaelmas 1289 and 1290.

The years 1250-1300 represent the most prosperous period of the see during the middle ages. The level of economic activity is indicated by the growth of other markets and fairs within the locality. In 1255 Henry III granted to 'Richard Pauncefot and his heirs a weekly market on Tuesday at his manor of Cowarne . . . and of an annual fair there on the vigil, the feast and the morrow of St Michael', 29 September. In 1284, Edward I granted 'Richard [Swinfield] bishop of Hereford and his successors, a weekly market on Tuesday at his manor of Credeleye, and of a yearly fair there on the vigil, the feast and the morrow of St Barnabas', 11 June.(81) It was probably Swinfield who established the market and the little borough by the church and palace at Bosbury. The remains of the burgage plots can yet be seen on the south side of the church. Unlike Capella's borough it never grew. The chill winds of the 14th century petrified the foundation.

The predominance of Ledbury's markets and fairs was so secure by the 13th century, that these grants represented no threat. In 1234, Ledbury fair, held on the feast of St Matthias, 21 September, and the three days following, was worth £7 to the bishop. This compares favourably with the £20 he received from St Ethelbert's fair at Hereford in 1275.(82)

After Swinfield's death, the see and its tenants experienced increasingly bleak times. Symptoms of demographic decline were visible even before the Black Death. The acute shortage of labour after the outbreaks of 1348-50 and 1361, and the consequent collapse of rents and rise in labour costs, forced drastic economies on Bishop Trilleck.

In April 1356, a general chapter agreed that the palaces at Ledbury, Bromyard, Ross, Colwall and Bishops Frome, more than half of those in the county, were to be abandoned. Bishops Frome had not been used since Swinfield's death — a portent of things to come.(83) Only Hereford,

Sugwas, Bosbury and Whitbourne were to be kept in use. Thus, after 1356, the chase was only hunted from Bosbury, long an especially favoured residence, and the place where the old blind Saxon bishop Athelstan had died after the Welsh had burned down his new minster at Hereford in 1055.

The site at the Upper Cross became a scene of dereliction and remained so for more than two centuries, a grim reminder of the catastrophe which had struck the town and the country. When Leland made his antiquarian tour of England, between 1534 and 1543, the 'faire mansion place for the bysshope at Ledbury' was still to be seen, but 'all in ruyne'.(84)

The bishop's chase to the east of Ledbury was the setting chosen for one of the greatest works of mediaeval literature, William Langland's *Vision concerning Piers the Plowman.* A.H. Bright has suggested that the 'broad bank by a bourne side' where Piers 'went me to rest' was in the little valley just north and west of Wynds Point. The 'tower on a toft truly made' was the Norman keep built within the Herefordshire beacon Iron-age hill fort and the dungeon 'with deep ditch and dark, and dreadful of sight' was Old Castle just below, of which nothing now remains. The 'fair field full of folk. . . of all manner of men, the mean and the rich, working and wondering, as in the world we must' lay between.

The first printed edition of *Piers the Plowman* was published in 1550 by Robert Cowley who tells us in his preface that 'I have learned that the Autour was named Robert Langelande, a Shropshire man born in Cleybirie about VIII miles from the Malvern hills'. Bright has argued that 'Cleybirie' is a mistake and should read 'Ledbirie', which is precisely eight miles from the Malverns. He further suggested that the poet's surname came from Longlands on the boundaries of Colwall and Ledbury parishes and that Langland was ordained to acolyte's orders by Bishop John Trilleck at Bromyard in 1348.

Within the chase, Bronsil castle, erected by Richard Beauchamp, son of the 1st Lord Beauchamp of Powicke, who was given a licence to crenellate in 1449 and 1460. Engraving by S. & N. Buck, 1731.

ABOVE: View across the deer park to the Malverns. (HCL/WMC/582)
BELOW: Here on the Herefordshire side of the Malverns, according to A.H. Bright, William Langland, weary of wandering, went to sleep under a broad bank by the side of a little stream. Here came to him his remarkable vision of 'a tower on a hill, fairly fashioned, beneath it a dell, and in the dell a donjon with deep ditches and dark . . . and all between . . . a fair field full of folk'. (HCRO/AB48/B10)

ABOVE LEFT: Woodhouse Farm, probably the oldest domestic building in the parish, built not long after the ravages of the Black Death. (HCL/WMC/5173) RIGHT: Cruck truss of the hall in the bedroom. (HCL/WMC/5173) BELOW LEFT: Barn at Wall Hills Farm. (HCL/WMC/8771) RIGHT: The Homend, early 17th-century building incorporating earlier cruck truss. (HCL/WMC/5170)

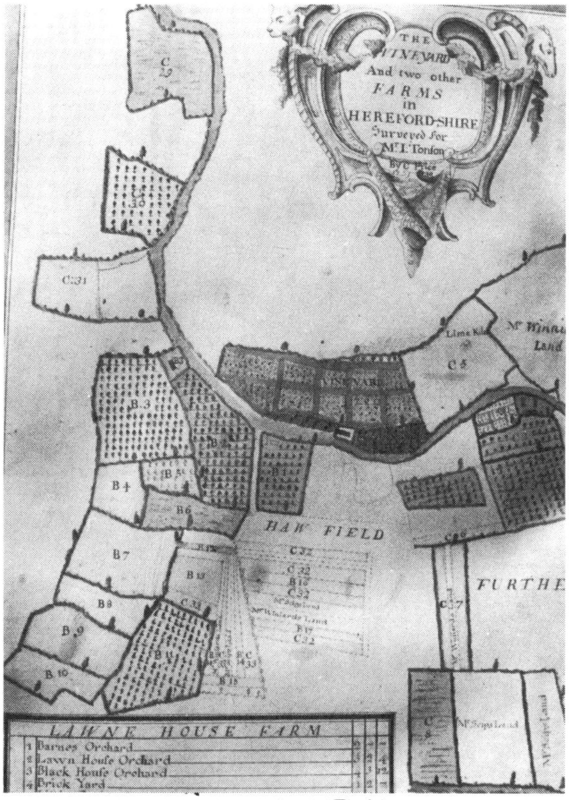

LEFT: The country's only cruck-framed public convenience? Due to sex discrimination on the part of the local council, the cruck blades can only be seen in the Ladies' section. RIGHT: The vineyard on the slopes of Wall Hills. Here Robert dressed vines in the days of Bishop Hugh Foliot (1148-63). In 1366, it was renewed on Thomas Cantilupe's order and in 1288 the 12-acre yard was valued at 100s yielding the equivalent of 2,000 bottles of white wine in 1298. C. Price's *Survey* of 1730. (HCRO/J95/1) BELOW: Bosbury, looking down the burgage plots from the Bell to the Crown Inn.

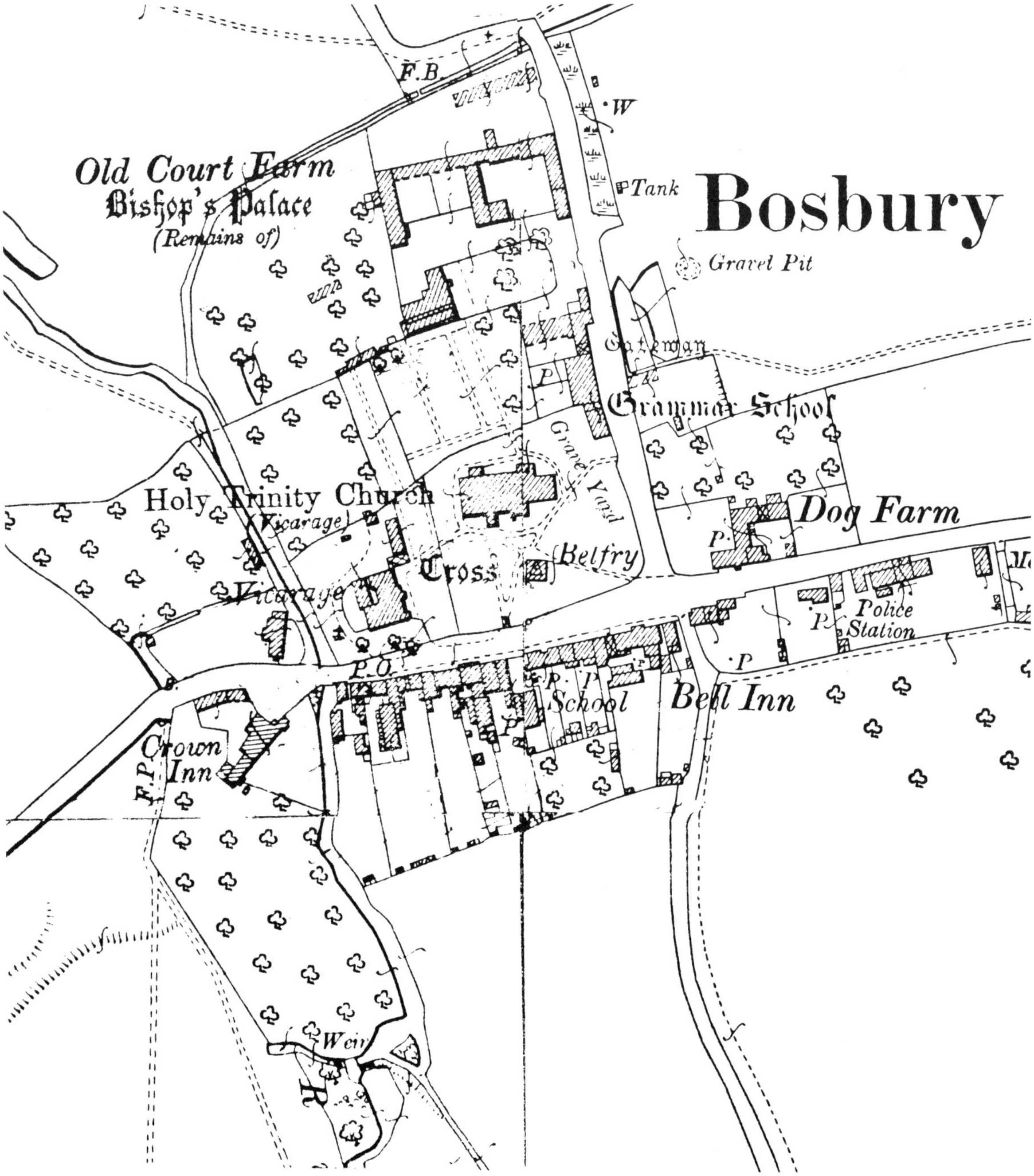

The palace site at Bosbury. Across the road to the south of the church can be seen the dozen or so burgage plots. However, the chill winds of the 14th century petrified Gilbert Swinfield's foundation. Crown Inn, home of the Harfords, to the left. 1st ed 25 ins OS (1887).

Coming of Age

Between 1540 and 1640, Ledbury came of age. Until the 16th century the authority of the church had always, in the last resort, been supreme within the town. The abandonment of the palace by the bishop in 1356 had little effect. The markets and fairs continued to be conducted by his officers and for his profit. His court was still held: in the Booth Hall until 1400, and afterwards in the new Court House in the Southend, built by Richard Glover. His influence extended far beyond borough and foreign, for the five largest neighbouring manors — Bishops Frome, Bosbury, Cradley, Colwall and Eastnor — were his as well. St Peter's remained the centre of ecclesiastical administration.

From the Upper and Lower Halls the church's control was further strengthened, for the two estates were possessed of considerable lands in and around the borough. Many of the portionists, sometimes residents but frequently absentees, were ecclesiastics of character and distinction, holding important offices within the diocese.

The reform of the church in the 16th century changed all this. By 1590, control of the town and much of the district had passed into the hands of a small group of families, closely linked by blood and economic interest. Some, such as the Skyppes, were new to the area while others, such as the Eltons and Skynners, were old-established. Almost all the lands of the church passed into the hands of this group. First the chantry lands and subsequently, by a series of complex transactions, the portionists' estates with their tithes, were acquired. The greater part of the bishop's demesne and his manorial rights, which had been seized by Elizabeth in 1559, were purchased in 1630.

The position of this dominant group was further strengthened by marriage into the wealthier merchant families of the town. The New House, built about 1590 and aptly named, is a dramatic monument to one such family, the Halls, who had recently arrived from Lincolnshire. It has been described as 'the grandest black and white house in the county'.(85) It certainly is the only one that could vie with the great clothiers' houses of Shrewsbury, such as the four-storeyed Ireland's mansions of 1576 in the High Street. The New House is the most important domestic building in the town, in terms not merely of its size but also of its position. At the Upper Cross, on the site of the bishop's palace, with the spacious grounds of Ledbury Park beyond, it dominated, yet was apart from the town. In this respect, it was a clear and unchallengeable symbol of the new order.

Death and marriage were ever changing the make-up of this group, but always at its centre were the three major estates of the borough and foreign — the Upper and Lower Hall and the Ledbury Park, now New House estates. The Upper Hall was held by the Skyppes until 1812 and by their successors, the Martins, until 1921. The Lower Hall belonged to a branch of the Eltons until 1756; while New House was in the hands of the Halls until 1680, when it passed to the Biddulphs, who lived there until it was sold to Horace Chapman, after the death of the 3rd Lord Biddulph, in 1949.

The Chantry Lands. It was not the measures of Henry VIII's reign but those of Edward VI and the first years of Elizabeth I's reign that ushered in this era of radical change for Ledbury. In 1547,

Parliament transferred to the king's majesty the possessions of all colleges, chantries and free chapels 'by reason of the superstition and errors . . . brought into the minds and estimations of Men by . . . devising and phantasying vain opinions of purgatory and masses . . . to be done for them which be departed'.

The chantry services in St Peters came to an end and their chaplains were pensioned off, not ungenerously. John Potter of the chantry of the Blessed Virgin Mary received a pension of £6 *per annum.* He also had the benefice of Tedstone Wafre near Bromyard, valued at £1 10s. 'Syr Gryffyth Fowler', who had served St Anne's chantry, received a pension of £5 and was a chaplain of St Katherine's. His burial is recorded in the parish register for 13 September 1559. Richard Wheeler, priest of the Trinity chantry received a pension of £6.

On 21 August 1549, Richard Willason of Ledbury, gentleman, and John Harford of Bosbury bought from the Crown:

'The lands in Ledbury, Tybbynge Sparowhawke, Morefeld and all other possessions of Trynite Chaunterye in these places and in Estenour and Michelfelde or elsewhere; the rent from Clerken Mille in Ledbury, from land called Watlyns in Estonour, also the messuage called Homehouse and land called Berbers and lands in Ledbury and Estonour and elsewhere of Saynt Anne Chauntery [all the gift of John and Joanna Hope in 1384]; the rents, messuages, burgages, cottages, shops, garden, mills, barns, lands and other possessions in Ledbury, Estonour and elsewhere of St Mary chantry.'(86)

They paid £957 6s 2d for the lands of these and 26 other chantries, including those at Clehonger, Stoke Edith, Mathon and Holmer in Herefordshire and All Saints and Saint Helen's in Worcester.

The Upper Hall Estate. While king and Parliament were engaged on the reform of the church and the sequestration of so much of its land and wealth, John Skyppe, a Norfolk man, held the see of Hereford (1539-52). He never married, but he did make careful provision for his family.

Bishop Skyppe's sister, Alice had married John Willason of Ledbury. Richard Willason was their son. In 1542, John Skyppe leased the Upper Hall estate and the Ledbury demesne lands to his nephew, Richard Willason, on highly favourable terms. Seven years later, Richard, jointly with John Harford, was able to purchase the Ledbury and other chantry lands from the Crown, and in 1551 leased the episcopal palace at Sugwas from John Skyppe. Richard Willason married Ann, the daughter of William Elton of Ledbury by his first wife, Mary, but died without heirs in 1574.(87)

He was buried at Madley, where his remarkable tomb, the work of the Hereford sculptor John Gildon, can still be seen. Ann, his widow, must have admired Gildon's tomb of John Harford, her late husband's partner in the purchase of the chantry lands. This equally elaborate monument had been erected by Harford's son in Bosbury church the previous year, 1573. At the top, in the position of honour, in a large triangular pediment, are the arms of Bishop Skyppe. Just across the road at the Crown Inn, which was originally the Harford mansion, Bishop Skyppe's arms can also be found, with a number of others, carved on the roof bosses of the principal ground floor room.(88)

Richard Willason left the Upper Hall estate to Edmund Skyppe but it was to be at the disposal of his widow, Ann, during her life. Edmund Skyppe, who enjoyed the lease of the episcopal estate at Bishops Frome, was another of the bishop's nephews. His son, John was the first of the Skyppes to reside at the Upper Hall. Edmund died in 1608 and under the terms of his will, John Skyppe was to have 'one standing bedstead with furniture, two bedsteads for servants, one table board with frame standing in the parlour, three forms, one square table, two little stools, one dripping pan and one brass pot, all at Ledbury', where his son had taken up residence. To his son George he left the lease on the manor of Bishops Frome and to his son Thomas, his lease of the Dean and 'Chamters' portion in Bishops Frome and the 'cupboard and deske in my chamber' and all his books.(89)

When John Skyppe died in 1619, as his son and heir was only 15 years old, he left to his widow, Johan, 'one half of the house where she now lives called the Upper Hall . . . and if she inhabits there . . . 10 loads of wood yearly to be sent there from the Frith of Conygre, as his overseer shall appoint . . . half his household stuff within his house, all the bees, two of the best kine, the best heifer, her own mare and colt, and the lower garden'.

From the 'True Inventorie of all the goods . . . and Chattells of John Skippe of the new hall within the parishe of Ledburie . . . gent., made and taken by Edward Elton, gent. Anthony Northen, gent. Roger Skippe, gent. and John Baldwine, yeoman, the xxist day of May Anno dmi. 1619' (90) we can reconstruct the Upper Hall as it was before it was destroyed in the Civil War. At ground floor level it had parlour, hall and buttery and above each was a chamber. It was therefore of the traditional H-plan, but the hall was not open to the roof as was the Mansion House of St Katherine's. Possibly John Skyppe had modernised it by building a chamber over the hall at first floor level. This would give further accommodation and make the hall below easier to keep warm.

John (1574-1619) was the first of the Skyppe dynasty at Ledbury. Subsequently, the Skyppes became one of the major county families. John Skyppe II (1604-84) was High Sheriff of Herefordshire in 1680. John Skyppe III (1679-1764) held the shrievalty in 1706, John IV (1707-1796) in 1772 and John V (1741-1812) in 1801. They retained and enjoyed the power and wealth acquired during the reform of the church until 1812 when, on the death of John Skyppe V, the Upper Hall estates passed by marriage of the heiress, Penelope, to John Martin of Overbury Court, near Tewkesbury, senior partner in the bank of that name 'at the sign of the Grasshopper', on the corner of Lombard Street and Change Alley. The Martins held the Upper Hall to this century when, in 1921, it was bought by the Herefordshire County Council for use as a mixed grammar school.

The Lower Hall Estate. It was William Elton, Richard Willason's father-in-law, who ultimately gained control of the Lower Hall estate.

William's elder brother, John, held the Lower Hall estate at Ledbury from 1517-47. He was a man of considerable influence who enjoyed a multitude of offices in the dioceses of Hereford and Salisbury; he was master of St Katherine's, canon of Hereford cathedral, archdeacon of Hereford, and chancellor of the diocese. As portionist he was able to present one of his brother William's younger sons, Edward, as vicar of Ledbury in 1520.

After John Elton's death Bishop Skyppe presented his kinsman, Richard Skyppe, to the portion with a long and advantageous lease on the Lower Hall. The estate was effectively his own; the lease had merely to be renewed on the original terms. In 1552 Richard Skyppe bequeathed 'all the said portion or rectory called Netherhall' to William Elton.

William Elton settled the estate on his younger son by his second marriage, Peter (d 1594), who was succeeded by his own son, Edward (1583-1652), his grandson John, who was also master of Pauncefort Court, Munsley, and his great grandson, George (d 1711). The last of the Eltons at the Lower Hall was George (d 1756). His father, George (1675-1753), had married his niece, Eleanor, whose unassuming monument, bearing the Elton arms, can still be seen in the church.(91)

The Hazle Estate. William Elton's eldest son, Anthony, was provided for out of the church's lands in a different way. The Hazle had been part of the manor of Ledbury since earliest times. In 1066 William I had returned it to the see after it had, in the words of Domesday Book, been 'unjustly held by earl (king) Harold'. In 1166 *Hugo de Hasla,* one of the bishop knights, held it but by the 13th century the Pauncefots, *Ricardus Pancevot* in 1210 and Grymbald Pauncefot in 1304, owed knights' service to the bishop for the Hazle. In 1332 Osmeric Pauncefot obtained a licence for mass to be said by a chaplain from St Katherine's in the Hazle chapel three times a week.(92) Then, for almost 200 years, it was in the hands of the Walwyns. Thomas Walwyn of Hellens Much Marcle held the lease at the time of his death in 1531, just before it was granted to Anthony Elton.

Anthony, who was securely enough established to marry Alice, daughter of John Scudamore of Kentchurch, died in 1587. He was succeeded at the Hazle by his eldest son, William, who died without issue in 1593. Anthony's second son, Ambrose inherited the estate. In 1630, he was to join with three others in the purchase of the manor of Ledbury and to secure his own position at the Hazle.(93) The monument to Ambrose and his wife Ann, in the south aisle of the church, records that before they died in 1659 and 1660 respectively they had 'three sons and 14 daughters; and from their own loins they lived to see above 120 children'. About 1720, the Hazle estate was purchased by Jacob Tonson, publisher of the works of Dryden, Congreve and Pope, who commissioned the splendid *Accurate Survey of the Hazle Manour in Hereford-shire* by Charles Price in 1730. The Elton arms can still be seen at the Hazle farm, above the early 18th century fireplace in the east wing.

The Royal onslaught on the ecclesiastical estates in Ledbury continued during the reign of Elizabeth I. In 1599, the Attorney-General filed a suit in the Exchequer, claiming that, as Bishop Trefnant had obtained a licence in 1401 to found a college of priests at Ledbury, the Upper and Lower Hall estates, with all their lands, tenements, tithes, etc, belonged to the queen under the 1547 Act for the suppression of colleges. A licence had been issued to Trefnant, but it had never been put into effect. As it could be clearly demonstrated that the two estates did not belong to a college with a seal expressing its corporate legal personality, the Crown lost the case.(94)

The irony is that the beneficiaries of this judgement were not the church, but the laymen who had forestalled the Crown. An act of 1558 had sought to prevent bishops from granting lands, except to the Crown as part of an 'exchange', 'other than for the term of xxi years or three lives'. It was through the abuse of such power that the Upper and Lower Hall and Hazle estates had fallen into lay hands.

The Manor and Demesne Lands. By the 1558 Act authority was given 'to the Queen's Majesty, upon the Avoidance of any Archbishopric or bishopric, to take into her hands certain of the temporal possessions thereof, recompensing the same with Parsonages impropriate and tenths'. The Crown was thus able to obtain such episcopal lands and estates as it desired. In return the bishops would receive from the Crown the right to a miscellaneous assortment of small and fixed payments from the clergy. These were difficult, often impossible, to collect.

Elizabeth's first appointment to the bench of bishops was that of John Scory, to the see of Hereford (1559-86). Mary Tudor had deprived him of the see of Chichester and he had sought to restore himself to favour with the catholic monarch by recanting his reformed ideas, renouncing his wife and doing penance for being married. This did not have the desired effect and eventually he fled to Calvin's Geneva. Knowing Scory to be a malleable man, Elizabeth would not confirm his appointment until he had agreed, under the terms of the new act, to the 'exchange' of 17 of the choicest manors of the see for 'decayed chancels, ruinous houses often overburdened with pensions of vicars and for tenths which could only be collected with difficulty from the poor and reluctant clergy of the diocese'. The deal cost the see half its revenue.(95)

Ledbury borough and foreign were among the 17 manors lost to the diocese in this 'exchange'. The demesne lands (some 500 acres in the *Red Book,* including the Denzein park, Coneygree wood and the palace site, the lordship of such knightly estates as Ockridge, Massington, Wellington, Donnington, Underdown, Wall Hills and the Hazle) together with all manorial rights, such as suit of court, passed into the hands of the Crown. If it is accepted that the manor had been part of St Mildburga's estate 'in the district called *Lydas*' which was given to the see, this represents the end of a lordship which had lasted for more than 700 years.

Given a determined group within the town, a start could now be made on consolidating the new order, for the Royal interest in Ledbury was merely financial. In 1584, the original charter being deemed 'obsolete', Elizabeth granted a new charter, at an appropriate fee, for a weekly market and two annual fairs. In 1592, an untainted supply of drinking water was secured for the town when lead pipes were laid down from Coneygree wood.

The manor remained in Royal hands until Charles I, having dismissed his third Parliament in 1629, found himself in the severest financial straits. He had now to live 'of his own'. In December of that year, the lordship and manor of Ledbury, with many others, were sold to the Corporation of London. Almost immediately, negotiations were entered into for their purchase by a consortium that included most of the major figures in the town — Ambrose Elton of the Hazle, Thomas Skynner of London (merchant), Thomas Hooper, Stephen Skynner, John Phillips (clothier), Richard Hall of the New House, Thomas Pirrock, John Woodward, Francis Skynner, Anthony Vobe, William Wheeler of Mockrill, Ledbury, and John Went. The lordship and manor were purchased for £1,400.

They were bought, in the words of a deed of 1635, 'to be at the disposition of the tenants', such as Ambrose Elton at the Hazle and Francis Hall of the New House, who already held their lands on long and advantageous leases. Francis Hall bought up the remainder of the lease on 'the park in Ledbury forren called Dingewood' from 'John Watts of Worcester, gent.'. John Skyppe II acquired William Wheeler's share in the manor in 1636 and added to his inheritance by purchasing further properties, including some of the demesne lands — the Lower Wall Hills estate with its vineyard. The Skynners, with numerous branches of the family in the town, and others at the Knapp, Pixley, the Burtons, Wellington and in London, now established themselves at Underdown.(96)

Bishop Scory, having lost half of the revenues of the see in the 'exchange' of 1558, looked elsewhere for some recompense. In 1569, under the terms of the 1547 Act, the queen granted him St Katherine's hospital as a 'deserted or relenquished hospital' which had been 'concealed and converted to the use of certain private men of sufficient wealth'. This was a reference to Edward Cooper, who had been appointed master by the dean and chapter in 1562, and such bedesmen as remained. This conflict over Scory's attempt to suppress St Katherine's became linked to another battle with the dean and chapter, over his claim to the right to visit, or inspect the cathedral.

Both claims were hard fought and both were ultimately lost by Scory. The St Katherine's dispute was referred from the court of Star Chamber to the court of the Exchequer. In 1580, after 11 years of litigation, this court accepted Hugh Foliot's foundation charter of 1232 as good cause for its continuance in perpetuity. Its decree 'in behalf of the poor almsfolk' was then confirmed by act of Parliament.

Cooper was vindicated and reinstated as master. John Baldwyn, the hospital's chaplain, said of him, 'He useth the poor better than he ever knewe them used — giving them meat and drink and a livery which he knew not Mr before give' and 'the Mr hath dispensed yearly £20 of his own revenue in defending the whole house'.(97)

King Edward VI Grammar School. Chantry lands and possessions, the 1547 Act suggested, might be used for 'such good and godly uses as the erecting of grammar schools to the education of youth in virtue and godliness'. Throughout the land, these intentions were frustrated. Powerful laymen, 'knowing that this was the last dish of the last course and that after chantries as after cheese, nothing was to be expected', seized the last opportunity for enrichment from the wealth of the church.

This did not pass without comment. Thomas Lever, master of St John's, Cambridge and leader of the extreme protestant reformers asked, in a sermon before Edward VI in 1550, 'How many grammar schools be taken, sold and made away to the grievous offence of the people, to the most miserable drowning of youth in ignorance?' On another occasion he demanded, 'For God's sake, you that be in authority, look upon it. For if you wink at such matters God will scowl upon you'. After Protector Somerset's fall in 1550, a programme of refoundation was begun which continued through the reign of Mary Tudor to that of Elizabeth I. Hence the number of ancient grammar schools that bear their names. The schools of chantry foundation at Ledbury, Bosbury and Bromyard were all saved in this way.

In their survey of the Trinity chantry at Ledbury, the Royal commissioners had reported: 'Sir Rychard Wheler, Stypendary there, of the age of 54 yeres, a man of god conversacion, and dayly occupied in teachyng of chylderne gramer, Whych hath for his salary, the clere Revenue of the same [£4 0s 16½d], And non other lyvyng, but the lytle rewarde of the Frendes of the Scolers'. The townsmen then petitioned the kings Council, beseeching their 'bountefull goodnes, to graunte that the saide scole maye ther styll be kepte, and the said Stipendary to Remayn for the maynteynying therof to the erudicion of yough, a charytable dede, for the Inhabitaunces of the same Have nott only Hade profytt and advauntage by the kepyng of a gramer scole there, as in bordynge and loggying His scolers, but also the countre therabowtes, in uttrying ther vytalles ther by mean of the said scollers'.

The petition was accepted and the Council ruled that 'the seid grammer Schole in Ledbury aforeseid shall contynue, and that Richard Wheler, Scholemaster ther, shall have and enjoye the rowme of Scholemaster there, and shall have for his wages, yerely, 71s 3d'. This sum continued to be paid by HM Commissioners of Woods and Forests to the school until it passed into oblivion in 1862.(98)

By 1585, when he gave evidence in a dispute over some of the lands of St Katherine's, Richard Wheeler was no longer schoolmaster, but vicar of Preston. His successor, Henry Hunt, who is described in the episcopal visitation books as *ludi magister,* was buried in the churchyard close to his school in 1586. According to the churchwarden's records, the vestry claimed the right 'as far as we lawfully can or may' to appoint the master. He was then licensed as suitable to teach by the bishop and his name was entered in the episcopal subscription books. Robert Symonds (1735), William Steele (1757), John Bennett (1785), William Giles (1795), William Humphreys (1799) and John Lodge (1800) are to be found among the entries.

By the 19th century, the school was failing. The premises which had served for some 300 years were 'completely built in, dark and unhealthy and in a very dilapidated state'. William Humphreys, master in 1822, was still serving in 1835, but five years later the post was vacant. By 1857, Thomas Perry had removed the school to Oakland House in the Homend. At Bromyard the grammar school faced similar difficulties but was rescued from without, by the London Goldsmiths' Company. Ledbury was not so fortunate. As a consequence of local indifference and perversity King Edward VI's grammar school just slipped into oblivion.(99)

ABOVE: Tomb of Richard (d1574) and Ann Willason at Madley. His mother was the sister of Bishop Skyppe. His wife was the daughter of William Elton of Ledbury. The Skyppe arms are omitted from his father's shield on the right. (HCL/WMC/11016) OPPOSITE LEFT: Tomb of John Harford at Bosbury. In a pediment above are the Skyppe arms. RIGHT: 'Here lyes the Body of Captain Samuel Skynner (d1725) who was no mean proficient in Maritime affairs having been conversant therein near forty years'. The ostentation of the Skynner monuments, especially their 'most prodigious wigs', amused John Byng in 1781. BELOW New House, c1590, a dramatic and aptly-named monument to one of the new families, the Halls, clothiers from Lincolnshire. 'The grandest black and white house in the county', it dominated yet was apart from the town. (HCL/WMC/6088).

TVMVLVS IOANIS HARFORDI QVEM SIBI SVVS FILIVS EREXIT RICHARDVS ANNO DOMINI 1573

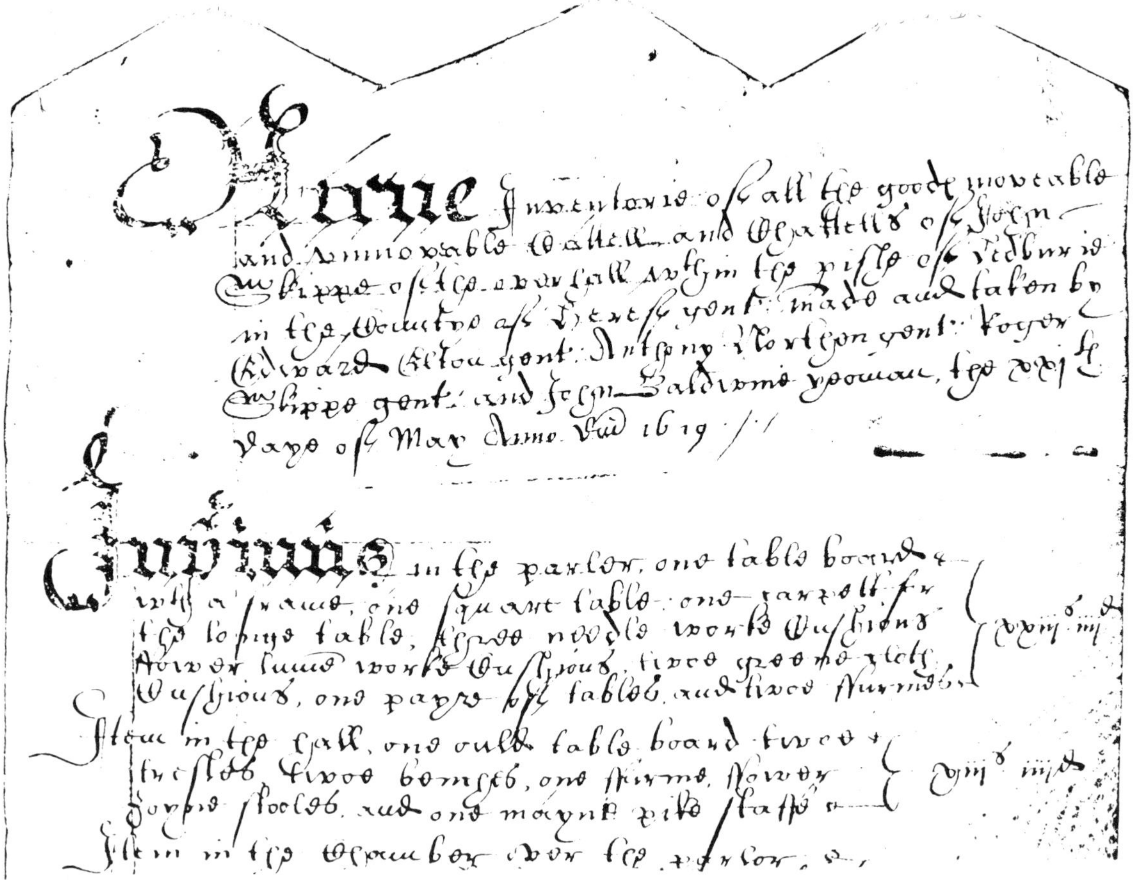

A True Inventorie of all the goods moveable and unmoveable Cattell and Chattells of John Skippe of the new hall within the parish of Ledburie in the Countie of Hereff gent. made and taken by Edward Elton gent. Anthony Northen gent. Roger Skippe gent. and John Baldwine yeoman, the xvij daye of May Anno Dni 1619

Imprimis in the parlor, one table board with a frame, one square table, one carpett for the longe table, three needle worke Cushions, fower turkie worke Cushions, two greene clothe Cushions, one payre of tables and two [illegible] — xxxiij^s iiij^d

Item in the hall, one ould table board two tressles, two benches, one chaire, fower joyned stooles, and one mayned pike staffe — xiij^s iiij^d

Item in the chamber over the parlor, [illegible]

ABOVE: 'True Inventorie of all the goods . . . and Chattells of John Skippe of the new hall within the parish of Ledbury, gent. . . . 1619'. BELOW: The Lower Hall, adjacent to the churchyard, indicating its origin as the house of one of the two portionists. Richard Skyppe bequeathed to William Elton in 1552, 'all the said portion or rectory called Netherhall'.

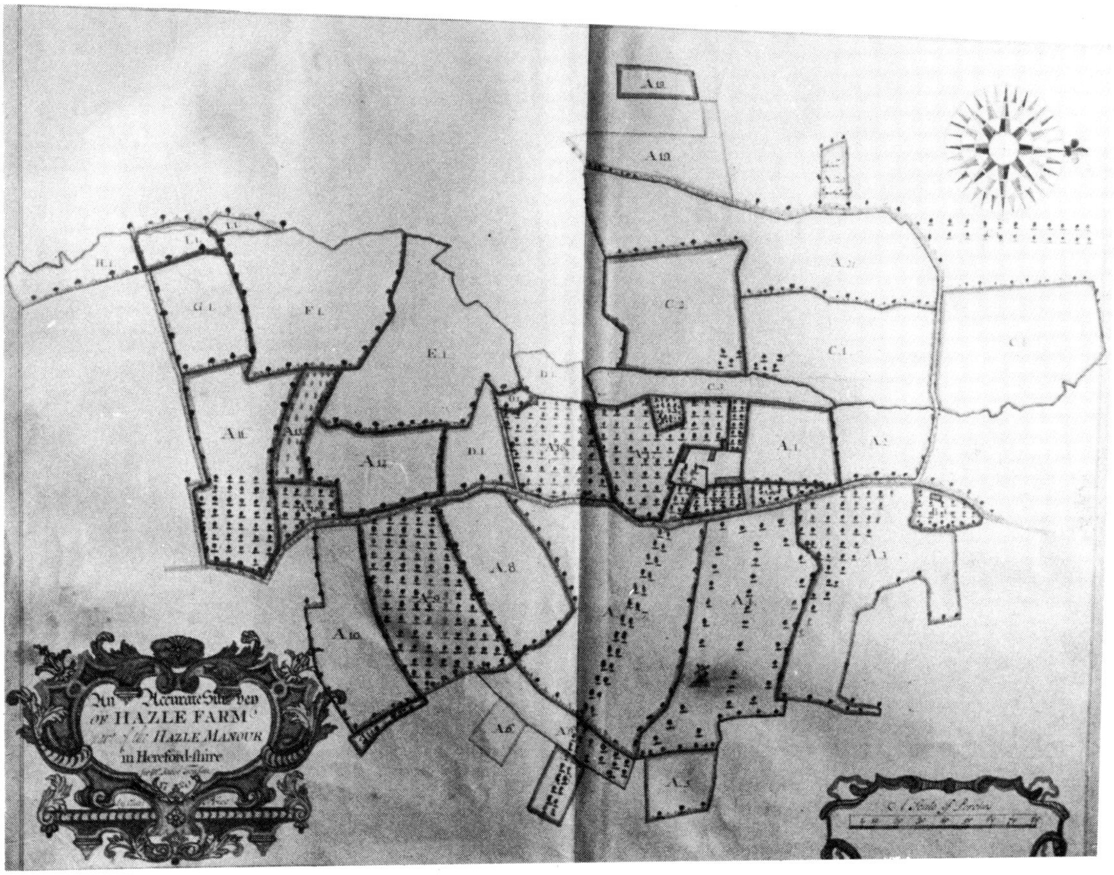

LEFT: The 18th-century facade of the Lower Hall. BELOW: About 1720, the Hazle estate was bought by Jacob Tonson, the publisher, for whom Price drew up this survey in 1730. (HCRO/J95/1) RIGHT: Edward Skynner, d1631, his wife and their 11 children. Legend has it that the 11th child (between them) was killed by the last wolf in the district.

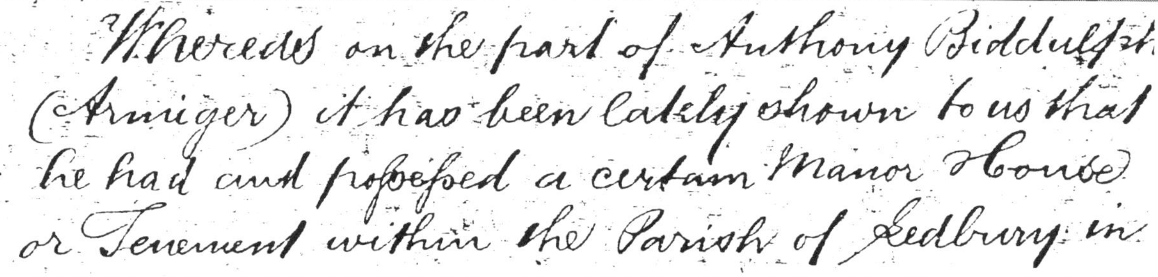

Whereas on the part of Anthony Biddulph
(Armiger) it has been lately shown to us that
he had and possessed a certain Manor House
or Tenement within the Parish of Ledbury in

LEFT: Anthony Biddulph, d1718, of the Inner Temple and first of the family at New House, which remained in the family for more than 250 years. RIGHT: Constance, eldest daughter and coheir of Francis Hall, d1706, brought New House and the Park to the Biddulph family after her father's death in 1680. CENTRE: Copy of deed granting a faculty for erecting a family pew to Anthony Biddulph, 1703. The pew came down in the restoration of 1895. (HCRO/92) BELOW: Celebration in stained glass of the alliance of Biddulph and Hall families.

A Considerable Clothing Town

After the dramatic reduction in the population of the town in the 14th century, recovery was slow. In the early 16th century, the number of tenancies was still almost 25 per cent down on the 1288 figure. The petition of 1552 to retain the grammar school stressed that 'the Toune of Ledbury ys a very pore toune'. This was in contrast to Bromyard and Leominster which described themselves in their respective petitions as 'a markett toune . . . greately Replenyshed with People' and 'a great Borough Toune . . . the greatest merket Toune within the Countie of Hereford'.

As the chantry certificates indicate the number of 'houseling' people, that is communicants, in each parish, a population table can be drawn up for Herefordshire market centres in Edward VI's reign.

Table 8. Communicants in Herefordshire, 1545

Leominster	Bromyard	Ledbury	Kington	Pembridge
1700	800	640	560	500
Eardisley	Bosbury	Kingsland	Weobley	
343	320	300	280	

The figures refer to the whole parish, the rural as well as the urban area. The communicants would be aged 15 years or more so, to obtain an estimate of the total population, we should add 40 per cent. There are no entries for Hereford or Ross.

Only two major buildings in Ledbury can be ascribed to the early Tudor period — further evidence of the condition of the town then. They are both in Church Lane and have in common such features as richly moulded bressumers and a bold jetty or overhang supported by deep brackets. They are the Council Offices and the Grammar School, now splendidly restored by the district council as an 'Heritage Centre'.

By about 1570 there had been a radical change. Ledbury was beginning to enjoy possibly its period of greatest prosperity. Almost all the mediaeval secular buildings were swept away in a great re-building of the town. A few may have been destroyed in the Civil War, such as the Upper Hall, or demolished subsequently. Certainly all that now remains is the fragment in the Chandos Cafe in Bye Street.

By contrast, a remarkable number of buildings of the late 16th and early 17th centuries still stands. In the 18th century, change did come but there are few major buildings entirely of that period. In many cases, all that could be achieved was a face-lift. The expansion of the town beyond its mediaeval bounds began about 1800. Yet the 19th and 20th centuries added little more than the 18th in terms of total reconstruction within those earlier bounds, even though, superficially, the brickwork of those centuries is a marked feature of the town. Just as the 12th and 13th centuries established Ledbury's street plan, so the late 16th and early 17th centuries are still the major elements in its streetscape.

The money which paid for the rebuilding in the years 1570-1620 came primarily from textiles but also from leather. The parish registers of William Davis, 1576-1612, frequently give occupations and thus indicate the range of trades in the town. Among those recorded for the years

1596-1602 are 'George Jerrome, wever; Thomas Hall, corveyser (shoemaker); Symon Willis, wever; Wm Meeke, tanner; John Willys, wever of the Homend; George Smith, glover; Philip Harries, taylor; Harry Averall, corveisor; Richard Jenkyns, currier; Anthony Skynner, clothier; John Bibb, wever; William Hooper, wever; Edward Skynner, clothier; Wm Sanford, milner; Richard Lawrence, corveyser; John Walcroft, mercer; Nycholas Stillin, sadler; Thomas Weeld, clothier'. Textiles predominate, leather trades follow and all the other trades together trail a long way behind — in marked contrast to the position in 1288 when the surnames indicated six main occupational categories (Table 2).

The growth of Ledbury's textile trade was part of a general expansion of the industry in the period. It is of particular interest because of the attempts in the 16th century to confine the industry to cities and corporate boroughs and to prevent its growth in market towns like Ledbury, or in the countryside.

According to Leland, writing in the reign of Henry VIII, 'no town in England maketh so many cloths yearly' as Worcester. It was renowned for both the quantity and quality of its cloth, made from Herefordshire and Shropshire wool. There were deep fears in the wool towns of rural competition based on cheaper labour. In 1533, to safeguard the industry in which half of Worcester's citizens were engaged, the manufacture of cloth was banned throughout the surrounding area, except in four specified towns.

Efforts to restrict the trade to the old centres were unsuccessful. An act of 1552, regulating the size and quality of various types of cloth, had referred to the white cloth 'made in the cities of Worcester and Coventry' but the 1606 Act, for 'the true making of woolen cloth', added Hereford. The industry was now fully accepted west of the Malverns, where the raw material was produced. There, non-corporate market towns, especially Ledbury, were able to take part in the boom in the textile industry. The change had been recognised by 1576, when an act was passed 'for the toleration of certain clothiers . . . to inhabit out of towns corporate'. In Ledbury the opportunities were seized by natives, such as the Skynners and Phillips, and newcomers, such as the Halls, who brought with them techniques used in more advanced eastern England.(100)

The deep religious and political controversies of the 17th century had little impact on Ledbury, in marked contrast to Bromyard, Leominster and Ross where there was much greater freedom of individual expression. The difference can be seen most clearly in the way the people of the four towns responded to the religious movement of the time. In all the towns except Ledbury, the sects and the new religious dissent flourished; Leominster was called the 'Little Geneva'. In all but Ledbury, the Society of Friends was firmly established, with regular meetings, within a few years of the Restoration of 1660.(101)

At Ledbury, the authority of the controlling group, which was essentially conservative, seems never to have been seriously challenged from within. The vicar, Henry Page, remained undisturbed throughout all the troubles of the Civil War and Protectorate, retaining office from 1631-63, for the 'new men' were the true heirs of the church. This is not surprising, given the origins of the Skyppes and Eltons. However, the Halls, who were clothiers and tanners and an essential element in the make-up of the controlling group, contrary to expectations, closely associated themselves from an early date with the church. It was Richard Hall who made the transcript of the parish register which was 'commenced in 1599' and 'diligently examined' by John Hall, tanner 'then being Church-Warden' and it was 'Francis Hall Esq of ye Toune of Ledbury . . . one of the Justices of the peace for this alottment and county of Hereford' who commenced the 'True Reiester of marriages' in 1654.(102)

There were no meetings of Friends at Ledbury. The only meetings of 'sectaries' took place, decently withdrawn from the public gaze, behind the premises of 3 High Street. According to a painted board, proudly displayed outside for many years but now destroyed, worship according to the reformed ideas had commenced here in 1607. After Charles II's restoration, worship continued, with joint meetings of congregationalists and presbyterians, in a half-timbered building similar, in all likelihood, to that down Baptist Alley in Tewkesbury. Until the 19th century, this was the solitary expression of dissent permitted within the town and was doubtless regarded as an adequate safety valve by those in control.

In 1852, it was rebuilt, rather grandly, in brick with Bath stone facings, thus suitably reflecting the new-found respectability of nonconformity, for the Baptists had built their chapel in the Homend in 1831 and the Wesleyans theirs in 1849. The alleyway, which for three and a half centuries had welcomed those who sought an alternative form of worship, is now boarded and barred at the very gates of the chapel. For the one institution of dissent accepted for so long by those in authority, our own age can find no use.

As it was situated at a strategic crossroads, Ledbury saw considerable action in the Civil War. Fortunately, the Parliamentary intention to fortify the town in 1644 was never implemented. Consequently the encounter between Prince Rupert and Col Massey, the Parliamentary governor of Gloucester, in Ledbury on 22 April of that year was brief and far less destructive than it might otherwise have been. Though the battle was short, it is well documented. There are accounts from both sides — one in the Royalist journal *Mercurius Aulicus* of 25 April, and the other in a letter from Massey to the Speaker of the House of Commons the same day.

Rupert, hearing of Massey's presence and marching through the night, surprised him at Ledbury. Some of the Royalists pushed through back gardens and orchards of the Homend and High Street to cut off Massey's line of retreat to Gloucester. Then 'the Rebels horse drew to armes, having barricadoed the streets with Carts etc . . . their horse kept out his Highnesse foot a while; but within halfe an houre the barricado was opened, and then the way was made for His Highnesse Horse to charge . . . Massies horse beaten out of the Towne (while the foot fell into the woods and enclosures) were persued up a very steepe hill . . . the Rebells having galloped their horse into Lard'.

Massey wrote that in the fight Prince Rupert 'sought me out, but knew not till after, no more than I knew him. But it seemes we charged each other, and he shot my horse under me, and I did as much for him'. According to tradition, Rupert made his headquarters at the New House. On display in the church is what purports to be the sword of Major Backhouse, 'that betrayed His Majesty in the delivery up of Gloucester' and who was mortally wounded in the battle.(103)

Ledbury saw action on other occasions. Prince Maurice rested with his troops here on his way from Tewkesbury to Ross in April 1643. On 12 February 1645, 60 of Scudamore's Royalists were charged through the streets by a small force under Major Hopton, and on 23 July the Scots army under Lord Leven rested in the town after successfully besieging Castle Frome. However, the town emerged virtually unscathed. John Skyppe II's Upper Hall seems to have been the only major casualty, but then he had distinguished himself on a number of occasions as an uncompromising Royalist — at the siege of Goodrich castle in June 1646, and in Henry Lingen's abortive Herefordshire Royalist rising of August 1648.

There is a wealth of information on the residents of the borough in the period immediately after the Restoration of Charles II in 1660. The hearth tax returns enable us to comment on the size and wealth of Ledbury in relation to the other Herefordshire market towns and on the distribution of wealth within the borough. (Tables 9 and 10). In terms of the total number of houses at Lady Day, 1664, Ledbury stands third among Herefordshire towns. Ross, with 226 houses and just one short of Ledbury's total, has gone through an impressive period of expansion since 1288 (Table 6), due primarily to the growth of the iron industry.(104)

However, the percentage of tax-exempt houses at Ledbury (occupied by those who did not pay church and poor rates, due to poverty or low rental value) was the highest in the county. Of the houses that were taxed, on the other hand, the percentage with four or more hearths was almost twice as great in Ledbury as in Ross, Kington or Leominster. Clearly a major characteristic of

Ledbury in the 1660s was a marked disparity in the distribution of wealth — a higher incidence of poverty than elsewhere and a greater concentration of wealth in the hands of quite a small group, some 33 households.

Table 9. Herefordshire Hearth Tax, Lady Day 1664

Boroughs	Charged: Hearths	Charged: Houses	Exempt: Hearths	Exempt: Houses	Total: Hearths	Total: Houses	Exempt houses as % of all houses
Hereford	1,230	361	498	357	1,728	718	50
Leominster	579	217	260	229	839	446	51
Ledbury	291	95	146	132	437	227	58
Ross	396	164	67	62	463	226	27
Bromyard	232	74	114	90	346	164	55
Kington	196	87		17		104	
Pembridge	78	41		51		92	

These households can easily be identified when the hearth tax returns are compared with the county militia assessments of 1663.[105] Clothiers, mercers and others linked to the textile trade predominate. Foremost was the clothier, Francis Hall senior, of New House, who was variously described as 'esquire' and 'gentleman'. He was one of three charged for nine hearths. When he died in 1668 he left cash to the considerable total of £1,300, as well as lands at Ledbury and Wormsley. His son, 'Francis Hall, jun. gent.', lived in a house with seven hearths in the Homend. John and Thomas Wilde, 'gent.' of Church Lane and New Street were also clothiers. The militia assessment for the latter relates to 'Stock worth £50'. John Hall and John Berrow, mercers, of High Street had stock rated at £50. So did Samuel Wilson and Robert Stone, who were both charged for nine hearths in the High Street, suggesting that they occupied premises now Hobbs the ironmongers and the Feathers.

Table 10. Number of Houses Charged in each Category
Herefordshire Hearth Tax, Lady Day 1664

Number of Hearths

Borough	11+	10	9	8	7	6	5	4	3	2	1	*charged*	*exempt*	*total*
Leominster	2		2	2	2	7	9	19	53	61	60	579	260	839
Ross	1		1		5	4	2	17	26	53	55	396	67	463
Ledbury			3	1	2	5	7	15	17	21	24	291	146	437
Bromyard	1		1	2	3	2	6	10	10	23	16	232	114	346
Kington				1	1	1	4	9	9	30	32	196		
Pembridge		1	1			1		2	2	5	29	78		

Tokens, issued by Ledbury merchants and tradesmen as a means of combatting the critical shortage of small change at the time, provide further details. In 1667 Richard Cox, clothier and designated 'gent.' in the militia assessment, issued 'his half peny'. Cox's house in New Street was charged at five hearths. Also in 1667, William Hooper and Thomas Page, weavers, issued 'their ½ peny in Ludbury'. They both lived in the Southend until 1665 when Hooper took up residence in the foreign in a house with nine hearths. 'Reighnald Randolph' issued 'his halfe penny' a year later at the Blacksmiths' Arms in High Street where his stock, assessed at £100, was by far the largest in the town. John Stone's undated 'halfe penny' bore the sign of the sugar loaf, seen outside his High

Street premises. Another halfpenny token was issued by the partners, Samuel Wilson and John White, whose houses, also in High Street, were respectively assessed at seven and two hearths. Farthing tokens bear the names of William Mathewes, at the sign of the earthen jar (1653), William Berrow, at the Grocers' Arms, both in High Street, and William Browne, at the Glaziers' Arms in the Homend.(106)

By the end of the century, Ledbury's era of outstanding prosperity, based on the manufacture of woollens, had gone. In 1720 the 'Gentlemen and other inhabitants' petitioned the Commons . . . 'in behalf of some Hundreds of Poor lately employed in the woollen manufacture in and about the said town . . . setting forth that the said Town of late a considerable clothing Town and therebye the Poor were maintained, but the Trade . . . is in effect, intirely lost in the said town, there being now but one Loom kept to work and that not constantly: That the poor have been forced to make application for relief to the respective parishes whereto they belong. The Reasons of the Decay of the clothing trade is occasioned by the wearing of calicoes and other East India Goods which hinder the consumption of the Raw Silks, which are imported in exchange of the woolen cloth exported into Turkey and other parts'.(107)

In the 18th century Ledbury had to readjust itself to becoming once more merely a market town. Memories of the golden age found expression in the duet for man and wife 'The Decayed Clothier of Ledbury'.

Only two major buildings can be ascribed to the early Tudor period, further evidence of the condition of the town at that time: LEFT: the Old Grammar School in 1880. (HCL/WMC/4246) RIGHT: The Council Chamber in 1981. The western half was built about 1500 and extended east a century later in a comparable style.

CAP. V.

An act touching the making of woolen clothes.

XXXI. Item, *Whereas divers ancient cities, boroughs and towns corporate within this realm of* England, *have been in times paſt well and ſubſtantially inhabited, occupied, maintained and upholden, as well by reaſon of making of broad woollen clothes and kerſies, as alſo by divers other artificers inhabiting then in the ſaid towns, at which time alſo the villages and huſband towns flouriſhed, and huſbandry and tillage was well maintained, to the great benefit of the realm and all the people therein:* (2) *Foraſmuch as divers years paſt, ſuch perſons as do uſe the feat or myſtery of cloth-making, not contented to live as artificers, and with the trade wherein they have been brought up, do daily plant themſelves in villages and towns, being no cities, boroughs nor corporate towns, and there occupying the feat and place of a huſbandman, do not only engroſs divers farms and paſtures into their hands, diſpleaſing the huſbandman, and decaying the ploughs and tillages, but alſo draw with them out of the cities, boroughs and towns corporate, all ſorts of artificers, whereby not only divers ancient cities, boroughs and towns corporate are utterly decayed, deſtroyed and depopulated, but alſo huſbandry and tillages very much decayed, to the great hurt, damage and prejudice of this realm and the people therein, if ſpeedy remedy be not foreſeen:* (3) *And foraſmuch alſo as the weavers and workmen of clothiers when they have been trained up in the trade of cloth-making and weaving three or four years, do forſake their maſters, and do become clothiers and occupiers for themſelves, without ſtock, ſkill or knowledge, to the great ſlander of the true cloth-making, beſides a great number of inconveniencies which do grow to the commonwealth of this realm thereby, as daily experience teacheth:*

CAP. VI.

An act for the true making of woollen cloth.

V. And that all and every white cloth and clothes which ſhall be made within the city of *Worceſter*, commonly called long *Worceſters*, and all like clothes of like making, made within the city of *Coventry* or elſewhere, after the ſaid feaſt, ſhall contain in length, being wet as is aforeſaid, betwixt nine and twenty and one and thirty yards the piece, and to every yard one inch of the ſtandard, and ſhall be of the breadth above ſpecified throughout and by all the length of the whole cloth, and liſted as hath been accuſtomed, and being well ſcowred, thicked, milled and fully dried, ſhall weigh fourſcore and four pound the piece at the leaſt.

CAP. II.

An act for the true making of woolen cloth.

FOR *the avoiding of many inconveniencies happening to his Highneſs ſubjects exerciſing the myſtery and trade of making and working of woolen clothes of divers names and natures, and that the buyers of ſuch clothes may have true and juſt commerce without fraud or deceit,* It pleaſeth his moſt excellent Majeſty, with the conſent of the lords ſpiritual and temporal, and the commons, in this preſent parliament aſſembled, that it be enacted,

II. And that every white cloth which ſhall be made within the cities of *Worceſter*, *Coventry* and *Hereford*, commonly called *Long-worceſters*, or elſewhere of like making, ſhall contain in length, being wet, between thirty and thirty-three ſuch ſaid yards and inches as is aforeſaid, and ſhall be in breadth ſeven quarters throughout all the whole cloth, and being clean ſcowred, thicked, milled, and fully dried, ſhall weigh ſeventy-eight pounds at the leaſt.

ABOVE LEFT: The Council Chamber in 1900. RIGHT: An act touching the making of woollen cloths, 1551. BELOW LEFT: An act for the true making of woolen cloth, 1552. An act for the true making of woolen cloth, 1606, and RIGHT: 17th century Ledbury trade tokens.

ABOVE LEFT: The only meeting of 'sectaries' at Ledbury took place, decently withdrawn from public gaze, behind 3 High Street. In 1852 it was rebuilt at a cost of £800. RIGHT: The Baptist Chapel, built in 1831. BELOW LEFT: The Wesleyan Methodist Chapel of 1849 expresses the exuberance of the new dissent. RIGHT: The Bye Street Mission Hall, founded by Lady Henry Somerset.

ABOVE: Charles Wesley Stephens, 'furnishing general ironmonger, iron and oil merchant, implement agent . . . and bellhanger, hot water fitter, swing bedstead and bedding warehouse', (now Hobbs) and Luke Tilley & Son (fourth from right), both plaster-faced. BELOW: The plaster peeled off such buildings. Evidence of side windows can be seen in the timbering of LEFT: Tilley's, High Street, and RIGHT: the Cinema House in the Homend.

The Great Rebuilding, 1570-1620

Ledbury's glory is its buildings of the late 16th and early 17th centuries. Houses of the great rebuild of 1570-1620 still dominate its streets. The only exception is Bye Street, although in 1898 Ellen Tilley's *Ledbury: A Concise Guide* drew the visitor's particular attention to this street on account of its 'many ancient houses'. Almost all have now gone, to make it, in conservation terms, Ledbury's only disaster area. Two-thirds of the buildings of the market place, other than St Katherine's, belong to this period, although some are tricked out in later garb. The same can be said of the pre-1815 sections of the Southend, the Homend and New Street.

Antipathy to half-timbered work was so strong in the 18th century and later that only the humblest structures were allowed to reveal themselves in such an indelicate state. All major buildings, such as New House, the Feathers and the Talbot, had to be decently clad in a suitable rendering. Windows were to be sash and, as far as possible, symmetrical in arrangement.

This can be clearly seen at Taylor's grocery, 10 High Street and Hobbs' ironmongery, no 21, which, despite their apparent Georgian facades, proclaim themselves to be half-timbered buildings by the jetties which are still visible. For a Georgian brick building, such an overhang was not only aesthetically unacceptable, it was physically impossible. Similar counterfeits can be seen in the Homend and elsewhere. Foster's, 9 High Street, has recently been cleared of such plasterwork and its original twin-gabled, close-studded facade has been revealed. The fine oakwork has not been covered with pitch or any of the other bituminous materials which were previously used to protect so many of the town's half-timbered buildings. It has been treated merely with a preservative, so that the rich texture of the oak can still be enjoyed.

Salmon's ironmongery, 8 High Street, has a heavier disguise. Yet disguise it is, for the Georgian facade is only skin-keep, a refronting in brick of a half-timbered structure of about 1600. Indeed, it is only with difficulty that it could be fitted into its new apparel. The canons of Georgian taste demanded that certain proportions be observed in the design of a facade. The windows of the first floor had to express its social superiority to that of the chamber floor above, but classical proportions and the *piano nobile* were concepts quite unknown to the builders in the vernacular tradition of timber houses. Thus, if one looks carefully at Salmon's, one can still descry the second floor of the earlier building in the heads of the Georgian windows at first floor level.

There are many other examples of such refacing in brick. The Royal Oak in the Southend is a late 16th century L-shaped half-timbered building which still retains some of its original panelling. Unfortunately, the splendid brick facade, grafted on in the 18th century, has now been disastrously rendered in an attempt to impart that specious brightness regarded by the large brewers today as an essential for their trade. Ledbury has thus lost for ever the rich patina of its Georgian brickwork.

The original building of the Feathers can be dated on stylistic grounds to about 1570. It was the first major structure of the era of the great rebuild. It was of three storeys, each projecting slightly above the other and divided into three bays, each marked off by architectural features. At ground floor, only one remains, a fluted pilaster with a leafed cap forming a bracket. Above, there are flowers in vases and, at the second floor, bulbous ionic columns on bases — a marked Renaissance feature. The facade is composed of close-set studs with pairs of horizontal timbers crossing at each storey.

An attic of five gables was added to this building when the house to the right was built, about 1600. Although less elaborately decorated, a conscious effort was made to relate this second building to its more imposing neighbour. It has the pairs of horizontals, albeit set wider apart. Each of the three bays is punctuated by brackets in pairs and each storey was slightly jettied, although the ground floor was subsequently built out.

In 1951, original wall paintings came to light in the course of alterations to the Feathers. Two are of a simple formal design of crosses. The third bears an intricate pattern resembling a series of receding arches. The colour used was something between green and black.(108)

Francis Hall's 'New House', commenced about 1590, is only out-matched by the Master's House of St Katherine's in terms of its styles and the range of its building periods. The original house, along the Southend, was divided into five bays and was originally of two storeys. The five great gables were added later. Before the outbreak of the Civil War in 1642, the north wing was constructed, along what was then Horse Lane, now Worcester Road. The remaining buildings are of the 18th and 19th centuries. The 17th century work has suffered from alteration and heavy-handed restoration. Although the original fenestration can be worked out, the windows onto the Southend are all modern, except for the 18th century sashes at first floor. Saddest of all, the original interior has been almost wholly lost.

The years about 1600 witnessed a frenzy of building activity within the town. The second stage of the Feathers, Church House, the Talbot, Abbey House and the Steppes are all attributable to this time.

Church House gives a clearer impression of the original appearance of a major town house of c1600. L-shaped in plan, it is of three jettied storeys, divided into four bays headed by four gables, with a cellar below. The gables retain their original moulded bargeboards. Between the gables there were three projecting rainwater gulleys. Much of the original fenestration remains at the first floor, where one room has a semi-octagonal projection forming a porch and giving the residents a view up and down Church Lane. The gable above carries its original pendants. Inside, there is an original plaster ceiling enlivened with lozenges containing birds, an elephant and a lion's face.

For the finest interior fittings of the period we have to go to the Talbot in New Street. It is of two builds. The line of the gables of the original building can be seen on the right. To this was added a twin-gabled extension and a porch, similar to that of Church House. The porch is carried on curved brackets and the doorway beneath is richly ornamented. On either side of this doorway are fluted Ionic pilasters which it is interesting to compare with those on the Feathers. Above, is an entablature with an elaborate strapwork frieze. With a proud disregard for its quality, this doorway has now been embellished with some of the cheap bric-a-brac of the modern brewer. The panelled door bears the initials I.A.F. and the date 1600.

On the right on entering is one of the splendours of Ledbury — a room with its original Elizabethan fittings. The wainscotting is panelled, with an entablature above, which has triglyph brackets and carved fox-heads on the western side. Surmounting it all is a carved frieze. The fireplace which was in the south wall has gone, but its overmantel remains. It is carried on two fluted Ionic pilasters and is divided into three arcaded panes by four figures in a caryatid-like posture. An Ionic pilaster on the west wall bears the date 1596 and the initials A.N.

Here, better than anywhere else in the town, we can get some impression of what the owners of these new houses were seeking in their frenzy of building activity. Above all, they sought comfort, privacy and the modest display of their new-found affluence. The great rebuilding was part of a revolution in housing standards — at least for Ledbury's more affluent citizens. For them, the open hall of the middle ages, with its smoke-blackened beams, shuttered, unglazed windows, its communal living with cooking smells and constant noise of servants from the adjacent service wing, was no longer acceptable. This was cogently expressed by William Langland in his *Vision concerning Piers the Plowman:*

> 'Elyng is the halle . vche daye in the wyke,
> There the lorde ne the lady . liketh nougte to sytte.
> Now hath vche riche a reule . to eten bi hym-selve
> In a pryve parloure . for pore mennes sake,
> Or in a chambre with a chymneye . and leve the chief halle,
> That was made for meles . men to eten inne;'(109)

Privacy was ensured by a wide range of rooms allocated different and quite specific functions. Each was well appointed. Comfort dictated the generous provision of fireplaces, leading, as William Harrison observed in his *Description of England* of 1577, to the 'multitude of chimneys lately erected'. It also dictated a 'great amendment of lodging'. Principal rooms were elaborately panelled in wood, as we can still see at the Talbot. The impact of the fireplace was heightened by the overmantel. Where panelling was not used, hangings and wall paintings, such as those in the Feathers, took their place. Ceilings, themselves an innovation, bore plaster decoration of which Church House has one of the few, and certainly one of the finest examples in Ledbury.

Equally important, large glazed windows ensured that rooms were well-lit, well-aired and, when the sun shone, warm. With the advent of cheap glass, available in small panes of varying shapes, it became possible in a timber-framed building to glaze wide areas of the outer walls without weakening the overall structure, something which is not possible in a brick or stone building without the use of reinforced steel joints. In some places, as at Speke Hall in Lancashire and in many of the merchants' town houses of this period in High Street and Church Street, Tewkesbury, glazing was carried along the whole length of a building by taking the weight-bearing uprights through the windows. This principal was applied, in a modest way, to the porch of Church House, but for the most part fenestration, like ornament generally, was restrained within the town.

Windows, at their most elaborate, usually consisted of projecting oriels of eight glazed lights, divided by upright mullions and a horizontal transom, within moulded frames. In their most simple form, they were a mere inset between vertical and horizontal timbers, as in the now blocked three-part light on the first floor of the Church Lane facade of 1 High Street. Tilley's, 17 High Street, retains its little side lights at first floor level. Traces of this feature, 'not normally found in Herefordshire', can be seen in a number of other Ledbury houses. The presence of a geared timber winch and the type of roof construction suggests that the attic was designed to be used for storage purposes.(110)

Within the spaces created by horizontals and uprights were placed fixed lattices of thin lead strips, H in section, called cames, in which the quarries were set in shapes, according to the fancy of the owner. A number of such quarries from the windows of the old Grammar School are on display there. An iron stanchion, to which the lattice could be tied with flexible lead tapes, was frequently fixed to the rear to give additional support. Each window usually had one or more casements made with an iron frame to open on iron hinges and locked by catches of varying and often elaborate design. There was, therefore, plenty of opportunity, even in a window, for the display, not only of craftsmanship, but also of affluence. Such a window required the collaboration of the masters of four distinct crafts — the carpenter, the glazier, the plumber and the smith. Sadly, the combination of changing fashion and decay through neglect has meant a poor survival rate for these windows in Ledbury.

Ledbury's principal public building, the Market Hall, was begun in 1617 when John Phillips, clothier, bought 'certain houses in the High Street' from Thomas Davis, alias Weaver, for £40. This was 'not the sole and proper money of him, the said John Phillips, but had been raised by the charitable contributions as well of himself as of divers other well disposed persons, in trust to be used and employed for the erecting of a market-house and market-place for the use of the town of Ledbury forever.'(111)

These 'certain houses', which had to be demolished before work could commence, were the ancient Shop Row, descended from the *seldae* or booths mentioned in the *Red Book.*

Hereford's magnificent market hall, completed about 1600, was the model for Ledbury's humbler structure. It has been suggested that the latter was the work of John Abel, the king's carpenter. Comparison with other work by Abel, such as the highly ornate market hall, now the Grange, erected at Leominster in 1633, and the florid timberwork he provided for the church restored by Lord Scudamore at Abbey Dore in 1634, would indicate otherwise. Nevertheless, the 16 beautifully moulded oak pillars which carry the upper chamber show that the original design was quite ambitious.

The market house 'was erected and built', but not completed, when John Phillips died in 1655. John Skyppe II and the other trustees decided in 1668 to disburse the £20 apiece which Richard Hall (d1631) and Francis Hall (d1645) had left for 'providing 12 coats or gowns for 12 poor people of the town', towards its completion. They decided 'to make and build several rooms, lofts or corn chambers, over the market house; and also two staircases to go up into the same , and one or two shops underneath the lower staircase, with a room or rooms boarded over'. The rents, it was hoped, would provide for all necessary repairs, as well as the 12 coats or gowns yearly and 'the overplus to be distributed to the poor'. Each year, the churchwardens were to provide 'a true and just account'. The wheat and oat grain, wool, hops and acorns found during the repairs carried out in 1939 amply confirmed its use for that purpose.(112) Grain which could not be accommodated in the hall was kept under penthouses in front of the shops nearby. However, in the mid-18th century, with the growth of turnpikes, grain came to be sold by sample, with serious implications for the vestry's finances.

Edward Cooper's accounts for work carried out at St Katherine's between 1585 and 1595 describe the source and the cost of the materials used and the techniques employed in the great rebuilding of the town. During his 15-year campaign of rebuilding and repair the Master's House was modernised according to the standards of the age. The ground floor room of the solar wing was completely refurbished and lined with panelling. The fireplace was flanked by pilasters. Above were four arcaded panels, similar to those at the Talbot, and the contemporary painting of Hugh Foliot, founder of the hospital, now to be seen in St Katherine's chapel.

Carved into the frieze were Cooper's initials, F.C., and the date, 1588. The accounts show that on 5 February of that year the two 'ioigners', Thomas Mayo and Richard Wood, received 22s 10d for 30 and 25 days' work respectively on the wainscotting — at a rate of 5d per day 'besides theire dyettes'.

The chapel and the houses of the brothers and sisters were repaired. New buildings included 'kytching'; 'preevie' and two 'howses of office'; stable; 'wayne', pigeon and 'saddell' houses; 'boulting howse'; 'mustmyll'; as well as 'oxe howse' and 'sheere' at the north end of the barn. A new well was sunk. The courtyard was paved. 'Servaunts' and 'maydens' chambers, 'deyhowse', 'malte milhowse', 'maulte' kiln, 'bruynge howse', 'mill howse' and garner were restored.(113)

Much of the material used was not local. Large quantities of timber came from Teddiswood near Ross. The Rudhalls of Brampton Abbotts received 43s for four timber trees, bought for wainscotting in the parlour. '4,000 tylestones bought and digged in Teddiswoode' cost 38s. The battering (trimming) of 3,000 tiles on site cost 3s. Carriage was expensive, for the materials had to be taken by the old route from Ross to Ledbury, which rose some 600 feet to the Old Gore before descending steeply by way of Yatton to Much Marcle. The servants of Henry Poole and

Christopher Matthews received 3s for bringing two loads of these tiles by wain from Teddiswood. In 1589 'fower yonge men w.[ch] brought boordes from Woolhope' received 8d. Three years earlier William Lucy had 3d for fetching punchings (upright timbers) from Fownhope to make the portal. Lime for building came from Newent and the Forest of Dean.

Specialist craftsmen had to be brought in. For October 1583 the accounts record 'to the goodwife Litle for 3 nights lodgings for 3 masons . . . 3d' and 18 months later Morgan the glazier was allowed 'his 1d bed in the towne'. In 1588 Richard Barrett received 4d for lodging the joiners Mayo and Wodd. Carpenters were brought in from Hereford. In 1589 Symon Jeoffreyes was given 12d 'in traveling from Heref. to Ledbury to vewe certern worke to be done over the stable'. Some years later a man was paid 14d for 'carring and recarreing to and from Hereford' the tools of two carpenters who put in the floor above the mill house.

As to prices — felling one elm was 4d, felling an oak at Dunbridge was 10d, while cutting, hewing and squaring seven elms cost 2s 6d. For the furnace eight plates of iron cost 8d and four plates of lead weighing 18 lb, 2s 2d. The glazier was paid 5s for solder, cane lead and setting 20 feet of glass, while an iron casement cost 18d. A 'locke and key for the Chamber dore where the Bailif of Husbandrie, and the hyndes doe laye' was 6d and 'locke, keye, and staple to the maydens' chamber', 8d.

Three houses of the great rebuild, nos 8, 9 and 10 High Street. Georgianisation was taken to the extreme with no 8. The windows of the *piano nobile* (of the first floor) show in their heads the joists of the second floor. Note also, first floor, original glazing and thick glazing bars on left; new windows on right.

LEFT: Old Talbot at turn of century. (HCL/WMC/572) BELOW: The Old Talbot revealed. Original gables and building line can be seen on right. Twin gabled extension with semi-octangular porch carried on large curved brackets to left. (HCRO/AB48/B10) RIGHT: The New House before 1897. (HCRO/AB48/B10).

LEFT: The New House in the early 1930s. (HCL/WMC/514) RIGHT: The Feathers at the turn of the century. The division into three bays can be seen clearly at second floor level. (HCRO/AB48/B10) BELOW: The disguise removed, showing the close-set timber studs with pairs of horizontals crossing at each storey. (HCRO/AB48/B10)

ABOVE LEFT: Behind this 18th- and 19th-century facade of the Master's House at St Katherine's is the H-shaped, half-timbered manor house of the 15th century. RIGHT: The Old Court house adjacent to Rutherglen, soon to disappear. A disguise only skin-deep. BELOW LEFT: Magistrates' Court roof structure showing provision for moving large commodities, probably bales of wool. RIGHT Church House. Original window over porch with moulded frames, transoms and mullions. Note detail on base, pendants and bargeboard of gable above.

ABOVE LEFT: Early 19th-century lithograph of Church House by T. Ballard. RIGHT: A porch similar to that of the Talbot gives views up and down the lane. (HCL/WMC/560). BELOW LEFT: The Steppes, New Street of c1600. RIGHT: Abbey House, the Homend, in 1931. L-shaped in plan, a small projecting bay has been added to the facade. (HCL/WMC/568)

LEFT: Details of fenestration. ABOVE: Church House: moulded and slightly projecting four-light window at first floor; one-light window beyond is modern. CENTRE: Windows of the period at their simplest: the blocked three-part light on the first floor of the Church Lane facade of 1 High Street, and council offices: projecting five-light moulded windows, with casement open, on chevron-decorated bracket. BELOW: Council House: projecting three-light window on similar bracket. Splendid detail of Old Talbot doorcase, 1600: ABOVE: entablature decorated with strapwork . . . CENTRE LEFT: . . . carried on two fluted Ionic pilasters with delicately carved heads overshadowed by the heavy brackets of the porch. CENTRE: The Feathers. Each of the three bays is marked off by architectural features — by flowers in vases at first floor and bulbous Ionic columns on bases at second. RIGHT: Much fine oakwork has been covered with pitch or other bitumenous materials. By contrast, at 9 High Street the rich texture of the oak can still be enjoyed. BELOW: Under the pitch, the carpenters' marks can still be seen on some half-timbered buildings. LEFT: The buildings were prefabricated so local variants on Roman numerals were used to facilitate assembly. RIGHT: Numbers were applied on a vertical plane, while the horizontal was denoted by circles, quadrants, etc. Here an inverted V and half circle, above a II and a quadrant.

Road and Riot

'The County of Hereford is equalled by few spots in the island of Great Britain for the production of every article that can contribute to the comfort, happiness and in some degree, the luxury of society', wrote John Clark in 1794.(114) The land about Ledbury has always been accounted the most productive in the shire. In the Domesday Survey of 1086, the number of plough teams per square mile varied from one, in the extreme west, to a maximum of five — about Ledbury.(115)

In 1586, Sir William Camden referred to the predominantly corn-animal husbandry of 'A Country (besides its pleasantness) both for feeding of Cattel, and produce of Corn, everywhere of an excellent soil; and admirably well provided with all necessaries for life. Insomuch that it may scorn to come behind any County in England for fruitfulness of soil. And therefore says that for three W — Wheat, Wooll and Water, it yieldeth to no Shire of England'.(116)

Later, with the decline in the demand for wool, the area between Ledbury and Hereford came to be called the Wheatlands. The production of wheat completely overshadowed all other grain crops. Under the old system of common field agriculture, there had been rotation of fallow, wheat, beans or pulse, and then fallow. After the enclosure of open fields in the 16th century and earlier, production rose. The heaviest wheat crops in the county were produced here, some 300 gallons an acre in the more favourable districts.(117)

The dominance of wheat did not prevent 'meadows, orchards, extended lawns and hop grounds satiating the eye by one continued scene of luxury'. When Celia Fiennes viewed 'Herrifordshire' from the top of the Malverns, she saw 'a Country off Gardens and Orchards, the whole country being very full of fruite trees, etc. it looks like nothing else, the apple and pear trees etc. are so thick even in their cornfields and hedgrows'.(118) Yet, in the midst of this plenty was poverty, for inadequate land transport prevented the effective export of much of the county's produce.

Herefordshire's roads, or ways as they are better described, were notorious. Lord Leven, the commander of the Scots army that took Canon Frome in July, 1645, commented that he had advanced from Bromyard to Ledbury 'with much difficulty, the waies are exceeding strait, and hard to passe on this side Severne, so that the Army is not able to march above eight miles a day, though they begin to march at the Sun rising, and continue till ten at night, and the carriages are so long in providing, that they are forced to drive all night'.(119)

For Celia Fiennes, 50 years later, 'the miles are here (in Herefordshire) very long so that at least it may be esteemed the last 20 miles as long as the 30 miles gone in the morning' (in Worcestershire).

Wherever possible, recourse was had to water transport for heavy goods. In 1695, after more than half a century of agitation, an act was passed to improve the navigation of the Wye from Monmouth to Hereford, by the levying of a county rate. The petitions to Parliament in favour of the navigation indicate the liabilities under which the county's economy laboured: 'Many useful commodities are become mere drugs . . . for the want of cheap carriage' (Petition of divers

Townships and Hamlets); 'by reason of the deepness of the roads our commodities are scarcely worth propagating' (Leominster); and 'the Price of Coals and Fuel which is now very dear will be reduced by one half . . . and the roads preserved which are almost unpassable' (Hereford).(120)

However, the parishes of Eastnor, Donnington, Colwall, Pixley, Cradley, Much and Little Marcle, under the leadership of Ledbury, petitioned against the proposed Wye navigation: 'being nearer Severn or using such other markets as that they will not have any occasion to use the river, whose navigation will bring other places to have the same ease of carriage to market and so take away the advantage these others now enjoy and it must needs be thought very unreasonable that that part of the country which will lose by the Navigation should be at any charge in carrying the navigation on'.(121)

In 1289, two of Richard Swinfield's squires had bought five tonnells of red wine for cash in Bristol and seen it delivered to the trows that plied the Severn. They left the casks in the custody of servants who had mats to keep off frost and rain. The consignment was unloaded at Upton for land carriage to Bosbury and Ledbury. The Churchwarden's accounts for 1774 include disbursement paid to '19 men for removing Snow to clear the Road in order to procure Coals from Upton'.(122) In 1794, W. Matthews' *Bristol Guide* listed the trows *Charlotte,* under Mr Ricketts, and the *Molly,* under Mr Pomfrey, as 'in and out every spring tide' from the 'Head of the Quay', carrying to Upton 'and Ledbury, etc.'.

The land passage between the town and Upton was essential to the growing grain trade. It was Ledbury's life line. Yet the maintenance of the route, under the Highways Acts of 1555 and 1562, was entrusted to the constables and churchwardens of the parishes through which it passed. They were to specify six days when the parishioners were to come together 'with the requisite implements and draught animals' for its repair, under the supervision of an elected and unpaid parish surveyor. The system of statute labour had been introduced when almost all travelled either by foot or horseback and most commodities went by packhorse. The only external pressure that could be brought to bear on recalcitrant parishes was an indictment before the justices, meeting in Quarter Sessions.

At the same time as they were petitioning 'in behalf of the woollen manufacturers in and about the town', the 'Gentlemen and other inhabitants of Ledbury' were also petitioning the Commons for a 'Bill to repair several roads leading thereto'. They claimed that the roads around the town were damaged by 'the heavy grain carriage' and by 'waggons carrying goods between the Wye and the Severn'.

The resulting Ledbury Turnpike Act of 1721 was remarkable. Not only was it the first such act for Herefordshire, it was only the third to be passed for the neighbouring counties of Gloucester, Worcester and Shropshire. Its two predecessors were the Gloucester-Birdlip Hill Act of 1697-98 and the Worcester-Droitwich Road Act of 1714. Each of these related to a specific section of one road, but the Ledbury Act established a town-based trust covering all roads entering the town. The 39 trustees named in the Act included Michael Biddulph of New House, John Skyppe III (1679-1764) of the Upper Hall, Jacob Tonson of the Hazle, Robert Biddulph, John Skyppe of Donnington, George Elton, Caleb Randolph, Samuel and John Skinner of Bickerton. The Act empowered the 'several trustees or any three of them to meet together at the sign of the Green Dragon in Ledbury . . . on or before 24th Day of July, 1721'. It gave them the authority to erect toll gates or bars and to levy tolls on nine of the roads 'leading from the town . . . to the several places therein mentioned for the repair of those several roads'.(123) The toll bars are shown on the 1824 and 1831 plans of Ledbury, the first edition 1 ins OS map of 1831 and A. Bryant's *Map of Herefordshire,* 1832-34.

The reaction from those who were to carry the main burden of the tolls levied under the act was slow. However, turnpike disturbances, which had been taking place in Gloucestershire for some years, spread to Ledbury in June 1734 and an act passed in July extended the death penalty to those convicted of 'cutting down turnpikes'. Nevertheless, indignation was so strong that on 21 September the next year, 'Rioters, who rather deserve the Name of Rebels, for they appeared a hundred in a Gang, arm'd with Guns and Swords, as well as Axes, to hew down the Turn-pikes, and were dressed in Women's Apparel, with High-crown'd Hats, and their faces blacken'd'.(124) John Skyppe III had to read the riot act and, with his servants and neighbours, went to defend the last turnpike. He took prisoners whom he secured for the night at the Upper Hall when 'the whole gang appeared and demanded the said prisoners threatening in the case of refusal, to pull his house down and burn his barns and stables'.

Later, two of the prisoners had to be transferred from Hereford to Worcester for trial, as the master of Hereford gaol feared for their security. When William Bithell and William Morgan were hanged at Worcester, 'the Turnpike Levellers having been very tumultuous at the trial, near 100 soldiers with bayonets fixed to the end of their muskets attended the execution'. Two other prisoners, Thomas Reynolds and James Bayley, were taken to London for a show trial before the Lord Chief Justice. Bayley turned king's evidence and Reynolds was hanged but, having shown signs of life after he had been put in his coffin, 'the mob favouring him, lest the officers should take and execute him again' carried the coffin away 'but by reason of cold and other mismanagement he died' and was buried by the Oxford Road.(125)

Although the authorities and the press attempted to dismiss these episodes as the work of 'rebels', 'rioters', 'mobs', 'gangs' or 'levellers', all the evidence makes it clear that discontent was both deep-seated and widespread throughout the county. The manner of their death shows that those executed were men of courage and good life. Bithell and Morgan, at Worcester, 'in the shrouds and hand in hand . . . made no confession but their behaviour was decent' and they met their death with prayers. Thomas Reynolds was of honest parents of Ledbury parish. His father was a farmer and 'bred him to his own way of country work'. His parents dying while he was young, 'he served a substantial farmer within a mile of Ledbury and had a good character for honesty and industry'. He had intended to marry and 'to take a convenient farm, if the humour which of late possessed a great many country people had not prevented him'. At Tyburn, 'he appeared very devout and serious, he forgave everybody and died in the faith of Christ. He was very attentive to prayers and the singing of psalms'.(126)

Unrest was strong in the countryside, reflecting deep distress amongst farmers and their labourers. English agriculture was in depression between 1730 and 1750. This was especially marked in the wheatland around Ledbury where the heavy clay gave little opportunity for diversification. The Ledbury turnpike riots were part of the 18th century process described by Eric Hobsbaum as 'collective bargaining by riot'. The deep distress expressed itself, despite draconian penalties, in riots against a system of which the toll bars were the most evident symbols.

Bithell, Morgan and Reynolds did not die in vain. The progress of the turnpikes was halted. After the riots, no other roads were turnpiked in Herefordshire until the Ross Roads Act of 1749. When the Ledbury Act came up for renewal in 1742, the toll on waggons was reduced from 1s to 6d, as 'the said Toll or Duty hath been found burdensome to such persons as frequently pass through the turnpikes erected by virtue of the said act'. This did not solve the problem and there were further riots, and troops sent to quell them were refused diet and quarters in the town. The town and the countryside continued to smoulder and it was some time before authority was fully restored.(127)

Although a new route was opened along Horse Lane which, with its gentler gradients, eased the passage of wheeled traffic out of the town to the east and to the Severn, the turnpikes did little to solve Ledbury's problems of communication with the world beyond. Despite further renewals of the act, not much more was achieved. Road surfaces in particular remained bad. In 1794, Clark could write that 'to say the roads are bad is, in fact, saying nothing . . . they are so in a very uncommon degree'.(128)

Towards the end of the century, it was hoped that a canal would succeed where the turnpikes had so signally failed. From 1774, a range of schemes was considered, to link Hereford, through Ledbury, with the Severn and thus with Birmingham and the industrial midlands and Bristol and the south-west. Ultimately, the line of the canal followed the valley of the Leadon from Over, near Gloucester, to Tibberton. There, a diversion from the original route, as shown on Clowes' and Halls' *Plan* of 1791, took it to the collieries near Newent. It rejoined the Leadon valley at Dymock. The section from Over to Newent and Oxenhall was opened in October 1795. The Oxenhall tunnel provided difficulties, both financial and structural, but on 30 March 1798, when the proprietors and others embarked at Newent for Ledbury, 'the banks of the canal were lined with spectators who hailed the boats with reiterated acclamations. It is supposed that upwards of 2,000 persons were present on their arrival at Ledbury . . . A dinner was provided at the George Inn, where the greatest conviviality prevailed and many appropriate toasts were drunk . . . Coals of the first quality are now delivered at the Wharf at 13s 6d . . . the former price was 24s per ton'.(129)

The arrival of the canal, with its wharf at the end of New Street, provided a welcome fillip to the economy of the town. Until a link was made with the Frome after 1830, the northern end was always short of water. Nevertheless, Ledbury was the only market town in the county to enjoy a canal link with the outside world and by 1812 the Canal Co had £1,200 in the bank and income had doubled since 1804. In 1822, although 'the supply of water being uncertain there is no regular trading', it did 'afford an opportunity of laying in stocks of coals, and facilitates the transit of cyder and timber'.(130)

Work was begun on the section to Hereford only in 1830, due in great measure to the interest and pressure of John Biddulph (1768-1845). It took 15 years to complete and, almost immediately, negotiations were entered into with a number of railway companies for its sale, but they came to nothing.

In 1830, Stephen Ballard, boat builder, had his premises at the wharf. Robson's *Directory* (1840) shows James Jones' Vinegar and Cider Works and the Biddulph Arms on the wharf and, not far away, the Gas Works. Hunt (1847) indicates that two coal merchants had arrived at the wharf, as well as three boat companies, each offering regular services two or three times a week to Hereford and Gloucester by 'water conveyance'. By 1850, Slater lists nine coal merchants at the New Wharf. This development marks the first major change in the pattern of growth established with the market place about 1120. Although Byng reported 'some well-built houses' on entering the town in 1781, the new Horse Lane route to the east attracted little commercial activity.

The opening of the railway line from Worcester to Hereford on 13 September 1861, with a station at Ledbury as well as Henwick, Bransford Road, Malvern Link, Great Malvern, Colwall, Ashperton, Stoke Edith and Withington, brought about a rapid change. Development now proceeded apace at the northern end of the Homend. By 1870, although there were still four barge owners in the town, all the coal merchants now had premises at the station. Eventually, the GWR took over the canal and the Gloucester to Ledbury railway, opened on 27 July 1885, was built, in part, on the line of the canal.(131)

A design for a Ledbury Tollhouse. (HCRO/G2)

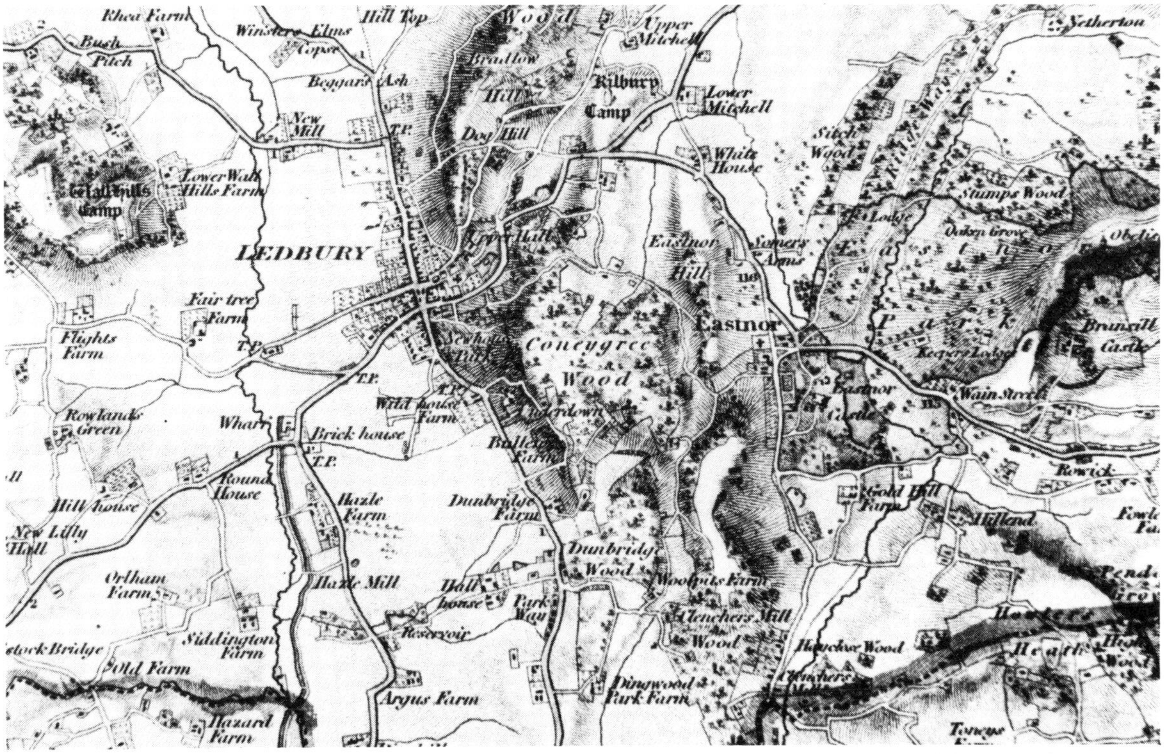

Anno Regni decimo quinto Georgii II. Regis.

And whereas by the said former Act, the Toll or Duty of One Shilling was laid on, and made payable for every Waggon, Wain, Car, Cart, or Carriage, drawn by Two Horses; which said Toll or Duty has been found burdensome to such Persons as frequently pass through the Turnpikes erected by virtue of the said Act; be it therefore enacted by the Authority aforesaid, That from and after the Twenty fourth Day of June, One thousand seven hundred and forty three, there shall be demanded and taken the Sum of Six Pence, and no more, during the Continuance of this Act, for every Waggon, Wain, Car, Cart, or Carriage, drawn only by Two Horses, Oxen, or Mares; any thing in the said former or this present Act to the contrary notwithstanding.

ABOVE: 1st impression of the 1 in Ordnance Survey map of Ledbury, 'published at the Tower of London, 29th Sept. 1831 by Lieut. Colonel Colby of the Royal Engineers'; showing turnpikes (TP). LEFT: The 2nd Ledbury Turnpike Act of 1742 reduced the toll on waggons drawn by two horses. RIGHT: Ledbury Turnpike Trust milestone by the playing fields on the road to Ross. The milestones are marked on the first and all subsequent editions of the 1 in Ordnance Survey maps.

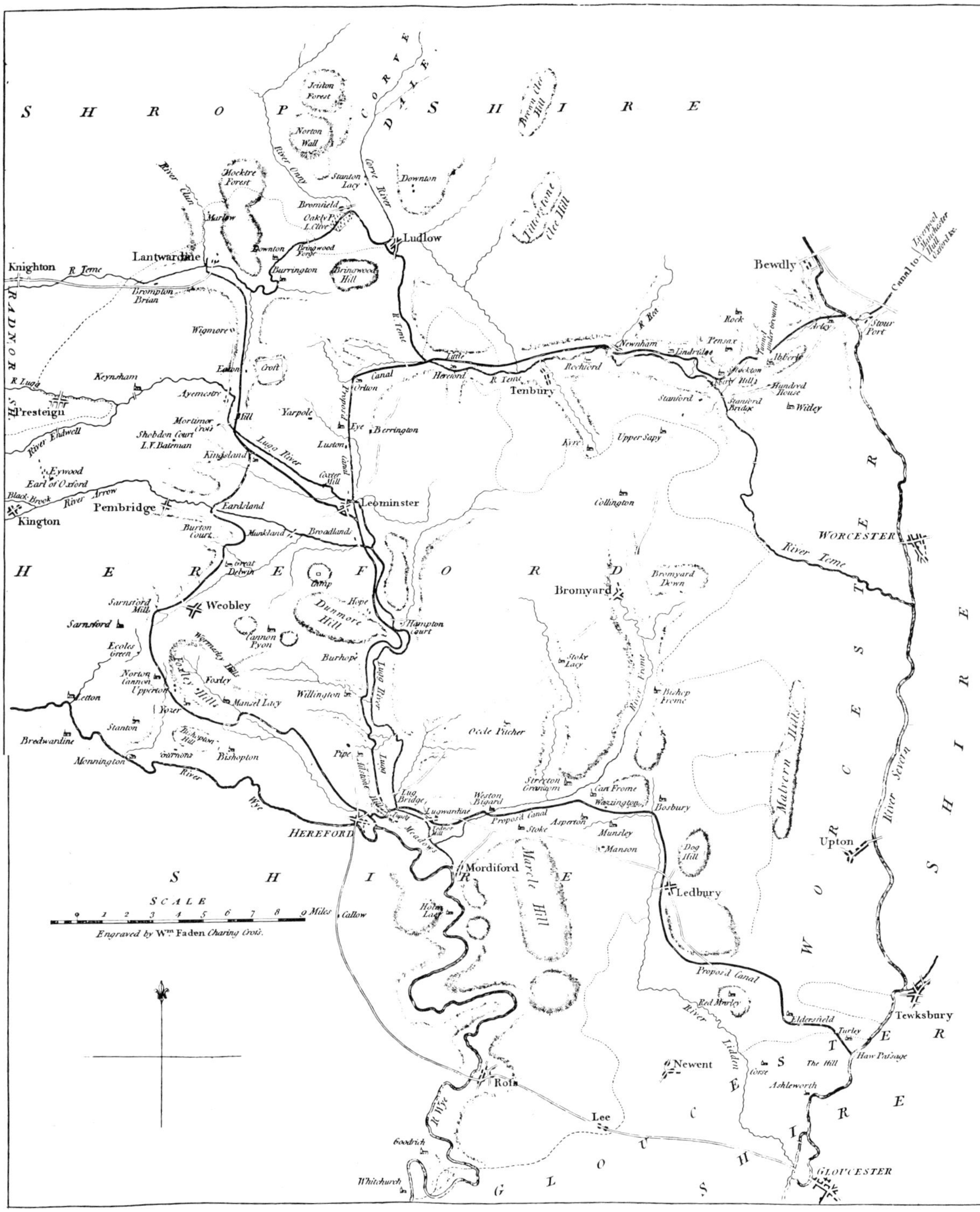

An early, and wildly ambitious canal scheme for Herefordshire. It proposed to bring Ludlow, Leintwardine, Leominster, and Weobley, as well as Hereford and Ledbury, into a comprehensive network which would link the county with the Severn at Stourport and the Haw. (HCRO/G2)

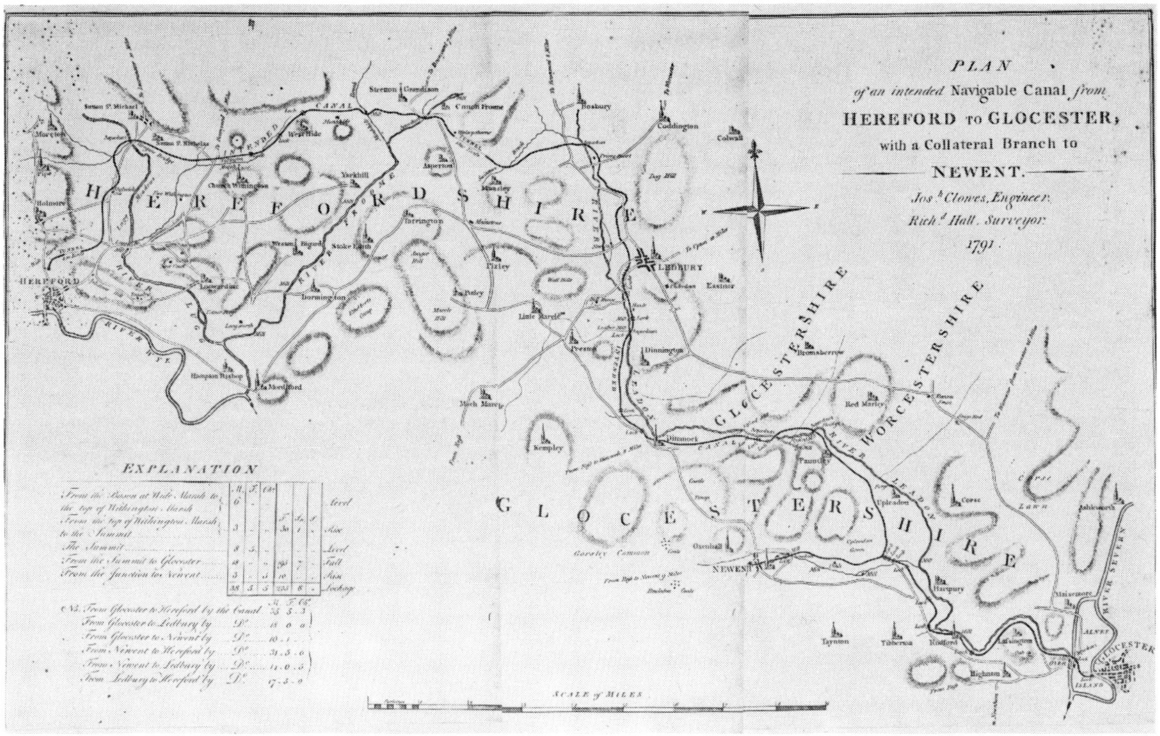

ABOVE: The first route proposed by Clowes and Hall for the Hereford and Gloucester Canal in 1791. As constructed, the canal left the Leadon at Tibberton to take it to the collieries near Newent. It could only regain the Leadon valley near Dymock by means of a tunnel at Oxenhall. (HCRO/G2) LEFT: The Ledbury Canal, photographed by Alfred Watkins during a two-day canoe trip along its entire length in 1880 or 1881. RIGHT: Bull and Boar Inn. (HCL/WMC/578)

ABOVE & CENTRE: The Ledbury railway during construction; mouth of the tunnel. (HCL/WMC/579) LEFT: Ledbury railway station. (HCRO/AB48/B10) RIGHT: Train at Colwall Station. (HCRO/AB48/B10)

Proportion and Symmetry

The first half of the 18th century, especially the 1730s and 1740s, when the turnpike riots presented such an open challenge to authority within the town, was a period of continuing stress for Ledbury. Building activity was restricted until after the end of the French wars, in 1815. However, not all the Georgian buildings belong to those later years.

Georgian architecture in the town is brick building, but the ample supply of good local timber means that brick was adopted late. The first major brick building in the town now forms the west wing of the Upper Hall. It was built by John II or George Skyppe in the late 17th century and has all the characteristics of the period — projecting modillion cornice to the eaves, casement and not sash windows, and a raised horizontal brick band between ground and first floor. Work of the same period can be found behind 12 and 14 High Street. Nevertheless, timber-framing was still being used for 27 High Street opposite, dated 1675, and the cruck-framed structure, now public conveniences, in Church Lane may well be of the 18th century.

Elegance and coherence were the hallmarks of the buildings of the period 1680-1830. These qualities came from an adherence to proportion and a regard for symmetry.

Only four of Ledbury's Georgian houses are intact. All the others have been altered, usually by the addition of shop fronts. Thus the coherence, the symmetry and proportions of the original designs have been lost. It is particularly disturbing that of the four houses that remain unaltered two should now be under threat — not from developers concerned with private gain, but the from District Council formulating its policies miles away in Malvern.

Rutherglen in Church Lane is of particular architectural interest. The facade, with its sash windows, thick glazing bars and crown glass panes, illustrates well the 18th century ideals of symmetry. Gravity is added to the composition by the treatment of the doorway. The strongly emphasised keystone and the rustication of the side panels indicate the influence of James Gibbs' pattern book, *The Book of Architecture* (1728). Not only the doorway but also the keystones and moulded sills of the windows are of stone, a rare touch of luxury for Ledbury. Internally the building has a number of unusual features. The chimney stacks are placed at the corners. The roof structure is carried by three pairs of raised crucks. In this respect Rutherglen represents a quite extraordinary combination of new and ancient traditions.

Despite its outstanding interest, Rutherglen has been almost totally neglected since 1973 — when Ledbury Rural District Council's plan to demolish it to create 'an interesting urban space' was frustrated.(132) Prolonged neglect has led to vandalism. The crown glass panes have been smashed, and thick glazing bars broken. Water pours inside from a large hole in the roof. Plans have now been submitted to gut the interior, including the original staircase and to 'restore' the exterior. But the failure to afford Rutherglen the care and attention which was its due now means unnecessary expense for the ratepayer and a sad pastiche for the town.

The Serjeant's house in Church Street shares with Rutherglen, the Lower Hall and the Shell House in the Homend the distinction of retaining its Georgian facade intact. Yet if Malvern Hills District Council has its way it will be demolished as 'it makes no useful contribution to the street scene other than overall massing'.(133)

There are other fine Georgian buildings in the town but all have been marred by the addition of later shop fronts. Of these only 10 the Homend was conceived on a grand scale. It has a slightly recessed central section of three bays surmounted by a brick pediment. This is flanked on either side by two bay units each with pediments above the first floor, an unusual design. The early 18th century house at 67 the Homend has been sadly mutilated. Four pilasters boldly divide the facade into three. A string course punctuates the division between ground and first floor. The proportions of the windows, tall and narrow, indicate an early date, similar to that of the Shell House opposite. Unfortunately the original panes and glazing bars, which gave so much to 18th century architectural composition, have been replaced by Victorian panes. The plastered front of 16 High Street, with its pair of tall and gracefully fluted Ionic pilasters, retains its blind cases to the heads of the windows. It would seem to be more at home in Cheltenham than Ledbury.

Although Ledbury has few major buildings of the period, the town is fortunate in that it still retains a wealth of unspoilt Georgian detail on minor buildings or mere facades. They provide an excellent foil to the work of the earlier half-timbered vernacular tradition. Great care will have to be taken to preserve this Georgian detail if the delicate balance between the two traditions, which gives Ledbury much of its charm, is to be maintained.

Glass and glazing bars are especially important and especially vulnerable. 18th and early 19th century glass can never be restored. The delightful eccentricities of its surface, once destroyed, are gone for ever. Glazing bars can be copied but rarely are with any degree of accuracy. As the period progressed, glazing bars became much finer. Advances in the techniques of glass production permitted them to be used much more adventurously, in doors and skylights, in house windows and above all in display windows for shops, of which Ledbury has some especially fine examples, such as 4 the Southend and 30 the Homend.

Building in the 18th century was also restricted outside the town. There were only two major developments. Dingwood Park, a five-bay structure of brick with hipped roof, was built about 1700. Castleditch was rebuilt by Charles Cocks, later 1st Lord Somers of Evesham, after he inherited the Eastnor estate from his cousin and ward James Cocks in 1758. Of plain white stone, it had a portico in front and projecting semi-circular wings.

The 19th century saw more activity, some of national importance. In 1809 Edward Moulton Barrett bought the 475-acre Hope End estate in Colwall from Sir Henry Tempest. He moved there with his three children. The eldest, Elizabeth, was only three years old. With a fortune derived from West Indian sugar he built a new Hope End and the old house was converted into a stable. The new Hope End was the work of John Claudius Loudon, the Scots landscape gardener and horticulturalist. He wrote of the 'extensive improvements to house and garden now executing from my design at Hope End'.(134) It was built in what was called the Hindoo style, although its inspiration was Islamic rather than Hindoo Indian. Sir Charles Cockerell's house at Sezincote, Gloucestershire (c1805) and the Prince Regent's Brighton Pavilion (1815-22) are further examples of this exotic taste. Domes, minarets and ogee-headed windows were its chief characteristics. Loudon laid out the grounds in what he called the 'gardenesque' style. Some of his planting remains. The park was the scene for Elizabeth Barrett's childish reminiscences found in such early poems as *Hector in the Garden, The Lost Bower* and *The Deserted Garden.*

Here, she began writing. An epic in four books, *The Battle of Marathon* was written when she was 11 and 12. Her father proudly had 50 copies printed 'because papa was bent upon spoiling me'. At 15 she suffered the riding accident which left her an invalid for the rest of her life. In 1828 her mother died and in 1831 John Biddulph wrote in his journal, 'from great opulence the Barretts are reduced to poverty. What will become of them?' Elizabeth's father's creditors foreclosed on the estate and the Barretts left Hope End. First they went to Sidmouth and ultimately to Wimpole Street whence Elizabeth was to elope in 1846 with Robert Browning. 'Even now', wrote Elizabeth 10 years later, 'I never say "Hope End" before him. He loved the place so'. It was equally important to her. 'Beautiful, beautiful hills and yet not for the whole world of beauty would I stand amongst the sunshine and shadow of them any more; it would be a mockery like the taking back of a broken flower to its stalk'.(135)

In 1873 the estate passed to C.A. Hewitt, who demolished the Barretts' home. The concrete minarets were so sturdy that they had to be blown up with gunpowder. All that now remains is the coach house and stable block, with its Saracenic gateway and minarets. This is now the Hope End Country House Hotel. Hewitt built a new Victorian Gothic mansion on a hillside nearby but this was gutted by fire in 1910. Only a small part survives.

Two years after Edward Moulton Barrett had begun his Islamic mansion at Hope End, work was begun, at a site near Castleditch, on the construction of Eastnor Castle. Robert Smirke's design was an early and adventurous essay in the Norman revival style. The great hall was 60 feet in length and 65 feet in height. The roof trusses were of iron.

Smirke was also the architect of Haffield House, Donnington, constructed in 1819. This, like his Shire Hall in Hereford (1817-19), was severely classical. Three years later he was brought in to supervise the reconstruction of St Katherine's almshouses but his efforts did not impress the Charity Commissioners; 'there is nothing in the appearance of the building which would lead to the supposition that a metropolitan architect had been employed at the expense of nearly £500'.(136)

ABOVE LEFT: Castleditch, home of the Clintons from about 1280 until it was sold to Richard Cocks, 'grocer' and alderman of London, in the reign of James I. He was appointed High Sheriff of the county in 1615. RIGHT: Charles Cocks (1725-1806), Lord Somers of Evesham from 1784, rebuilt Castleditch 'of plain white stone, having a portico in front and projecting semi-circular wings'. CENTRE: Eastnor castle, built on the Castleditch site by Robert Smirke for John, 1st Earl Somers, 1815. BELOW LEFT: Hope End, bought by Edward Barrett Moulton-Barrett from Sir Henry Tempest with its 475-acre estate in 1809. (HCL/WMC/3019) CENTRE: Hope End as remodelled 1809-15, with its concrete minarets, cast-iron domelets, ogee-headed upper windows. 'A chef-d'oeuvre, unrivalled in the kingdom', according to the 1831 sale catalogue. The circular-ended drawing room on the right. (HCL/WMC/585) RIGHT: Hope End, 'the magnificent mansion of Charles Archibald Hewitt, Esq. J.P., D.L., is entirely new but stands near the site of the former structure'. Littlebury's *Directory,* 1876. (HCL/WMC/590)

ABOVE LEFT: Rutherglen, Ledbury's finest intact Georgian house. A strictly symmetrical composition with windows inset to accommodate corner fireplaces. Gibbs doorway and stone trim. RIGHT: The Serjeant's House shares the distinction with Rutherglen and the Shell House of retaining its Georgian facade intact. Yet the District Council plans its demolition. BELOW LEFT: Timothy Spencer's bold facade for 3 the Homend, c1820. T. Ballard, Engraving. (HCL/PC) RIGHT: 1981. The late Georgian multi-paned shopwindow has been replaced, the small door to the right blocked and the parapet altered.

ABOVE: Some of Ledbury's Georgian doorways: LEFT TO RIGHT: Rutherglen: an early Georgian doorway to Gibbs' design, built of stone, an unusual touch of luxury for Ledbury. The Shell House: door with six raised and fielded panels and moulded case. Ledbury Farmers, New Street: door of six raised and fielded panels, above, a cantilevered canopy. The Steppes, New Street. CENTRE LEFT: The Homend, Bayliss House c1930. RIGHT: 1 Church Street. A simple fanlight above the robust eight-paned door; CENTRE: The Shell House, 36 the Homend. BELOW: Commercial premises: LEFT TO RIGHT: 2 New Street; fanlight and glazed door, typical of shops of the late Georgian period. 4 the Southend; doorway to the house; the curved panes illustrate the advance in glass-making. The Feathers: note the marvellous play of light on the original panes; light above door has been replaced.

ABOVE: 4 the Southend, double-fronted shop, a perfect example of the Regency builder's art. BELOW LEFT: 30 the Homend, one of a pair of projecting windows in original black livery. CENTRE: 67 the Homend, a sadly mutilated Georgian brick facade. RIGHT: 16 High Street; the plastered front seems to be more Cheltenham than Ledbury.

ABOVE LEFT: Georgian twilight: 33 the Homend, a humble yet pleasing late Georgian composition. RIGHT: 203-21 the Homend — variety within a convention. CENTRE LEFT TO RIGHT: 207 the Homend, 205 the Homend, 225 the Homend; steps and houses now lost, and BELOW (HCL/WMC/570) (HCM) steps in the Homend. As the land rises steeply behind the premises on the east side of the street, the ground floor had to be built well above street level. RIGHT: 35 the Homend: Abbey Cottage, door knocker.

COMMITTEE ROOM, OCTOBER 30th. 1820.

AT

A MEETING

OF THE

INHABITANTS OF LEDBURY,

HELD THIS DAY, FOR THE PURPOSE OF TAKING INTO CONSIDERATION THE EXPEDIENCY OF

OPENING A SUBSCRIPTION,

FOR TAKING DOWN

THE BUTCHER ROW.

JOHN BIDDULPH, ESQ. IN THE CHAIR.

Resolved,--That the said Row is an unsightly mass of building, and, that the houses, composing the same, are inconvenient habitations, without proper offices, and are particularly ill-calculated for the business of Butchers; as the practice of slaughtering animals in shops, fronting the street, is offensive, disgusting, and unwholesome, and ought not to be conducted in the centre of a populous town.

That the removal of the Row would conduce to the cleanliness, salubrity, and respectability of the Town, and to its general improvement, that the labourer, artisan, and mechanic, would be materially profitted by the employment that would arise from the measure, and the inhabitants at large generally benefitted.

That, the centre of the town being occupied by the Row, the thoroughfare is rendered inconvenient and dangerous to travellers, particularly at the time when the business of slaughtering animals is carried on.

Resolved,--That a Subscription be opened for the purpose of removing the said Row, in aid of which the inhabitants of the town and all persons connected therewith, by birth, property, preferment, or otherwise, be invited to assist, and, that, for the reason mentioned in the last resolution, the solicitation be extended to the Members for the County, and to all the Nobility, Gentry, and Clergy of the vicinity, who may occasionally travel through the town, or attend on business therein.

That as it may be more convenient to many well wishers to the plan to pay the sums subscribed, by instalments, and may also induce them to give more largely,--Resolved,--that all Subscriptions may be paid at the time of subscription or by four annual payments, at the option of the donors.

That a Committee be appointed to promote the business of this meeting, and that such Committee do meet monthly for that purpose, and, also, report their proceedings, at a general meeting of subscribers, to be held annually on the first Monday in June; and, that Messrs. Webb be appointed Treasurers to the Fund.

That the Committee do consist of John Biddulph, Esq. the Rev. James Watts, W. E. Saunders, Samuel Cooper, Thomas Webb, jun. Richard Webb, and James Holbrook, Esquires, Mr. Benj. Mutlow, Mr. John Edy, and Mr. Thomas Baylis; and that any three be a quorum.

A Meeting of the Inhabitants of Ledbury, 1820. (HCRO/G2)

The Age of Improvement

The reconstruction of St Katherine's was part of a wider campaign to improve the centre of the town. The guiding figure in this movement was John Biddulph (1768-1845), great grandson of that Anthony Biddulph of the Inner Temple who had acquired New House and Ledbury Park in 1688 after his marriage to Constance, daughter and co-heiress of Francis Hall. The reclining figures of Anthony and Constance Biddulph at the western end of the parish church form an apt memorial to the founders of a dynasty which played a leading role in the town for more than two and a half centuries.

John Biddulph's uncle, Francis established a banking house in the city of London. In 1757 Francis Biddulph asked Charles Cocks, who rebuilt Castleditch, if he could send someone to London to assist him. Charles Cocks sent his brothers James and Thomas Cocks. It was in this way that the Cocks, Biddulph Bank was founded. In 1759 the firm moved from St Paul's Churchyard to 43 Charing Cross, later called 16 Whitehall. Here it remained until it was taken over in 1919 by Martins Bank which itself later amalgamated with Barclays. It is still known as the Cocks, Biddulph branch.

Because of its West End site, most of the bank's clients were drawn from the official and fashionable circles, not from city merchants. The most august of these clients was King Edward VII whose account, as Duke of Cornwall, was opened in 1841 and remained on the books until his death in 1910.

Cocks, Biddulph & Co also had important links with Wales and the west. Account holders included Hereford Infirmary and the Dean and Chapter of Worcester. It was the London agent for such country banks as Joseph Berwick & Co's Old Worcester Bank, the Monmouth Bank, the Chepstow Old Bank, the Newport Old Bank, the Pembroke Bank and the Carmarthen Bank. It also acted as London agents for Mutlow and Rankin's Ledbury Bank at the end of the 18th century. William Mutlow had started in business as a tanner but at one stage his bank was clearing nearly £6,000 of notes a month with Cocks, Biddulph & Co. In the 19th century Webbs, later Webb, Spencer & Co, the Ledbury Old Bank of High Street also drew on Cocks, Biddulph. Country banks such as these were founded to serve the immediate locality. They played a major role in the financing of local improvements in agriculture, transport (especially canals), trade and industry.

From the earliest days there had been a close connection between Cocks, Biddulph's Bank and Martin's Bank at the sign of the Grasshopper on the corner of Lombard Street and Change Alley. The former was not a member of the Clearing House but operated through the agency of the latter. In 1757 James Martin I gave Michael Biddulph a long case clock as a present on the occasion of his marriage to Penelope, daughter of John Dandridge, It was through the Biddulph and Ledbury connection that the marriage of James Martin II was arranged with Penelope, daughter and ultimately heiress of John Skyppe IV. When John Skyppe V died in 1812 the Upper Hall estate passed to John Martin IV (1805-80), senior partner at the sign of the Grasshopper (1844-75), who was to play a major role in Ledbury affairs.

John's brother, James lived at Old Colwall, next door to Hope End. His wife remained a life-long friend and correspondent of Elizabeth Barrett Browning and invited her to stay at Old Colwall when the Brownings returned to England for a visit in 1850. The offer was declined; 'I could as soon open a coffin as do it'.

The bond between the Martins and Biddulphs was further strengthened in 1837 by the marriage of John Biddulph's daughter, Mary Ann, to Robert Martin, the younger brother of John Martin IV. The children of this union, Richard Biddulph Martin and John Biddulph Martin were the most important members of the fifth generation of the family. Sir Richard Biddulph Martin was senior partner, 1878-91 and when the firm went public as Martins Bank Ltd in 1891 he was the first chairman, an office he held until his death in 1917, only a year before the two banks merged.(137)

The close alliance of Biddulph and Martin families constituted a formidable local combination, but on many occasions it found its match in the equally formidable combination of lethargy and obduracy which characterised much of the opposition of Ledbury tradespeople, and of parochial and other officers to John Biddulph's programme of improvements for the town. After some 30 years of struggle he concluded: 'never was there a people so blind to their interests as the people of Herefordshire. They seem to wish to remain behind all the world'. He underestimated his own powers, for in that time he had transformed the face of Ledbury and had ensured that it was provided with that range of public facilities which came to be regarded as essential before the end of the century.(138)

John Biddulph was the second son. As he was not expected to inherit the family estate, he was able to indulge his somewhat unorthodox tastes in travel. In his early 20s he visited India, the West and East Indies, serving on small craft, on one occasion as the first and on another as the second mate. In 1797 he married Augusta Roberts, who brought with her a considerable fortune. In 1801 his elder brother, Robert married Charlotte, co-heiress of the Myddletons of Chirk Castle, and adopted that name with a large part of the estate: John thus succeeded to Ledbury Park. He also joined the Cocks, Biddulph Bank as a partner. Subsequently he divided his time between his business in London and his affairs in Ledbury.

The Age of Improvement was ushered in by the Ledbury Enclosure Act of 1813. The freeholders of the borough had certain rights on Bradlow Common. These were to be sold and after defraying expenses the residue was to be paid to 'Lord Somers, John Martin, John Biddulph, the Rev John Napleton (Master of St Katherine's, 1808-17), the Rev James Watts (Vicar 1810-47) and others in trust to be applied and disposed of in cleansing and otherwise improving the said Town . . . in such manner as they . . . or the major part of them think most advisable and expedient'.(139)

The Act received the Royal assent on 21 May, and on 24 June John Biddulph submitted a report to 'The Trustees for Improving the Town of Ledbury' which put forward specific and detailed recommendations street by street. This opened the campaign for improvement. It took more than 20 years to implement the programme in full.

The first major success was the removal of the Upper Market House which stood in the middle of the Southend, just beyond the Upper Cross. It is clearly shown on Lydiard's *Plan* of 1788. In 1814 the Toll Shop, next to the Market Hall, and in 1818 the Butter Market were taken down. The latter is shown on Lydiard's *Plan* at the southern end of the Butchers Row.

John Biddulph and John Martin were not merely concerned with the physical appearance of the town but, like John Skyppe III almost a century earlier, with the improvement of communications. The introduction by John Palmer of the *Mail Diligence* on the London-Bristol route in 1784 had transformed road travel. By 1791 mail coaches were covering some two and a half million miles a year, and by the 1820s competition in terms of price and speed was intense. It has been estimated that there were 15 times as many coach travellers in the mid-1830s as there had been in the 1790s.(140) All self-respecting towns vied to be on a mail route. To John Martin and John Biddulph it was essential.

In 1791 the Hereford stage coach, which left London at 9 am on Mondays, Wednesday and Saturdays, passed through Ledbury. By 1793 a coach left the Bolt-in-Tun in Fleet Street at noon every Tuesday and Friday for Ledbury. The service had improved little 30 years later. The *Cambrian* from Carmarthen left Ledbury at 5.30 am for London three days a week. There was, in addition, a connection with the Royal Mail at Gloucester which left Ledbury at 8 am on the other three weekdays, but no direct Mail coach.(141)

In 1816, now that two carriages could meet without danger at the Upper Cross, John Biddulph turned his attention to the Lower Cross where 'several persons had lost their lives' to the removal of 'that unsightly row of houses, called the Butchers Row'. He had a number of conversations with John Martin and promised to subscribe £50 if St Katherine's would take down the three houses in the row belonging to them. 'If other persons will subscribe I will give £100.'

The 1819 Act, which empowered the Dean and Chapter of Hereford cathedral to rebuildSt Katherine's almshouses, provided for the demolition of their properties in the Butchers Row which overshadowed the site. In 1820 the Improvement Trustees resolved to apply the funds in hand towards the taking down of other houses in the Row. They solicited the aid of 'the gentry of the neighbourhood and the inhabitants of the town'.

'The advantage of removing this obstruction will be very great, not only in widening the Street, which is the principal thoroughfare, but, also, in getting rid of the disgusting custom of slaughtering animals in the public street, when the gutters are, literally, running with blood: and the noisome smell from so many privies and slaughtering rooms, in the centre of the town, is, also, very disgusting and unwholesome'.(142)

By 1821 eight of the 15 buildings, including those belonging to St Katherine's, had been demolished. Materials were sold and a number were re-erected behind existing buildings in the town. One of these has been rescued by the Ledbury and District Society, carefully restored and erected once again. It is now the Butcher Row House Museum in Church Lane.

As the four northernmost houses of the Butchers Row were now demolished, the passage of the High Street was much easier and when the Royal Mail route was extended to Hereford it passed through Ledbury. The London Mail called at the Feathers at four each evening and the Hereford Mail at ten in the morning. They travelled by way of Tewkesbury, Cheltenham, Oxford and Henley. The *Telegraph* also made the same journey each day.(143)

The momentum of 1819-20 was not maintained. The Butter Market was removed but the vestry could not be pushed into action, and nothing else happened until 1830, when the visit to Ledbury of the Duchess of Kent and the Princess Victoria seems to have precipitated further activity. A 'Society for effecting the removal of the Butchers Row' was founded, with Mr Timothy Spencer as chairman, but little was achieved until the passing of the Ledbury Improvement Act of 1835. As the preamble states, 'In consequence of legal difficulties that exist in purchasing the remaining houses and of raising the requisite funds for that purpose, the same could not be effected without the aid and authority of Parliament'. Put simply, owners would not sell and Ledburians would not pay for demolition.

Under the terms of the Act, special commissioners, with John Biddulph at their head, were appointed with powers to levy a rate for this especial purpose, and to take any parties that refused to treat to the Quarter Sessions. The seven remaining shops, the weighing machine and the machine house were now taken down. No longer 'from October to January would the noise occasioned by the killing of pigs, and the danger to passengers from the fires for singeing them, deter travellers from passing through the Town'.

After more than 600 years the market encroachment had gone and the market place was, apart from the Market Hall, once more an open space, as it had been when first laid out by Richard de Capella's surveyor in the 1120s.

Although the 1820s witnessed a lull in the battle to remove the Butchers Row, there was considerable activity on other fronts. In 1821 'many persons in the High Street being very anxious to have the street paved with a flagstone for the convenience of Ladies, and others, attending their shops', a flagged pavement, three feet wide, was laid down with pitching stones on the inside and with covered drains from the houses to the gutter. In 1823 Thomas Taylor submitted an estimate for street lamps 'make and size of ye Feathers Lamp [which is still there] about £3 10s 0d'. Each lamp, it was calculated, would consume a pint of oil in six or seven hours and the 'total expense of Oil, Trimming and Lighting each lamp for 6 Months' would be £4 4s 0d. By contrast, the first of Hereford's four Lamp Acts had been passed in 1774 and the 1787 Hereford Paving Act had provided a commission for paving, repairing, cleaning and lighting the town. Pall Mall was lit by gas in 1809 and Westminster Bridge in 1813.

Matters relating to public health — an untainted water supply, effective drainage, medical care for the impoverished — played a key part in the campaign for improving the town. In 1808 the vestry had repaired Church Street and had made 'the open brook [which flowed from the Upper Hall] into a covered drain'. The serious outbreak of typhoid in the town in 1826 was attributed by the medical officer to 'effluvia rising from the brook' in its yet uncovered section in Bye Street, but it was three years before a parish meeting was prodded into culverting these lower reaches of the brook, 'heretofore such a disgusting nuisance'. The main sewer and all drains from the houses in the Homend and the Southend were also covered — something Biddulph had pressed for in his 1813 Report. By 1828 new reservoirs had been put in Coneygree Wood and the noisy and nasty public pump in the Southend and all necessity for resorting to it were done away with, by laying pipes to carry water to every house. Bromyard, without such firm leadership, only got a piped supply in 1900.(144)

The Public Dispensary, established in 1824 with a parish grant of £60 pa, was to serve the poor of the parish in place of the inefficient and expensive parish doctor. Its success was reflected in attendance figures — 861 in the first year; over 2,000 in 1834. The Dispensary Surgeon, Mr, later Dr Selwyn was assisted by two qualified midwives who kept child-bed linen and other comforts for the needy, and attended some 58 married women a year.

Great benefits, subscribers were told, resulted from the attention paid to vaccination. John Biddulph noted in 1831 that 211 people had been vaccinated. To this he attributed the absence of smallpox in the town, 'though it has been very violent in the neighbourhood'. In the same year, despite the campaign against water-borne disease, there was a typhus outbreak. Although 260 cases of fever were reported, a policy of public vaccination kept the death toll low — only seven died. When cholera raged at Gloucester and Worcester in 1832, John Biddulph spent much time persuading the townspeople to adopt suitable precautions. A Board of Health was established, and a hospital, but they were not needed. Vaccination and improved sanitation kept the town free of the epidemic. The parish signified its gratitude to the Dispensary in 1835 by withdrawing its grant and John Biddulph faced many disputes over the new waterworks.(145)

It was principally due to pressure from John Biddulph that work was recommenced on the Hereford and Gloucester canal in 1830. In October 1829 he had explained his views on substituting a rail road for the canal to Stephen Ballard, Clerk of the Canal Company, but the committee at their next meeting decided against the scheme. When he confided to his *Journal,* 'a Rail Road would have been a better thing', he was quite right. Within a year of the completion of the Ledbury-Hereford section in 1844, the committee had accepted the Welsh Midland Railway Co's £130,000 bid to convert the canal to a railway. John Biddulph was better informed than anyone in the county about the potential of the new railways, for his son, John was planning to produce rails for the Stephensons at his works in Wales. In June 1830, a year after the Rainhill trials and just three months before the opening of the Liverpool and Manchester Railway, George Stephenson's son, Robert, stayed at Ledbury Park on his journey to Wales to advise on production.

On occasions John Biddulph was overcome by despair. Noting the decline in trade at Ledbury fair in 1829 he wrote, 'I cannot but feel that my family are falling. I had elevated my House too high, all was prosperity till 1812 [the war years], and we have been sinking ever since and I fear never to rise again in my time. I can no longer exert myself and see no prospect for any of my sons'. Nevertheless by June of the preceding year he had spent £20,000 altering New House and repairing farms on the Ledbury Park estate. The major work was undertaken in 1818-19, when the service and stable block behind the old house was rebuilt for domestic use. The south or lawn front was altered and a suite of rooms added. The impressive Worcester Road entrance was built then, and the adjacent dovecote was converted into a lodge.

The Biddulphs were actively involved in politics over a number of generations. John's father, Robert had sat in the Commons as a Whig member for the county from 1796-1802. John himself was active in politics, particularly during the crisis which led to the passing of the First Reform Act. In 1831 his son, Robert won Hereford City for the Whigs on the parliamentary reform ticket and was received in triumph in Ledbury. However, he was not able to retain the seat in 1837, and his father attributed his defeat to the fear on the part of many tradesmen voters, at a time when there was no secret ballot, of 'offending the clergy and gentry tories who deal with them'. Later, John's grandson, Michael Biddulph held one of the county seats as a Liberal from 1865 until the Redistribution of Seats Act, 1885, when Herefordshire was divided into North and South, each with one seat.

John Biddulph believed that the limited extension of the Parliamentary franchise would act as a safety valve but he shared the fears of the neighbouring gentry of the spirit of revolt and mob rule. With reports of violence and rick-burning in the vicinity in 1830, he took measures to prevent rioting and fight incendiarism. In 1834, when Gloucester trades unionists sent delegates to Ledbury to swear in members, the whole town was in confusion. The trades unions, he believed, 'if not stopped soon will ruin the country'. Ledburians who joined were discharged by their masters and left in a body of about 30 for Worcester and Birmingham saying that 'they would be back'. He was almost as shocked by the waltzing that he witnessed at a ball in the Feathers Assembly Room in the winter of 1836, especially as his daughters indulged in it.

At the beginning of 1840 (while planning the building of a Crescent in Ledbury) he had a slight stroke. He was in bed until his birthday, 17 March, when he made the final entry in the *Journal* he had kept since 1787: 'this is the last day of my journal — writing affects my hand'. He lived on until December 1845, when the *Hereford Journal* recorded that: 'the mortal remains of this universally beloved and respected gentleman were gathered to those of his ancestors . . . The shutters of most of the shops and private houses in the town were either partly or wholly closed and a deep feeling of grief seemed to imbue the minds of all classes of the inhabitants. We may truly say that one of the best and noblest spirits in Ledbury has taken its flight, that the poor of the town and neighbourhood have lost one of their truest friends and benefactors'.

The condition of the poor was of perennial concern to the parish and by the late 18th century had assumed crisis proportions. Elizabethan legislation placed the responsibility for the poor on the parish, and established a pattern of relief which remained unchanged in its essentials, until the passing of the Poor Law Amendment Act of 1834. Out-relief, money payments, were made to the poor. In 1695 the Ledbury Overseers ordered that 'each poore person who shall Receive monthly pay, house rent or Coales at the charge of the Parish shall weare such bagge'.(146) The brass badge bore the inscription, 'This signifieth that I am reduced to poverty and receive alms from Ledbury'.

The first reference to in-relief, to a parish workhouse, is found in the Workhouse Minute Book for 1733, which records the payment of a rate of 5s 1d for the workhouse in Church Lane. In 1737 a Union was formed with Cradley which undertook to pay £8 pa, a third of the cost of upkeep, to provide bedding and clothes and pay funeral expenses for each of its paupers sent there.(146)

Part of the workhouse was converted to a house of industry at a cost of £1,000 in 1786. The children of the poor were employed in such activities as pin-heading and rope-making. By 1817 the factory had been closed. Many men were set to work at the quarry in Coneygree Wood. In 1821 it was resolved that labourers 'out of employ and chargeable to the parish do work from six o'clock in the morning till six in the evening or their pay to be discontinued'. In 1830 the overseers entered into a contract with the Canal Co for the employment of paupers in cutting part of the new line to Hereford. A year later the overseers were still concerned that 'a certain class of men will always prefer working for the Parish at easy labour rather than seeking for a master under whom they must work hard'. Work should whenever possible be task work 'at such prices as they must do an honest and hard days work'. Despite the intense pressure placed on the overseers by the size of their problem, (between 1813-15 the annual cost of poor relief to the parish was about £2,500), they frequently showed great understanding. Thus in 1829 they resolved that: 'James Hill be assisted with a sufficient sum . . . to discharge a years rent in consequence of . . . having been confined to three months' imprisonment under a charge of illegally pursuing game, by which means he lost the earnings of the harvest months, and is still very ill from an attack of pleurisy'.(147)

The professed aim of the 1834 Poor Law Amendment Act was to terminate out-relief for the able-bodied. Relief was now only to be available in a workhouse, and that under a strict regime. Policy was to be controlled by Poor Law Commissioners in London, and parishes were to be grouped together into Unions for poor law purposes, these to be supervised by elected Boards of Guardians. The Ledbury Union was made up of 20 parishes and covered an area of some 50,000 acres.

The Guardians moved quickly with their first task, the construction of a new workhouse. A site at Belle Orchard was chosen and the contract was signed on 2 August 1836 with John Matthews of Ledbury, only eight weeks after E.W. Head had published his report on the operation of the new poor law in the county. It was to be built to the design of George Wilkinson of Witney, Oxon, who was also the architect for the Weobley and Bromyard workhouses, and was to hold 150 people. The cost was to be £3,500. The committee's attention having been drawn to '12 small tanks to hold only 6 gallons of water each, provided for in the specification, [they] learned from the contractor the special use of those cisterns'. Despite such innovations as water closets, John Biddulph was deeply concerned about the regime proposed for the inmates. The new workhouse opened in February 1837 with James Hughes as master and his wife, Ann as matron.(148)

A large part of the old workhouse in Church Street was used as a school for 300 boys.(149) This was the National School for Promoting the Education of the Poor in the Principles of the Established Church with Richard Webb Taylor master and Mary Bowkett mistress. About 1850, the girls and infants moved to new premises opposite the Lower Hall. Later the boys' department was provided with a new site in the Homend by John Martin IV, where the new school and master's house were erected in 1868. The burden of maintaining these two voluntary schools seems to have been too great for the local Anglicans; thus in 1894 a School Board was established for what were now the urban and rural civil parishes of Ledbury. The Board assumed responsibility for the schools under the terms of the 1870 Education Act, and was able to levy a rate on both parishes for that purpose. The 1902 Education Act transferred that responsibility to the local education authority — the County Council. The Girls' and Infants' department is now the County Junior School and the Boys' department has become the County Infant School. Onto the foundations laid in the 19th century our own century has added secondary education: a Grammar School at the Upper Hall in 1923 and a Secondary School, after the end of World War II, in Mables Furlong — now amalgamated as the Masefield School.

The National Society, and later the Board and the local education authority, catered for the majority of Ledbury children but the range of schooling in the town was extremely diverse. The ancient Grammar School, despite the efforts of John Biddulph, passed into oblivion, and its funds were transferred to the National School, but the school for girls founded by Elizabeth Hall in 1708 flourished in the Southend well into the 20th century, under the protective eye of the Biddulphs. Frequently referred to as the Cookery School, it was in fact concerned with all the domestic crafts

— sewing and knitting, washing and ironing, cleaning and dusting — as well as the basics of reading, writing and numbers. Rebuilt in 1910, the original seat of the mistress, with its tall back and pediment carrying the Hall arms, was carefully restored in the lecture kitchen. It has since been lost.

In the 1860s there was a Ragged School in Back Lane for 30 poor boys and girls and, for a short time, a school run according to the principles of the British and Foreign Schools Society in the Homend. The School of Industry in the old workhouse was replaced by a school in the new Union workhouse in Belle Orchard. Private boarders and day schools, or academies as they liked to call themselves, flourished. There were eight in 1835, taking in children, especially girls, from the whole district, to teach them 'the accomplishments'. The most renowned were George Dunn's Academy in New Street, shown on Gibbs' 1831 *Plan,* the Misses Davies' Academy at the Lower Hall and the Ladies 'Seminary' at Linden House, New Street. The needs of the boys were evidently not sufficiently met, for in 1899 the Russell Endowed Middle Class Boys School was opened in the Southend 'to provide a sound education for the sons of professional and business men'.

The pace of improvement slackened after 1850. The police force under a superintendent replaced the watch. At a meeting called to consider that 'almost indispensable desideratum', a new corn exchange, the mayor acknowledged it 'a well known fact' that Ledbury's markets had 'for many years been in a dull and unprogressive state. If farmers went to Leominster there is a spacious new market. If they go to Ross there is a good one being built'. No new corn exchange was built; all that could be provided was accommodation behind the Feathers, but Ledbury, following its rivals, established an off-street cattle market in Bye Street before the end of the century.

A cemetery was opened in Ross Road in 1861. The Ledbury Gas Coke and Coal Co built a new gas works in New Street in 1875. New premises were provided for the Cottage Hospital, originally founded in the Homend in 1873, by Michael Biddulph, to commemorate the coming-of-age of his eldest son in 1891. The Royal Hall adjacent to the Royal Oak in the Southend could accommodate 500 people for plays and other entertainments.

Since the 13th century a tannery had stood at the Lower Cross. In 1895 this was replaced by the Barrett Browning Memorial Institute. The cost of £3,000 was met by public subscription. A reading room, library and meeting rooms were provided. Brightwen Binyon chose a Tudor revival style to complement the Market Hall across the road.(150)

A year earlier one of the most remarkable of modern houses was completed at Colwall. Perrycroft, just off the road from the Herefordshire Beacon to the Wyche, was the first large house to be designed by C.F.A. Voysey. Completed in 1894, it exhibits all the characteristics to be seen in his later buildings — overall horizontal proportions, massive unbroken sweeps of roof, exaggerated chimneys and buttresses, cleanly designed external rough cast walls, with horizontal bands of leaded light windows. Only the slight timbering on top of the tower looks backward. Perrycroft rejects classical forms and seeks to give a sense of oneness with its surroundings. With the houses of Norman Shaw, Lethaby and Lutyens it points firmly to the 20th century and through the writings of Hermann Muthesius these architects were to have a profound influence on continental practice.(151)

It was in 1894 that John Masefield returned, briefly, to Ledbury after leaving the *Gilcruix,* the ship on which he had served as an apprentice, at the Chilean nitrate port of Iquique. Later he was to write at length about the 'little town of ancient grace' where he had been born and brought up until, at the age of 13, he joined the training ship *Conway. The Everlasting Mercy* (1911), *The Widow in Bye Street* (1912), *The Daffodil Fields* (1913), *Reynard the Fox* (1919), *Wonderings* (1943) and *St Katherine of Ledbury and other Ledbury Papers* (1951) shed a powerful light on the town as he knew it during childhood years. Until he was seven he lived at the house his father had built in the Homend, the Knapp, but after the death of his mother and the serious illness of his father, he was adopted by his uncle, William Masefield, and moved to the Priory in Church Lane.

Life was still hard for many in Ledbury at the end of the 19th century despite the improvements of the years since 1820.

I never crossed the town without the sight
Of withered children suffering from blight . . .
And starving groups in rags, with boots unsoled,
Blear eyed, and singing ballads in the cold.
I saw filthy alleys, close and dark,
Where few could read or write, but made their mark,
Where men and women lived and died in tetter,
So little human that the dogs were better.(152)

Masefield's view of Ledbury in the 1880s is vividly supplemented by the photographs of Alfred Watkins.(153) As the representative of his father's Hereford Brewery, the young Alfred Watkins knew well many of the dark alleys and back street public houses to which Masefield so often alluded. His early passion for the camera has thus left us a remarkable photographic record of the town in those years.(154)

Notwithstanding the arrival of the railway in 1861, Ledbury continued to be firmly rooted in the countryside. This was fully acknowledged when local government was reformed in 1894. The establishment of elective county councils in 1888 which assumed local government powers previously exercised by the magistracy, began a process of reform that was completed by H.H. Fowler's Local Government Act of 1894. This introduced the Rural District Council to fulfil those functions of local government not granted to county or parish. The bounds of the new Rural District were the same as those of the Poor Law Union set up in 1834, except that West Malvern, which was part of the Union, was not included within the District as it was outside Herefordshire. The Union, with minor modifications in the west, was based on the hundred of Radlow. Ledbury Rural District had a long and proud lineage going back to the 12th century. Local government reorganisation at the end of the 19th century thus recognised the vital bond between the small market town and the district it served. At Ledbury it was more than 1,000 years old.

Peter Walker, MP for Worcester, and the authors of the Local Government Act of 1972 cut right across this bond. At a time when the scope of local government was wider than ever, the vital decisions affecting the future of the town and district were henceforth to be taken at Malvern and Worcester.

Timothy Spencer's new bowed brick facade looking onto the Homend c1820. Pentices of the Butchers Row on the left. T. Ballard, Engraving. (HCL/PC)

Copy of a letter written by HRH The Duchess of Kent.

Buckingham Palace
28 March 1838.

Sir,

I have this day given directions for the repayment of the loan I owe to your friendly feeling. It is due to that feeling to announce this to you myself; but it is still more so, that I should offer you my cordial and grateful thanks and acknowledgments for your kind and considerate attention in aiding me to provide for expenses, caused by the exertions I made to connect the Queen with the Country by the Tours which I made for that purpose.

Believe me to be
with esteem & regard
Sir,
Your sincere friend
Victoria

Robert Biddulph Esq.

His Royal Highness
Albert Edward
Prince of Wales.

Marlborough House.
Pall Mall S.W.

11th May 1877

Gentlemen,

I desire that you will open an account in my name, subject to the sole orders of Major General Sir Dighton Macnaghten Probyn KCSI. CB. VC whom I have appointed my Treasurer and Comptroller.

Albert Edward P.

Messrs Biddulph & Cocks
43 Charing Cross.

ABOVE: Cheque of the Cocks, Biddulph and Co Bank, founded by Francis Biddulph of New House and St Paul's Churchyard in 1757 when he was joined by James and Thomas Cocks of Eastnor. They moved to 43 Charing Cross, now 16 Whitehall, SW1, in 1759. Merged with Martins, 1920, now part of Barclays. BELOW LEFT: Copy of letter from Queen Victoria's mother, the Duchess of Kent, thanking Robert Biddulph for a loan of £10,000, and RIGHT: Letter from Edward VII, as Prince of Wales, opening a private account with the Biddulph and Cocks Bank on 11 May 1877. This account remained with the bank until Edward's death in 1910.

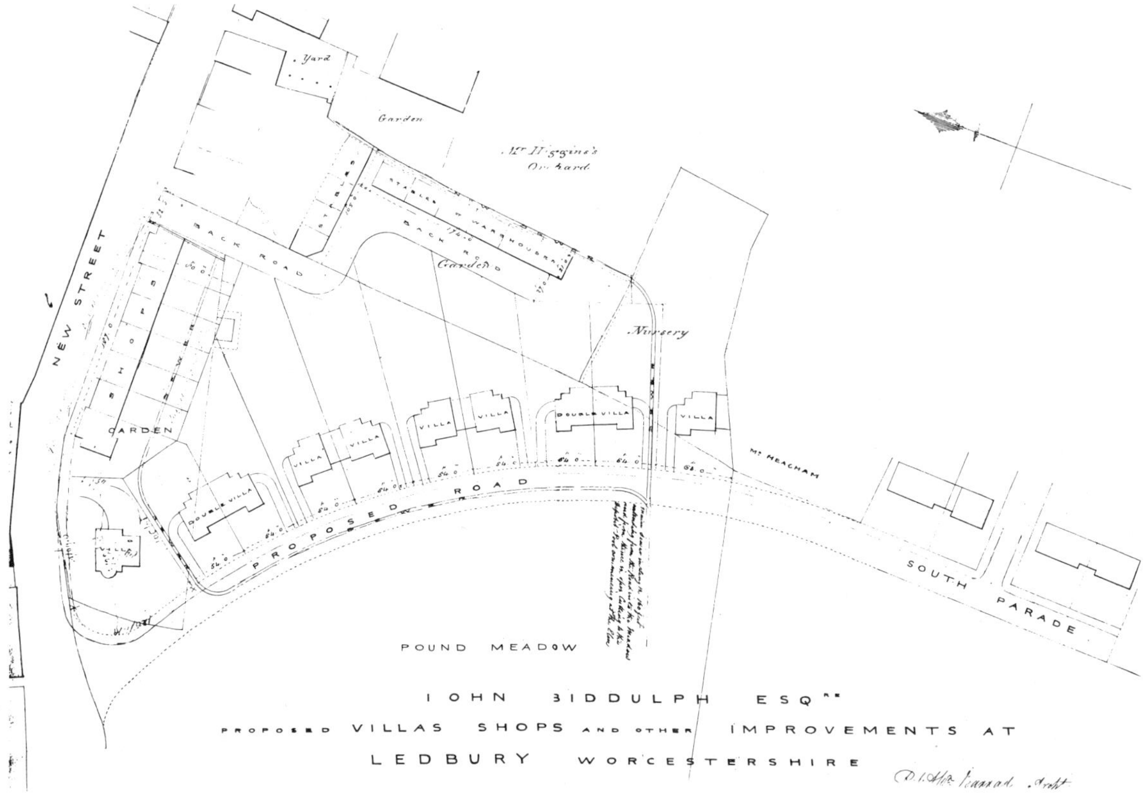

ABOVE: Property development in Ledbury 150 years ago: proposal by John Biddulph to link South Parade and New Street. (HCRO/G2) BELOW LEFT: The Boys' Church of England School, erected in 1868 on a site given by John Martin IV of the Upper Hall, senior partner in the Bank at the Sign of the Grasshopper in Lombard Street, 1844-75. RIGHT: The Mistress's High Seat of 1708, carefully restored when the 'Cookery School' was rebuilt on its original site in the Southend in 1910. The curved pediment carried the Hall coat of arms. (HCRO/AB48/B10)

Remnants of the Butchers Row: LEFT: The 'Butchers Row House' on its former site behind Boots, 14 High Street. It has now been re-erected by the Ledbury and District Society in Church Lane, and RIGHT: a remnant behind 22 the Homend. CENTRE: The Knapp, built by Edward Masefield. Here, his son John was born on 1 June 1878. When John was eight, he moved to his uncle William's house at the Priory with its grounds adjacent to the churchyard. BELOW: 1 the Homend is transformed. But the market hurdles remain. (HCRO/AB48/B10)

Text Notes

Abbreviations

BL	British Library	HCRO	Herefordshire County Record Office
Cal S P Dom	Calendar of State Papers (Domestic)	HD & CR	Hereford Dean and Chapter Records
HCM	Hereford City Museum	PRO	Public Record Office
RCHM	Royal Commission on Historical Monuments		
Reg	Registers of the bishops of Hereford, published jointly by Cantilupe Society and Canterbury and York Society (1906-21)		
Tr WNFC	Transactions of the Wolhope Naturalists Field Club (1852-1979)		

1 J. Hillaby, 'The Origins of the Diocese of Hereford', *Tr WNFC*, XLII (i) (1976), 16-52
2 Bede, *Epistle to Bishop Egbert*, c.8
3 For the Iron Age Hill-Forts of the area see S.C. Stanford, *The Malvern Hill-Forts* (1973) and S.C. Stanford, *Midsummer Hill* (1981)
4 H.P.R. Finberg, *Early Charters of the West Midlands* (1961), 202 and 205
5 E. Ekwall, *Concise Oxford Dictionary of English Place-Names* (1959), 293; E. Ekwall, *English River-Names* (1928), 241-2
6 F.M. Stenton, 'The Historical Bearing of Place-Name Studies: The Place of Women in Anglo-Saxon Society', *Tr Royal Hist Soc*, 4S, XXX(1943), 1-13
7 A. Morey and C.N.L. Brooke (eds), *Letters and Charters of Gilbert Foliot* (1967), 300
8 *Reg. Swinfield*, 464-7
9 *Reg. Trilleck*, 40-1
10 C.B. Andrews (ed), *The Torrington Diaries: Tours through England and Wales of Hon John Byng*, I (1934), 43
11 Bede,*History of the English Church and People*, trans L. Sherley-Price (1955), 86
12 Sir William Dugdale, *Antiquities of Warwickshire* (1730), II, 682
13 *Reg. Gilbert*, 90-1
14 *Victoria County History of Herefordshire*, I, 322
15 H.A. Cronne and R.H.C. Davis (eds), *Regesta Regum Anglo-Normannorum, 1066-1154*, III (1963), 148
16 William of Wycumb, *De Vita Roberti Betun, Episcope Herefordensis*, c. 21 in J. Wharton (ed), *Anglia Sacra* (1691), II, 312
17 J. Hillaby, ' "The Saint that Never Slept": Robert de Bethune, Bishop of Hereford, 1131-48', *Report of the Friends of Hereford Cathedral*, XLVI (1980), 21-42
18 Not printed in Wharton's edition of Wycumb's *Life*, it was one of the miracles which he believed 'the fastidious reader' might reject. See BL, Cotton MS. Julia DX or Lambeth Palace Library MS. 475, c.19
19 C. Johnson and H.A. Cronne (eds), *Regesta Regum Anglo-Normannorum, 1066-1154*, II (1956), 159
20 L. Toulmin Smith (ed), *The Itinerary of John Leland, in or about 1535-43* (1910), V, 184 and 187
21 M.D. Lobel (ed), *Historic Towns*, I (1969), 'Hereford', 4-5
22 HD and CR, 1658a
23 HCRO, HE/1/133677. *The Red Book of the Bishops of Hereford*
24 *Red Book*, pa. 137
25 For general discussion see J. Hillaby, 'The Boroughs of the Bishops of Hereford in the late 13th century', *Tr WNFC*, XL(i) (1970), 10-35
26 A. Ballard and J. Tait, *British Borough Charters, 1216-1307* (1923), 51-62
27 W.W. Capes (ed), *Charters and Records of Hereford Cathedral* (1908), 69
28 *Red Book*, pa. 122
29 A.T. Bannister, 'A Descriptive Catalogue of Manuscripts dealing with St Katherine's, Ledbury', *Tr WNFC* (1923), 231-53, catalogues some of the grants, leases etc. The originals are to be found amongst the Dean and Chapter's Records. The deeds are referred to below, first by the number in Bannister's printed catalogue and then by the HD and CR reference number
30 Bannister (1923), 92. HD and CR, A3742
31 *RCHM*, II (1932), 113
32 *Red Book*, pa. 119-42
33 For surname origins etc see F.H. Reaney, *Origins of Engligh Surnames* (1967) and R. McKinley, *Surnames of Oxfordshire* (1977)
34 R. Burn, *Ecclesiastical Law*, II (1781), 395
35 J.C. Cox, *Parish Registers of England* (1910), 79, quoting from the parish register of Cottenham, Cambs
36 *Patent Rolls*, 1244-1325
37 Bannister (1923), 15 and 16, HD and CR, A3255 and A3256

38 *Patent Rolls,* 1324
39 Bannister (1923), 97. HD and CR, A3747
40 J. Stow, *Survey of London* (Everyman, 1912 ed), 306-7 and 309
41 Bannister (1923), 69 and 83. HD and CR, A3320 and A3733
42 *Patent Rolls,* 1365
43 Bannister (1923), 151 and 96. HD and CR, A3692 and A3746
44 *Reg. Spofford,* 245
45 *Patent Rolls,* 1390
46 *Patent Rolls,* 1328
47 Bannister (1923), 76. HD and CR, A3327
48 *Reg. Trefnant,* 163-4
49 *Red Book,* pa. 141
50 See 19th century *Directories.* Here at the end of the century lived G.H. Piper who transcribed the parish registers 1556-76 for publication in 1899
51 J.C. Russell, *British Medieval Population* (1948). Z. Razi, *Life, Marriage and Death in a Medieval Parish: Economy, Society and Demography in Halesowen, 1270-1400* (1980) 83-92 and C. Dyer, *Lords and Peasants in a Changing Society: The Estates of the Bishopric of Worcester, 680-1540* (1980), 230-2 interpret material for neighbouring rural areas
52 *Reg. Trilleck,* 410-511
53 Razi (1980), 151
54 M.M. Postan, 'Mediaeval Agrarian Society in its Prime, 7. England'. *Camb Ec Hist of Europe,* I (1966), 570
55 Capes (1908), 68-72. HD and CR, 1389 and 2098
56 *Reg. Lewis Charlton,* 14-17
57 HD and CR, 1658a
58 Capes (1908), 199
59 *Reg. Trilleck,* 196 and 240
60 *Reg. Gilbert,* 42
61 Bannister (1923), 82
62 *Report of the Commissioners for Inquiring concerning Charities: Herefordshire* (1819-37), 111-22
63 *Reg. Cantilupe,* 309-12; *Reg. Lewis Charlton,* 106-7, 116-8; *Reg. Courtenay,* 22-3; *Reg. Gilbert,* 163-5; *Reg. Trilleck,* 410-9, 419-25, 445-58
64 *Reg. Gilbert,* 48-54; *Patent Rolls,* 1387
65 St Clair Baddeley, 'The 15th Century Effigy of an Unknown Lady at Ledbury', *Tr WNFC* (1929), 214-7
66 R.K. Morris, 'The Local Influence of Hereford Cathedral in the Decorated Period', *Tr WNFC* (1973), 48-67
67 N. Pevsner, *Herefordshire* (1963), 34 and 216
68 Printed in A.T. Bannister, 'The Visitation Returns of the Diocese of Hereford in 1397', *Eng Hist Rev,* XLV (1930), 92-101
69 *Reg. Cantilupe, Swinfield* and *Trilleck*
70 *Patent Rolls,* 1231, 1256, 1326 and 1332; R.M. Haines, *The Church and Politics in 14th-Century England: The Career of Adam Orleton c1275-1345* (1978), 161-80
71 For bishop's household etc see J. Webb (ed), 'Household Roll of Richard de Swinfield, 1289-90' *Camden Soc,* OS, LXII (1855)
72 *Letters and Charters of Gilbert Foliot* (1967), 372
73 *Red Book,* pa. 138
74 *Diary of George Skyppe of the Upper Hall, 1668-90;* T.W.M. Johnson, 'The Diary of George Skyppe of Ledbury', *Tr WNFC* (1953), 54-62
75 HCRO, J95/1
76 T. Wright (ed), 'Political Songs of England from John to Edward II', *Camden Soc,* OS, VI (1839)
77 *Reg. Cantilupe,* 52, 227-8. For Cantilupe's life and miracles, R. Strange, *Life and Gests of St Thomas Cantilupe* (1879 ed) is useful and M. Jancey, *St Thomas of Hereford* (1978)
78 *Reg. Cantilupe,* 69-70; *Reg. Trillick,* 85-6; *Reg. Trefnant, 166-9*
79 *Reg. Trilleck,* 164-6. HCRO, Silas Taylor's MS. f. 103
80 *Reg. Trilleck,* 83
81 *Charter Rolls,* I, 447 and II, 258 and 281
82 PRO, (Pipe Rolls), E372/80 m 2 and E372/120 m 22
83 Capes (1908), 226-9
84 A.H. Bright, *New Light on Piers Plowman* (1928), 33-57, A.H. Bright, 'Colwall and the Neighbourhood', *Tr WNFC* (1923), 178-80 and D. Pearsall, *Piers Plowman by William Langland* (1978), 9-20
85 Pevsner (1963), 219
86 *Patent Rolls,* 1549
87 For early history of Skyppe family and Willason connection see HCRO Skyppe collection (B38) especially B38/1-11

88 A. Harford, 'The Harfords of Bosbury', *Archaeologia Cambrensis* (1909), 283-301; F.C. Morgan, 'John Guildon or Gildon', *Tr WNFC* (1935), 113-8; L. Butler, 'John Gildon of Hereford', *Archaeological Journal,* CXXIX (1972), 148-53

89 HCRO, B38/13

90 HCRO, B38/14-5

91 HD and CR, 822 and 1163; *Reg. Mayhew,* 283; *Reg. Bothe,* 331, 339-41, 346, 348; C.H. Mayo, *A Genealogical Account of the Mayo and Elton Families* (1882), 6-34

92 E. Hall (ed), *Red Book of the Exchequer* (1896), 278, 496; *Reg. Swinfield,* 403; J. O'Donnell, 'A Border Knight: Sir Grimbald Pauncefot', *Tr WNFC,* XLI(i) (1973), 39-47; *Patent Rolls,* 1332

93 Mayo (1882), 13-8

94 *Reg. Gilbert,* 60-1; *Patent Rolls,* 1399 and 1401; *Reg. Mascall, 170 and 176;* A.J. Winnington-Ingram, 'The Constitution of the Church of Ledbury', *Tr WNFC* (1942), 70-4. There was a parallel case at St Peter's Bromyard. See J. Hillaby and E. Pearson (eds), *Bromyard, A Local History* (1970), 10-11

95 1 Elizabeth I, c19; J. Bacon, *Liber Regis* (1786), vii-viii; *Cal S. P. Dom,* Eliz XVII, 32. A.T. Bannister, *The Cathedral Church of Hereford* (1924), 85-92 and H.W. Phillott, *Diocesan History of Hereford* (1888), 178)87 give some account of Scory's episcopacy

96 HCRO, B36/26, 28-9

97 A.J. Winnington-Ingram, 'Edward Cooper or Cowper, 1528-1596', *Tr WNFC* (1948), xciii-civ

98 Survey, petition and and school continuance warrant are all printed in A.F. Leach, *English Schools at the Reformation* (1896), 92-3, 106-7; *Charity Commissioners' Reports: Herefordshire* (1819-37), 122

99 Herefordshire *Directories* (various)

100 Leland (1910 ed), II, 91; 4 and 5 Philip and Mary c 5; 5 and 6 Edward VI c 6; 18 Elizabeth I c 16. Also see A.D. Dyer, *The City of Worcester in the Sixteenth Century* (1973), 93-119 and D.C. Coleman, *The Economy of England, 1450-1750* (1977), 75-82

101 N. Penney (ed), *The First Publishers of Truth* (1907), 115-27; J. Bisse, *Sufferings of the People called Quakers.* I (1753), 254-61; Hillaby and Pearson (1970), 83-98

102 G.H. Piper (transcriber), *The Registers of Ledbury* (1899), v-xi discusses the registers

103 Reprinted in J. Webb, *Memorials of the Civil War . . . in Herefordshire,* II (1879), 177-82

104 PRO E179/119/492. See also M.A. Faraday, 'The Hearth Tax in Herefordshire', *Tr WNFC* XLI(i) (1973), gives total of charged hearths and houses, by parishes, 1662-73

105 Printed in M.A. Faraday, 'Herefordshire Militia Assessments of 1663', *Camden Soc,* 4S, X (1972), 97-99

106 G.C. Williamson, *Trade Tokens Issued in the Seventeenth Century,* I (1889), 287-89; J.W. Lloyd, 'Herefordshire Tokens of the Seventeenth Century', *Tr WNFC* (1884), 183-209

107 *Commons Journal,* XIX, 12 Dec 1720

108 I. Cohen, 'Report on Archaeology for 1952', *Tr WNFC (1952), 33-4*

109 W.W. Skeat (ed), *The Vision of Piers the Plowman,* I (1886), B Text Passus X, 94-9

110 J. Tonkin, 'Buildings, 1972', *Tr WNFC* (1972), 397

111 *Charity Commissioners' Reports: Herefordshire* (1819-37), 129-30

112 E.J. Bettington, 'The Recent Renovations of Ledbury Market Hall', *Tr WNFC* (1939), xxv-xxvi

113 A.J. Winnington-Ingram, 'Edward Cooper or Cowper, 1528-1596', *Tr WNFC* (1948), xciii-civ; F.C. Morgan and A.J. Winnington-Ingram, 'The Accounts of St Katherine's Hospital, Ledbury, 1584-95', *Tr WNFC* (1953), 88-132. In the text, howses of office / privy; boulting howse / house in which meal is sifted; must / pulp of the cider apple. In the 17th century the best sorts of apple for cider were the redstreak, the white and the green must; deyhowse / dairy; bruynge howse / brew house

114 J. Clark, *General View of the Agriculture of the County of Hereford* (1794), 8

115 C.W. Atkin, 'Herefordshire', in H.C. Darby and I.B. Terrett, *The Domesday Geography of Midland England* (2nd ed, 1971), 78-83

116 W. Camden, *Britannia* (1586), 574

117 Clark (1794), 17-20

118 C. Morris (ed), *The Journal of Celia Fiennes* (1949), 43. For the agriculture of the county in the 17th to 19th centuries, see E.L. Jones, 'Agricultural Conditions and Changes in Herefordshire, 1660-1850', *Tr WNFC* (1961), 32-55 and J. Hillaby, 'Introduction' to P. Williams, *Whitbourne: A Bishop's Manor* (1979), 1-12

119 Webb (1879), II, 379

120 *Commons Journal,* 11 Jan 1695/6

121 J. Lloyd, *Papers relating to the History of the Wye and Lugg Navigation* (1873), 20-1

122 Swinfield's *Household Roll* (1855), cx-cxi

123 7 Geo. I, c 23

124 *Daily Gazeteer,* 8 October 1735

125 *Worcester Postman,* 16-23 April 1736; *Gentleman's Magazine,* 9 April 1736, 229

126 Ordinary of Newgate, *Account of Behaviour, Confession and Dying Words of the Malefactors who were Executed at Tyburn,* 26 July 1736; 11 August 1736. For wider discussion see E.P. Thompson, *Whigs and Hunters: The Origins of the Black Act* (1975), 219-69

127 15 Geo. II, c 17; *Gentleman's Magazine,* March 1742, 117-8

128 Clark (1794), 51-2

129 *Hereford Journal,* 4 April 1798

130 J. Pigot & Co, *Directory* (1822), 76-7

131 See E.T. MacDermott, *History of the Great Western Railway,* I, 1833-63 (1927) and J.E. Norris 'The Worcester and Hereford Railway', *Railway Magazine* (June 1959), 445-55 and 'The Gloucester and Ledbury Branch', *Railway Magazine* (April 1958), 228-32. A short account of the Gloucester and Ledbury branch by J.E. Norris is also to be found in D.E. Bick, *The Hereford and Gloucester Canal* (1979)

132 J. Hillaby to H. Adams, Herefordshire County Planning Officer, 27 May 1973; D.R. Howe, Chief Executive, Ledbury Rural District Council to J. Hillaby, 14 June 1973

133 Malvern Hills District Council, *Church Lane Study* (1975), 17. A Department of the Environment Inquiry was held into Malvern Hills DC application for listed building consent to gut Rutherglen and to demolish the Magistrates' Court, the Serjeant's House and the adjacent house on 27 October 1981. All four of the Council's applications were rejected. The inspector's report describes Rutherglen as 'this outstanding and most unusual building' and of the Council's proposed development states 'this architectural solecism is out of place in a highly sensitive location such as this'.

134 This information was supplied by David Whitehead

135 S.R.T. Mayer (ed), *Letters of E.B. Browning to R.H. Horne,* I (1877), 158-61. She wrote to Mrs Martin from Sidmouth, 'They told us of our having past your carriage in Ledbury. I cannot dwell upon the pain of that first hour of our journey . . . The painful circumstances made Papa shrink from society of any kind . . . He would not even attend the religious societies in Ledbury which he was so much pledged to support.' F.G. Kenyon (ed), *Letters of Elizabeth Barrett Browning,* I (1897), 1-15

136 *Charity Commissioners' Reports: Herefordshire* (1819-37), 115

137 G. Chandler, *Four Centuries of Banking* (1964); Martins Bank Ltd, *Cocks, Biddulph & Company, 1759-1920* (1948); J.B. Martin, *'The Grasshopper' in Lombard Street* (1892); L.S. Pressnell, *Country Banking in the Industrial Revolution* (1956)

138 HCRO, G2 *Biddulph Papers,* especially John Biddulph's *Journals* 1787-1840 and *Diaries,* 1795-1841. On his building programme HCRO D51/1-97

139 On town improvements HCRO, K13/17-18

140 P.S. Bagwell, *The Transport Revolution from 1770* (1974), 43

141 *Universal British Directory,* 1st ed (1791); 2nd ed (1793); Pigot's *Directory* (1822)

142 Thomas Bibbs, Clerk to the Trustees, *Letter to Subscribers* (Nov 1820), HCRO K13/17

143 Pigot's *Directory* (1830)

144 J. Hillaby and E. Pearson (eds), *Bromyard: A Local History* (1970), 122-33

145 *Report of the Ledbury Dispensary* (1837)

146 *Ledbury Workhouse Minute Books* (1733-43)

147 *Ledbury Vestry Minutes* (1829)

148 *Ledbury Poor Law Union, Board of Guardians Minute Book* (1836/7)

149 *Ledbury Churchwardens' Accounts* (1837)

150 Ledbury entries, Herefordshire *Directories* (1820-1902)

151 H. Muthesius, *Das englishce Haus,* 3 vols, (1908-10)

152 J. Masefield, *Wonderings* (1943), 16

153 Most of these Ledbury photographs, in the form of plate negatives or slides, are to be found in the remarkable *Watkins Collection* in the Hereford City Library

154 Alfred Watkins, whose fame now rests on *The Old Straight Track* (1925) which itself contains a remarkable series of photographs, recollected 'The Ledbury of John Masefield' in a paper in *Tr WNFC* (1934), xl-xliii

Tables

Further Reading

Babington Smith, C., *John Masefield, A Life,* 1978
Baddeley, St Clair, 'The 15th Century Effigy of an Unknown Lady at Ledbury co Hereford', *Tr WNFC* (1929), 214-7
Ball, E., 'Fruit Trees planted by George Skyppe and his Son (?) at Upper Hall, Ledbury, 1676-1705', *Tr WNFC* (1954), 268-73
Ballard, Stephen, *Treatise on the Nature of Trees,* 1833
Bannister, A.T., 'A Descriptive Catalogue of Manuscripts dealing with St Katherine's, Ledbury', *Tr WNFC* (1923), 231-53
Bannister, A.T., 'The Hospital of St Katherine at Ledbury', *Tr WNFC* (1918), 62-70
Bentley, S., *History and Description of the Parish of Bosbury,* 1891
Berridge, E., ed, *The Barretts at Hope End: The Early Diary of Elizabeth Barrett Browning,* 1974
Bettington, E.J., 'The Recent Renovation of Ledbury Market Hall', *Tr WNFC* (1939), xxv-xxvi
Bick, D.E., *The Hereford and Gloucester Canal,* 1979 (includes the Gloucester and Ledbury Railway by J.E. Norris)
Bright, A.H., 'Colwall and the Neighbourhood', *Tr WNFC* (1923), 178-84
Bright, A.H., *New Light on 'Piers Plowman',* 1928
Chandler, G., *Four Centuries of Banking, as Illustrated by . . . the Constituent Banks of Martins Bank Limited,* 1964
Clark, J., *General View of the Agriculture of the County of Hereford,* 1794
Cohen, I., 'The Herefordshire and Gloucestershire Canal', *Tr WNFC* (1959), 167-79
Cocks, Biddulph & Company, 1759-1920, Martins Bank Ltd, 1948
Duncumb, J., *General View of the Agriculture of the County of Hereford,* 1805
Hadfield, C., *Canals of South Wales and the Border,* 1960
Hannah, G.W., 'John Trilleck, Bishop of Hereford', *Tr WNFC* (1974), 173-9
Hillaby, J., 'The Boroughs of the Bishops of Hereford in the late 13th Century', *Tr WNFC* (1970), 10-35
Hillaby, J., 'The Origins of the Diocese of Hereford', *Tr WNFC* (1976), 16-52
Hillaby, J., '"The Saint that never Slept": Robert de Bethune, Bishop of Hereford, 1131-48', *Report of the Friends of Hereford Cathedral,* 1980, 21-42
Hillaby, J. and Pearson, E., eds, *Bromyard: A Local History,* 1970
Jackson, J., *Architecture of Ledbury Church,* 1881
Johnson, T.W.M., 'The Diary of George Skyppe of Ledbury', *Tr WNFC* (1953), 54-62
Jones, E.L., 'Agricultural Conditions and Changes in Herefordshire, 1660-1850', *Tr WNFC* (1961), 32-55
Jones, E.L., 'Hereford Cattle and Ryeland Sheep, Economic Aspects of Breed Changes, 1780-1870', *Tr WNFC* (1964), 36-48
Kelly, P. and Hudson, R., eds, *Diary by E.B.B.: The Unpublished Diary of Elizabeth Barrett Browning, 1831-1832,* 1969
MacDermott, E.T., *History of the Great Western Railway,* vol 1, 1833-63, 1927
Masefield, G., *Old Records of Ledbury Church,* 1858
Masefield, J., *Reynard the Fox or the Ghost Heath Run,* 1919
Masefield, J., *St Katherine of Ledbury and other Ledbury Papers,* 1951
Masefield, J., *The Daffodil Fields,* 1913
Masefield, J., *The Everlasting Mercy,* 1911
Masefield, J., *The Widow in the Bye Street,* 1912
Masefield, J., *Wonderings (Between One and Six Years),* 1943
Mayo, C.H., *A Genealogical Account of the Mayo and Elton Families,* 1882
Morgan, F.C. and Winnington-Ingram, A.J., 'The Accounts of St Katherine's Hospital, Ledbury, 1584-95', *Tr WNFC* (1953), 88-132
Morgan, P., 'The Heraldry on the Willason Tomb in Madley Church, Herefordshire', *Tr WNFC* (1952), 288-90
Morris, R.K., 'The Local Influence of Hereford Cathedral in the Decorated Period', *Tr WNFC* (1973), 48-67
Norris, J.E., 'The Gloucester and Ledbury Branch', *Railway Magazine* (April 1958), 228-32
Norris, J.E., 'The Worcester and Hereford Railway', *Railway Magazine* (July 1959), 445-55; (August 1959), 533-8
O'Donnell, J., 'A Border Knight, Sir Grimbald Pauncefot', *Tr WNFC* (1973), 39-47
Parr, F., *Historical Notes on Old Ledbury,* n.d. (reprinted from *Hereford Times,* 19 January-24 May 1884)
Pearsall, D., *Piers Plowman by William Langland,* 1978
Piper, G.H., transcriber, and Mayo, C.H., ed, *The Registers of Ledbury, co Hereford, 1556-76,* 1899
Report of the Commissioners for Inquiring concerning Charities: County of Hereford, 1819-37 (Hundred of Radlow, Parish of Ledbury, 111-33)
Skeat, W.W., ed, *The Vision Concerning Piers the Plowman in Three Parallel Texts,* 2 vols, 1886
Smith, B.S., *A History of Malvern,* 1964
Somers-Cocks, H.L., *Eastnor and its Malvern Hills,* 1923
Spark, M., *John Masefield,* 1962
Stanford, S.C., *Midsummer Hill, an Iron Age Hillfort on the Malverns,* 1981
Stanford, S.C., *The Malvern Hillforts, Midsummer Hill and British Camp,* 1973
Thompson, L., *Robert Frost: The Early Years, 1874-1915,* 1967 (esp chs 32 and 33)

Watkins, A., 'Elizabeth Barrett and Hope End', *Tr WNFC* (1924/25), 104-9
Watkins, A., 'The Ledbury of John Masefield', *Tr WNFC* (1934), xl-xliii
Watkins, M.G., *Collections Towards the History and Antiquities of the County of Hereford in Continuation of Duncumb's History*, vol IV, 1902
Winnington-Ingram, A.J., 'Edward Cooper or Cowper, 1528-1596', *Tr WNFC* (1948), xciii-civ
Winnington-Ingram, A.J., 'The Constitution of the Church of Ledbury', *Tr WNFC* (1942), 70-4
Winnington-Ingram, A.J., 'Thomas Thorneton', *Tr WNFC* (1957), 207-22

Guides

Ledbury Guide, 'sold by John Devereux', 1824
Ledbury Guide, 'printed and sold by T.B. Watkins of Hereford', 1831
Hints of Old Ledbury, 'by a native Inhabitant (J.W. Gibbs?) and sold by T. Ward, S. Thackway and J. Gibbs, Land Surveyor', 1831
Freeman, E., *A Guide to Ledbury,* Jakeman and Carver, Hereford, 1892
Tilley, Ellen F., *Ledbury: A Concise Guide for Visitors,* 1898 (still in print, last edition 1980)

Newspapers

Ledbury Diary or Weekly Magazine, nos 1-5, March-April 1817 (published by H. Holder of Butchers Row)
Ledbury Free Press, nos 1-1805, 1870-18 August 1908 (published by Luke Tilley, printed by George William's Press, Worcester)
Ledbury Guardian and Herefordshire Advertiser, nos 1806-2543, 22 August 1908-2 July 1921
Ledbury Reporter and Farmers' Gazette, nos 1-1284, 1896-2 July 1921 (published by Thomas Vaughan, printed in Church Lane)
Ledbury Reporter and Guardian, nos 2544-5052, 9 July 1921-14 June 1967 (an amalgamation of the *Guardian* and the *Reporter;* between 14 June 1967 and 25 March 1970, incorporated with the *Hereford Times)*
Ledbury Reporter, nos 5053-, 6 November 1968- (subsequently incorporated with the *Malvern Gazette)*

Directories

Bailey's Western and Midland, 1783; Universal British Directory, 1791, 1793-98; Pigot, 1822; Pigot, 1830; Pigot, 1835; Robson, 1840; Hunt, 1847; Slater, 1850; Lascelles, 1851; Kelly, 1856; Cassey, 1858; Slater, 1859; Morris, 1862; Kelly, 1863; Littlebury, 1867; Kelly, 1870; Littlebury, 1876; Kelly, 1879; Kelly 1885; Wells and Manton, 1888; Jakeman and Carver, 1890; Kelly 1891; Kelly, 1895; Jakeman and Carver, 1895; Kelly, 1896; Kelly, 1900; Jakeman and Carver, 1902

Maps and Plans

Index

Subscribers

Presentation Copies

1 Ledbury Town Council
2 Malvern Hills District Council
3 County Council of Hereford & Worcester
4 Ledbury Library
5 Hereford Library
6 Ross-on-Wye Library
7 Bromyard Library
8 Malvern Library
9 The Rt Rev J.R.G. Eastaugh, Bishop of Hereford
10 Miss L.M. Tilley
11 Mr & Mrs F. Druce

12 Joe Hillaby
13 Clive & Carolyn Birch
14 Vincent Clayton
15 E.A. Roper
16 Keith Wilfred Francis
17 R.G. Bennett
18 T.E. Bennett
19 Miss M.E. Wiles
20 B.J. Barnett
21 Anthony James Hickey
22 Mrs W.F. Causier
23 Tony Watts
24 Mrs M. Clarke
25 C.J. Edwards
26 D. Budd
27 B. McGibbon
28 J.F. Cooper
29
30 Mrs M.E. Garlick
31 Mrs I. Dryburgh
32 Mr & Mrs Charles Smith
33 D.C. Baldwin
34 Mrs E.E. Bayliss
35 Mrs E. Bill
36 Peter Chard
37 Mr & Mrs I. Mustafic
38 Malcolm Read
39 Wg Cdr W.R.F. Cooney
40 B.S. Kiek
41 Mrs Anne P. Hobbs
42 Mrs E. Russell
43 K.W. Bullard
44 Mrs Edna Martin
45 D.H. Quick
46 P.J.R. Carter
47 Mrs E.M. Colman
48 Mrs G.P. Haines
49 Mrs A.T.S. Street
50 P.J.R. Carter
51 S.B. Bell
52 C.R. Bennett
53 D.H.M. Desmond
54 A. Thomas
55 R.J. Evans
56 Canon R.G. Lunt
57 R.J. May
58 Mrs M. Davies
59 Mrs M.E. Whittal Williams
60 Mrs B.A. Gladwin
61 Mrs Judith Lenore Scholefield
62 Mrs M.I.A. Jones
63 Mrs I.A.J. Price
64 Geraldine Wadley
65 Mrs K. Heslop
66 Mrs C. Burchell
67 M.D. Thomas
68 David A. Toombs
69 Mrs E. Keatley
70 Michael Handford
71 B.J. Meadows
72 J.L. Cale
73 Mrs S.M. Wells
74 L. Dunn
75 Mrs Mary Wilson
76 J. Edwards
77 M.H. Somers
78 Malcolm & Ann Dorsett
79 Peter Young
80 Anne Thatcher
81 Miss A. Hopkins
82 Mrs Catherine Hall
83 Miss A.C. Davies
84 Mrs Audrey P. Briggs
85 Andrew W. Perry
86 Mrs Ann Hodges
87 T.W. Watson
88 Mrs E.L. Keen
89 Mrs W.G. Davies
90 Miss D. Hamblin
91 W.L. Congreve
92 R.G. Bennett
93 J.H. Davis
94 E.W. Spring
95 Mrs P. Bottomley
96 Mrs Janice R. Davies
97 B.C. Butler
98 P.K.S. Griffin
99 Mrs A.D. Beard
100 W.F. Ritchie
101 M. Collins
102 Mrs Nicholas
103 Miss J.A. Baker
104 S.G. Powell
105 Linda Heath
106 Peter Constantine
107 Miss E.A. Warren
108 Mrs E.W. Lee
109 Miss M.A. Harris
110 P.E. Tector
111 J.J. Davis
112 Mrs M.A. Bunn
113 Miss E. Underwood
114 Mrs M. Miles
115 S.S. Churchill
116 Mrs F.J. Powell
117 D. Leyshon Williams
118 F.W.J. Gunter
119 Mrs M. Davies
120 Mrs B.J. Watkins
121 Mrs A. Bartleman
122 History Department John Masefield High School
123 Mr & Mrs A.L.A. Hissink
124 R.E. Deeley
125 J.M. Ireland
126 Miss C. Haines
127 Mrs E.M. Lloyd
128 Mrs E. Ballard
129 F.E.A. Armes
130 Dudley C. Brook
131 Dennis H. Tatler
132 Mrs M.E. Holland
133 Philip Holland
134 Frances Bradley
135 Miss Ann Watkins
136 Miss Marjorie Wheelock
137 G.P. Hunt
138 Mrs Susan Andrew
139 J.D. Denington
140 Mrs M.C. Salmon
141 David J. Windmill
142 Jane George
143 Jon B. Morris
144 Mrs V. Peate
145 Vera Winifred Evans
146 Mrs H. Sharpe
147 Robert J. Wreford
148 Mr & Mrs R. Wooding
149 J.R. Cutler
150 Hilda Lee Partridge
151 Mrs G.A. Newey
152 Dominic Hugh Shorthouse
153 Derek Shorthouse
154 D.E.G. Lewis
155 Mrs M.B. Gill
156 H.J. Cheale
157 Mrs J.H. Hooper
158 Mr & Mrs W.E. Phillips
159 Miss G.M. Hamilton
160 Miss E.M. Philpott
161 Brian F. Speakman
162 Miss Sheila Staunton
163 N.J. Howes
164 Mrs E. Bisem
165 Mrs P.A. Porter
166 Rev C.M. Oldroyd
167 Mr & Mrs J. Reed
168 Barton Yates
169 Miss B. Dearden
170 Mrs C.L. Cale
171
172 A.J. Gough
173 Mrs J.E. Morris
174 D.L. Carver
175 Major G.W.E. Farrow
176 G. Griffiths
177 P.B. Ranger
178 Mrs R.G. Perry
179 J. Barnes
180 Mrs R.H. Hickin
181 F.V. Winchurch
182 G.R. Morris
183 C.W. Turner
184 Mrs Morris
185 Miss K.M. Manistre
186 Mrs E.M. Stephenson
187
188 John Hegarty
189 Mrs E.M. Hunt
190 E.E. Bass
191 Martin Williams
192 Geoffrey & Rene Marklove
193 Earle & Irene Masterson
194 Jack & Margo Wallace
195 Mrs Vera M. Price
196 G.A. Shotbolt
197 Mrs Hilda Hawcutt
198 Mrs J. Ruddock
199 Miss Minnie Edwards
200 Mrs B. Hemingway
201 P.T. Garnett

202 C. Stephens
203 R.J. Bond
204 R.I. Barker
205 G. Perry
206 John Rogers
207 D. Davies
208 Major P.L. Brough
209 James H. Large
210 Mrs A.M. Hailwood
211 Miss I. Kirk
212 D.R. Neale
213 Roger Grimley
214 J. Hobby
215 Joan Caley
216 Miss K.E. Hart
217 Mrs J. Wheeler
218 Miss Grace Clemence
219 W.J. Heath
220 C.F. Brooke
221 R.B. Tremayne
222 Rev Canon N. Panter
223 Miss U. Palairet
224 H.D.R. Mitchell
225 W.H. Davies
226 Mrs T. Noot
227 A.S. Furnival
228 Stephen Jones
229 Mrs J.M. Hammill
230 C.W. Walker
231 Mrs H.V. Whatmore
232 Graham John Boyce
233 Mrs E.A. Moore
234 Miss D.E. Meadows
235 Mrs Jill Bray
236 Pamela Hurle
237 Mrs V.M. McNeill
238 J.H. Syrett
239
240 John Masfield High School
241 Mrs Betty L. Goode
242 Margaret & Brian Richards
243 Mr & Mrs J.G. Calderbank
244 B. Thomas
245 Ms P. Meredith
246 Mrs E. Farrington
247 W.J.S. Parry
248 Mr & Mrs J.M. Acheson
249 Mrs R.E. Skelton
250 H.H.J. Aubrey
251 B.F. Voss
252 Greg Unwin
253 P.R. Jackson
254 Mrs C. Rojjer
255 C.E. Attfield
256 Dick Sharpe
257 N.C. Reeves
258 Mae Irene Williams
259 Mrs D. Westoby
260 E.J. Godwin
261 Mrs A. Berry Ottaway
262 J.W. Martin
263 Miss Penelope E. Morgan
264 D.G. Pedersen
265 Basil Butcher
266 W.E. Preece
267 A.C. Lloyd
268 R.K. Watkins
269
270 Gwent County Library
271 A. Mac C. Armstrong
272 A.G. Welch
273 P.C. Judge
274 Mrs M.H. Brook
275 N.C. Reeves
276 G. Cerins
277 Miss A.M. Maddison Barnes
278 L. Bayliss
279 Richard John Sharpe
280 Powys County Library
281 Miss W. Lindsay Scott
282 Dick & Daphne Davies
283 J.W.M. & P.M. Caine
284 Mrs Sowdon
285 M.F.J. Peet
286 A.S. Parry
287 John Drew
288 Derek Foxton
289 Edward Ball
290 J.W. & M. Tonkin
291 C.E. Attfield
292 Roy Massey
293 G.E. Aylmer
294 F.M. Kendrick
295 Miriam M. Evans
296 Christopher George Noel
297 Chris Over
298 Nigel S. Carter
299 Estelle Davies
300 J.G. Calderbank
301 David Apperley
302 Manley Power
303 S.H. Pontin
304 Gillian Bulmer
305 Muriel E. John
306 W. Hugh Davies
307 H.J. Lloyd-Johnes OBE, TD, LLD, FSA
308 Mrs M. Griffiths
309 Hereford Educational Development Centre
310 Christopher Harley
311 Jeanette H. Miners
312 Bernard F. Voss
313 Mrs Shirley Preece
314 S.C. Stanford
315 Philip Charleton
316 J.M. Rees
317 Pershore High School
318 Jon & Heather Hurley
319 David Whitehead
320 Mr & Mrs A. Clark
321 Gp Capt J.B. Lewis
322 Fred Druce
323 G.K. Harper
324 F.S.A. Doran
325 Gwenyth J. Kalmar
326 Mrs Barbara J. Wyatt
327 D.A. Roberts
328 A. Huckerby
329 Mrs D. Belcher
330 Scott Brinded
331 R.S. Vivian
332 Alan & Barbara Denton
333 Richard Hodgkinson
334 B.R. Taylor
335 Morton Lloyd
336 M.T. Anderson
337 Mrs R.G. Perry
338 P.H. Shepherd
339 Mrs J. Preece
340 Mrs A.P. Williams
341 H. Worrall
342 K.C. Davies
343 Mrs C.M. Potter
344 R.G. Sheldrake
345 R.J. Hackett
346 M.H. Tovey
347 B.W. Waters
348 Mrs L. Gobey
349 Sandra Brookes
350 E.T. Lewis
351 Mrs G.A. Powell
352 Dudley C. Brook
353 Rev Ronald Smith
354 Mrs J.L. Ardrey
355 Mrs P.D. Williams
356 Pamela Hurle
357 Mrs D. Fletcher
358 Mrs J. Cerins
359 John G. Keely
360 S.P. Glennie-Smith
361 G.B. Underwood
362 Mrs. J.B. Eager
363 L.W. Jones
364 Frank E. Skinner
365 N.E. Lewis
366 Mrs J.L. Stevens
367 R.G.K. Camp
368 Martin A. Colman
369 Rodney H. Bennett
370 Claudia M. Daniel
371
372 Ledbury Trust
373 S. & C. Quan
374 Patrick Desmond
375 Mrs A. Cadbury
376 Mrs D.G. Redeser
377 J.A. Stratton
378 Richard Brooks
379 S.T. Walker
380 Gillian Madge
381 Marshall Wilson
382 County Museum of Hereford & Worcester
383 Mrs D. Lane-Hall
384 County of Hereford & Worcester, Library Dept
425
426
427 Mrs C. Grundy
428
429 Derek T. Preece
430 Extramural Library, Univ of Birmingham
431
432
433 Mrs Diana Merry
434
436 Mrs K. Hodgetts
437
439 L.W. Webb
440 I.D. Mackenzie
441 C.E. Attfield
442 A.N. Taylor
443 R.E. Deeley
444 Mr & Mrs J.L. Everett
445 C. Watkins
446 Sandra M. Peate
447 Victoria & Albert Museum

Remaining names unlisted

ENDPAPERS: FRONT — *Map of Ledbury and Environs,* 1831, by W. Gibbs, Surveyor. BACK — *Ledbury Tithe Map,* 1841

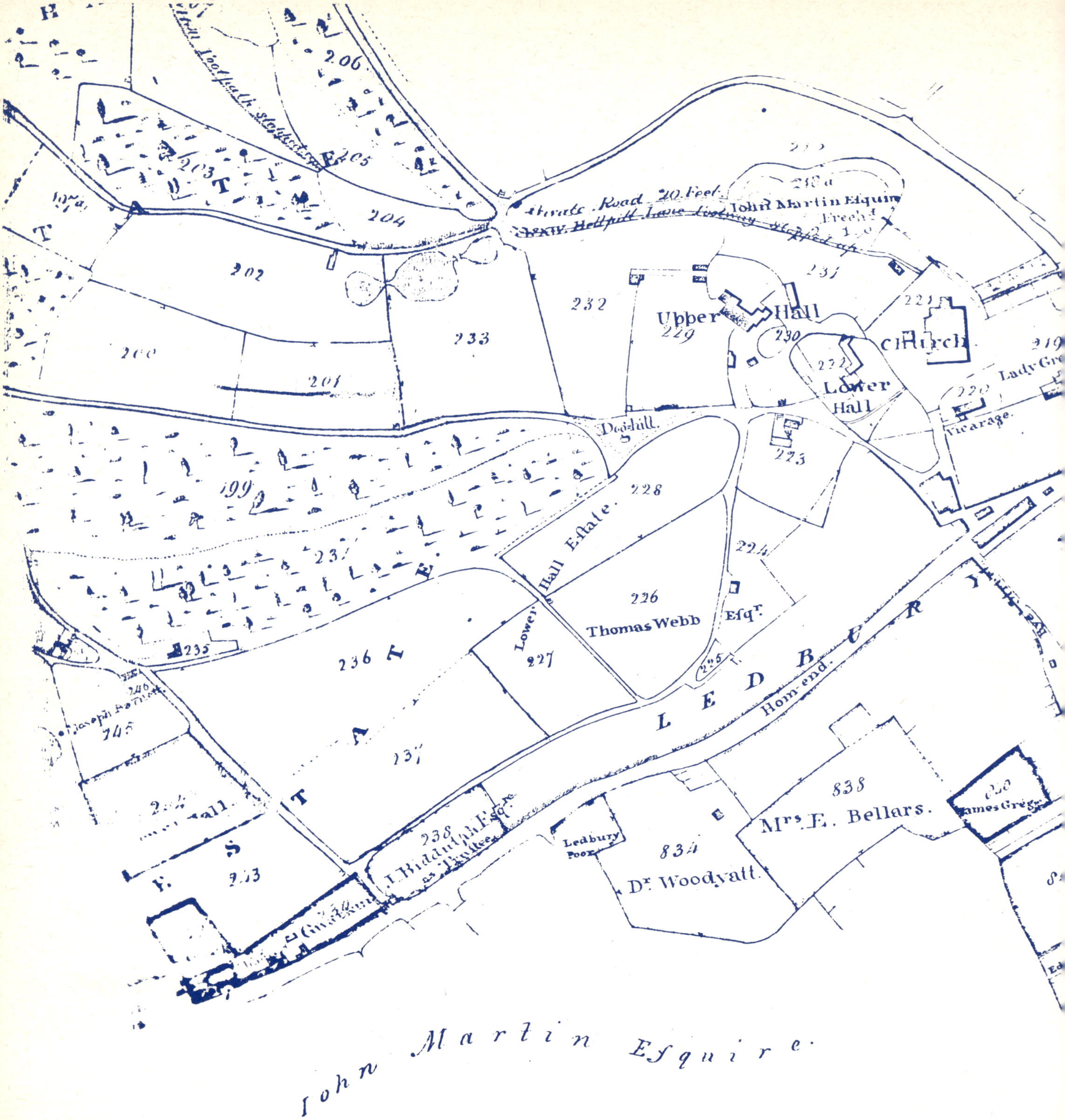
206
205
203
204
202
200
201
233
232
Private Road 20 Feet
John Martin Esquire
Upper Hall
229
230
Church
Lower Hall
Vicarage
Lady Gre
220
223
Dog-hill
199
228
Hall Estate
224
226
Thomas Webb Esqr.
Lower
227
225
236
235
Joseph Barrett
245
LEDBURY
Horn-end
838
Mrs. E. Bellars
834
Dr. Woodyatt
Ledbury Poor
238
J. Biddulph Esqr.
223
John Martin Esquire